Media, Ethics and Law

Preface

The Indian constitutional guarantees of free press and free expression have ensured a press largely without governmental regulation. Free media is an essential source of the information that is at the heart of a free society. This critical role endows the media with its own power, which, when used irresponsibly, can threaten a free society. This does not mean media without standards. In India, the government takes on the role of primary regulator of the media. It has established specific laws not only to regulate media activities but also to protect their freedom. This book explores the central role of media ethics as the core values which shape the functioning of Indian journalism.

The free media is an essential source of the information that is at the heart of a free society. This critical role endows the media with its own power, which, when used irresponsibly, can threaten a free society. Journalism ethics provide a process by which individual mistakes and excesses are corrected without jeopardizing the ultimate objective of a free media — to provide a healthy check on centres of power in order to maintain a free and enlightened society. Broadcast media and the internet have created a new set of challenges that are on occasion addressed in the India in a governmental regulatory framework, but always in the context of basic constitutional principles and protections of our free press.

Journalists everywhere have a vital role to provide the public with knowledge and understanding. But as they practice their craft in a world that is both technologically and geographically changing, systematic standards must guide their work. Only in that way will journalists serve their society in an ethically responsible and constructive fashion.

Naval Prabhakar
Narendra Basu

Contents

1

Media and Freedom of Expression

Freedom of speech, of the press, of association, of assembly and petition—this set of guarantees, protected by the Constitution, comprises what we refer to as freedom of expression.

Freedom of Speech

Freedom of speech is the right to freely say what you please, as well as the related right to hear what others have stated. It is self-explanatory. Recently, it has been commonly understood as encompassing full freedom of expression, including the freedom to create and distribute movies, pictures, songs, dances, and all other forms of expressive communication. Freedom of speech is often regarded as an integral concept in modern democracies, where it is understood to outlaw government censorship. Thus states may still punish (but not prohibit) certain damaging types of expressions, notably sedition, defamation, publishing secrets regarding matters of state security, etc.

People may be hesitant to speak freely not because of fear of government retribution but because of social pressures. When an individual announces an unpopular opinion, he or she may face the disdain of their community or even be subjected to violent reactions. While this type of suppression of speech is even more difficult to prevent than government suppression, there are questions about whether it truly falls within the ambit of freedom of speech, which is typically regarded as a civil liberty, or freedom from government action.

Theories of free speech

Self-governance

One theory is that freedom of speech is crucial in any democracy, because open discussions of candidates are essential for voters to make informed elections decisions during elections. It is through speech that people can influence their government's choice of policies. Also, public officials are held accountable through criticisms that can pave the way for their replacement. Some suggest that when citizens refrain from voicing their discontent because they fear retribution, the government can no longer be responsive to them, thus it is less accountable for its actions.

Defenders of free speech often allege that this is the main reason why governments suppress free speech--to avoid accountability. Alternatively, it may be argued that some restrictions on freedom of speech may be compatible with democracy or necessary to protect it. For example, such arguments are used to justify restrictions on support of Nazi ideas in post-war Germany.

Discovering truth

A classic argument for protecting freedom of speech as a fundamental right is that it is essential for the discovery of truth. The best test of truth is the power of the thought to get itself accepted in the competition of the market, and that truth is the only ground upon which their wishes safely can be carried out. The marketplace of ideas rationale for freedom of speech has been criticized by scholars on the grounds that it is wrong to assume all ideas will enter the marketplace of ideas, and even if they do, some ideas may drown out others merely because they enjoy dissemination through superior resources.

The marketplace is also criticized for its assumption that truth will necessarily triumph over falsehood. We can see throughout history that people may be swayed by emotion rather than reason, and even if truth ultimately prevails, enormous harm can occur in the interim. However, even if these weaknesses of the marketplace of ideas are acknowledged, supporters argue that the alternative of government determination of truth and censorship of falsehoods is worse.

Advancing autonomy

Another rationale is that it is an essential aspect of personhood and autonomy. Professor Baker said that "to engage voluntarily in a speech act is to engage in self-definition or expression. A Vietnam war protester may explain that when she chants 'Stop This War Now' at a demonstration, she does so without any expectation that her speech will affect continuance of the war... rather, she participates and chants in order to define herself publicly in opposition to the war. This war protester provides a dramatic illustration of the importance of this self-expressive use of speech, independent of any effective communication to others, for self-fulfillment or self-realization." This view suggests a rationale for the protection of acts of expression that are not obviously political or vital to self-government, such as abstract art, music, or dance.

Protecting speech because it aids the political process or furthers the search for truth emphasizes the instrumental values of expression. Justice Thurgood Marshall wrote that "the First Amendment serves not only the needs of the polity but also those of the human spirit -- a spirit that demands self-expression." Critics of this view argue that there is no inherent reason to find speech to be a fundamental right compared with countless other activities that might be regarded as a part of autonomy or that could advance self-fulfillment.

Promoting tolerance

Another explanation is that it is integral to tolerance, which should be a basic value in our society. Professor Lee Bollinger is an advocate of this view and argues that "the free speech principle involves a special act of carving out one area of social interaction for extraordinary self-restraint, the purpose of which is to develop and demonstrate a social capacity to control feelings evoked by a host of social encounters." The free speech principle is left with the concern of nothing less than helping to shape "the intellectual character of the society."

This claim is to say that tolerance is a desirable, if not essential, value, and that protecting unpopular speech is itself an act of tolerance. Such tolerance serves as a model that encourages more tolerance throughout society. Critics argue that society need not be tolerant of the intolerance of others, such as those who advocate great harm, even genocide. Preventing such harms is claimed to be much more important than being tolerant of those who argue for them.

The importance of free speech as a basic and valuable characteristic of western society cannot be underestimated.

As well as emphasizing the value of free speech, it is proposed to make an evaluation of some of the traditional restrictions on what may be freely said or published, such as the defamation laws, contempt of court, national security and so on. The approach is one which makes the case for free speech, since the world is now a place where people's unfettered freedoms are by and large in retreat. One of the difficulties inherent in discussing freedom of speech is that it contains what libertarians often describe as the paradox of freedom.

Unless we ensure to the enemies of freedom the liberties which they are keen to abuse, then we deny the essence of what we ultimately stand for and are therefore no better than those to whom we are opposed. Or as Voltaire has been paraphrased, "I disapprove of what you say, but I will defend to the death your right to say it."

On a more practical plane, freedom of speech serves many functions. One of its most important functions is that decision-making at all levels is preceded by discussion and consideration of a representative range of views. A decision made after adequate consultation is likely to be a better one which less imperfectly mirrors the opinions, interests and needs of all concerned, than a decision taken with little or no consultation. Thus freedom of speech is important at all levels in society. Yet it is most important for government. A government which does not know what the people feel and think is in a dangerous position. The government that muzzles free speech runs a risk of destroying the creative instincts of its people.

Freedom of speech is also important to governments because when criticisms of a government are freely voiced, the government has the opportunity to respond to answer unfair comments and criticisms about its actions. On the other hand, when freedom of speech is restricted, rumours, unfair criticisms, comments and downright falsehoods are circulated by word of mouth. These have a habit of spreading across the length and breadth of the country through conversation and surreptitiously circulated writings. The government is in no position to answer these views, because they are not publicly stated. It is in a government's interest to have criticisms in the public arena where it can answer its critics and correct its mistakes.

The government generally has access to electronic and printing communication far in excess of individuals and groups. It is able to present its view only if the opposing views are in the open and known. Finally, the freedom of speech is the single most important political right of citizens, although private property is required for its operation. Without free speech no political action is possible and no resistance to injustice and oppression is possible. Without free speech elections would have no meaning at all. Policies of contestants become known to the public and become responsive to public opinion only by virtue of free speech. Between elections the freely expressed opinions of citizens help restrain oppressive rule. Without this freedom it is futile to expect political freedom or consequently economic freedom. The sine qua non of a democratic society is the freedom of speech. Freedom of speech involves toleration of a great deal of nonsense, and even of matters which are in bad taste.

Free speech is simply what is left when many other things are taken out. One of those things is the effect of defamation laws, which seek to protect an individual's reputation. The central problem is to reconcile this purpose with the competing demands of free speech or to put the problem another way: It is really about how far individuals in society should be protected against what they perceive as the excessive power of those - like the press - who can command a large audience. In practice, defamation law is about the ability of the media to expose an individual to the public on a grand scale.

In a free society there is a strong presumption that people should be able to speak freely, especially in relation to public issues and an individual's behaviour in relation to these issues. However, the reality of potential for abuse of this freedom remains and so with it the need for defamation laws. In an action for defamation, there has for a long time been the defence of truthfulness but the onus is on the defence (the defamer) to prove it. The truth of all material statements contained in the libel must be proven.

There is also the legal defence of "absolute privilege". In simple language this means that whatever is said (however defamatory) is "absolutely privileged" and no action can be maintained. "Absolute privilege" attaches to whatever is said in Parliament or during evidence given in the course of judicial proceedings. There is also the defence of "qualified privileged" which is where an action cannot be maintained unless there is malice, such as in the reporting by the media of matters in respect of which "absolute privilege" exists. Privilege is often justified on the ground that "fear of liability might induce caution destructive of the frankness that the public has a right to expect." But, adds Fleming "unfortunately, demagogues who abuse the privilege are rarely brought to book by their own Chamber".

It is in view of these often extreme abuses of Parliamentary Privilege that there is good reason for exposing parliamentarians to the same liability as anyone else. Truth of the statements should be a complete defence. Perhaps a balance could be struck that those with privilege not carry the burden of proof. Rather, they would be liable if the plaintiff proved the untruthfulness of the statement. In the United States a person holding political or public office has no right to sue for defamation. The reason given is that a person who enters public office, unlike the private citizen, should come under unrestrained public scrutiny. This is considered essential to the workings of the US democracy. Thus the law of defamation offers no refuge to the holder of public office. There is an important lesson here for Australia.

However, last year the Attorney General proposed new Uniform Defamation Laws which would place much greater restrictions on freedom of speech than do Australia's already restrictive laws. The most severe aspect was that truth would not be a sufficient defence, as it is in Victoria, nor truth and public interest, as it is in New South Wales; rather, truth and public benefit would have to be proved. Of course, none of these new restrictions applied to Parliamentarians or others with Absolute Privilege. In view of the criticisms which the draft Bill received from the media, it now appears to have been put to one side. While there may be a need to codify the law of defamation which at present is in a very disorganised state, it should not be taken as an opportunity to impose further constraints on freedom of speech.

The proposed amendment to the Racial Discrimination Act is not the only proposal to restrict freedom of speech associated with the present government A proposed Uniform Defamation Law, floated last year, has been withdrawn in the light of the belting it received from the media, but it has not been scrapped. Much publicity has already been given to many of its provisions which, if implemented, would have given Australia, already suffering an international reputation for restrictive defamation laws, the most restrictive defamation laws in the English speaking world. The draft legislation which is now in limbo was originally presented in a curiously disjunctive form. Parliamentarians would have been free to pick and choose which provisions of varying degree of illiberality they would seek to impose uniformly throughout Australia.

Among the options was one that would give the dead a right to sue (through their living representative) for up to three years, thus finally ending the career of the honest obituary writer. Moreover truth would not be a sufficient defence, as it is in Victoria, nor truth and public interest, as in New South Wales; rather, under one proposed option, truth and public benefit would have to be proved. This last idea is a complete reversal of the fundamental principle of freedom of expression as set out by John Stuart Mill. The traditional principle is one which presumed the right to express oneself as one wishes unless some substantial harm to innocent people will result.

Under the proposed "reform" in one of the draft options in the uniform Defamation Law the presumption would be that you should not make statements about identifiable living or recently dead people unless some public good will be furthered. Many people have made useful and sound criticisms of this proposed legislation, and yet I think it has been insufficiently realized how profoundly questionable are the principles implicit in it. What the proposed amendment to the Racial Discrimination Act and the more restrictive proposed provisions of the uniform Defamation law have in common is a "wetter" view than Mill would ever have countenanced as to what constitutes a sufficient degree of harm to innocent people, or indeed how "innocent" they need be, to justify restricting freedom of expression.

Privacy - the value which the uniform Defamation law is really attempting to protect - was not seen as an important competitor. Indeed it was not until later in the nineteenth century that the American Judge Cooley and later Judges Warren and Brandeis, writing in the Harvard Law Review made privacy - what Judge Cooley had called "the right to be let alone" - an intellectual issue. Mill's famous principle that it is only the prevention of harm to others which justifies the state in restricting our voluntary conduct - a principle derived from Kant - has always caused practical problems because of the vagueness of the notion of harm. Some have attempted to give a "Millian" justification for the proposed anti-racist and defamation laws under discussion on the ground that the restrictions they introduce are motivated by a desire to prevent harm; the deep feeling of hurt in having one's racial ancestry denigrated, or the dignity and embarrassment of having what one thought were private shames publicised. But plainly this is not good enough.

The issue is thus not whether some people are profoundly hurt by what others are now permitted to say and write freely, but rather whether this hurt is so great as to justify curtailing by law the present right to do things which may produce it. The issue is not whether people engage in ethnic defamation and outrageous intrusions of privacy. It is whether, and if so in what circumstances, the real hurt that such people can and do sometimes produce is a sufficiently great evil to justify further curtailing that freedom of expression for which Voltaire, Milton, and Mill spoke so eloquently and passionately.

Relative Freedom Of Speech

It is well to remember that in spite of the valid criticisms which can be made of the way western societies have allowed governments to place restrictions upon freedom of speech, it virtually pales into insignificance when a comparison is made with the countries which lie between the Elbe and the China Sea.

One vivid example is the care which the leader of the Polish trade union Solidarity, Lech Walesa, has had to employ in any "statement" which he makes about the problems confronting that country. It is all the more of concern because it seems clear that it is only the threat of criticism from the international media which has prevented this episode from being dealt with in the usual way. A similar problem has been shown recently in the USSR by the controversy surrounding the health of the Soviet dissident, Sakharov.

This association of restrictions with socialism and freedom with capitalism, is no matter of chance. Capitalism is, with all its faults, a pluralist system. Power within it is dispersed and various, and it is this pluralism which is the necessary though not sufficient condition for freedom's existence and continuance. Socialism, on the other hand, is a highly centralized system, with political and economic power concentrated in very few hands.

Freedom of speech in the Socialist bloc is all the more restricted where all causes must bend to the Communist doctrine. A common justification for the restrictions upon the liberty of individuals is the supposedly overriding interests of efficient government and the public benefit. It is conveniently overlooked that what constitutes "efficient government" and "public benefit" are subjective concepts, the interpretation of which will be in the hands of legislators, bureaucrats and judges with human failings and feelings, lack of vision, imperfect knowledge and understanding, subjective views and personal prejudices.

However, while public benefit is an important factor, the test for allowing further restrictions upon free speech should strive to be somewhat more stringent. Legal restraints upon individual freedom of speech should only be tolerated where they are absolutely necessary to prevent infliction of actual harm or to secure the liberties of others. A more or less remote possibility that someone will be harmed or unbased claims that the stability of society will be undermined is not sufficient justification for legal prohibition. A balance must be struck between the ability of individuals to be unrestricted in the free expression of thoughts and ideas, and the need to ensure that governments are able to efficiently carry out their function of administration, law and order, and preserving the rights of individuals vis-a-vis each other.

Freedom of Speech in World Countries

The Constitution of India guarantees to all Indian citizens the right to express one's convictions and opinions freely. Freedom of speech and expression, which is an integral component that ensures the functioning of democracy, is a fundamental right enshrined in the Constitution of India. The mode or manner of expression could vary from speech to writing, printing, picture, electronic media or in any other manner. Electronic media would include communication through the net, a popular mode of communication in today's world of advancing technology. Freedom of expression would also include the freedom to propagate ideas, publish and circulate them and defend such ideas.

However this right, like all rights is subject to certain reasonable restrictions. The grounds on which this right could be restricted are:

1. *In the interest of sovereignity and integrity*: This ground was inserted as a ground by the 16th amendment to the Constitution in the year 1963, to enable India to combat cries for secession from organizations and their activities which could not be restricted otherwise.

2. *In the interest of security of state*: Under this ground only that expression which could give rise to serious and aggravated forms of public disorder, as distinguished from ordinary breaches of public safety or public order, can be restricted.

3. *In the interest of friendly relations with foreign States*: The intent behind inserting this as a ground was to prevent libels against foreign States, in the interest of maintaining friendly relations with them.

4. *In the interest of public order*: This ground was introduced by the first amendment to the Constitution in the year 1951. This followed the decision of the apex Court in Ramesh Thapar's case, wherein the Court had held that ordinary or local breaches of public order were not grounds for restricting freedom of expression. This was followed by several such cases in which, the Court upheld the contention that incitement to murder or promotion of disaffection among classes did not tend to affect the security of state and therefore was not punishable under the Constitution of India.

5. *In the interest of decency or morality*: This was engrafted as a ground to restrict speeches or publications, which tend to undermine public morals.

6. *Contempt of Court*: The freedom of speech and expression does not include interference with due course of justice or lowering the prestige or authority of the Court. However criticism about the judicial system or judges would be welcomed, if it does not hamper the administration of justice.

7. *Defamation*: Introduced as a ground as everyone also has a right to his reputation, which is regarded as property.

8. *Incitement to an offence*: instigating any person to commit an offence.

However restrictions on freedom of speech and expression, must also conform to the test of reasonableness. Only reasonable restrictions would be upheld in a Court of law.

In the United States freedom of expression is protected by the First Amendment to the United States Constitution. There are many exceptions to this general rule, including copyright protection, the Miller test for obscenity and greater regulation of so-called commercial speech, such as advertising. The Miller test in particular rarely comes into effect. The principle of freedom of speech promotes dialogues on public issues, but it is most relevant to speech which is unpopular at the time it is made. As a Pennsylvania state legislator, Rep. Mark B. Cohen of Philadelphia, once argued in a legislative debate, "Freedom of speech which is limited to freedom to say whatever a majority of the Pennsylvania legislature agrees with is not real freedom of speech".

Generally, the U.S. has the most liberal policy on freedom of expression in the world, with no formal government censorship of the news media (with the exception of broadcast media) or creative arts. Even when expressive content is held to lie beyond the protection of the First Amendment, the finding is usually made by a court during a prosecution after the content is published or publicly exhibited. A crucial goal of current First Amendment jurisprudence is to prevent "chilling effects" upon legitimate protected speech.

Americans deeply cherish their right of free speech and take it for granted. They are usually shocked when they learn that the governments of most First World countries exercise direct censorship powers over their publishers. However, also see Free speech zone. Like all other constitutional freedoms, freedom of speech is more a contested terrain than an absolute principle. The repeal of the fairness doctrine limited the right to reply to television opinions, but the proliferation of new media outlets has expanded media access.

The ever increasing cost of purchasing a newspaper, television station, or radio station has limited free speech, but the Internet and new forms of low power radio stations have increased it. What steps the courts of the United States will take to enforce freedom of speech depends somewhat on the identity of the judges appointed and the advocates for clients who appear before them. Within the U.S., the state of California permits its citizens the broadest possible range of free speech under the state constitution (which includes an affirmative right to free speech in addition to a negative right paralleling the federal prohibition on laws that abridge the freedom of speech).

The European Convention on Human Rights, when signed on 4 November 1950, proclaimed a broad range of human rights already in existence in the signatories countries. These rights include Article 10, which entitles all citizens to free expression. "Everyone has the right to freedom of expression. This right shall include freedom to hold opinions and to receive and impart information and ideas without interference by public authority and regardless of frontiers. This article shall not prevent States from requiring the licensing of broadcasting, television or cinema enterprises."

It also included some other restrictions: "The exercise of these freedoms, since it carries with it duties and responsibilities, may be subject to such formalities, conditions, restrictions or penalties as are prescribed by law and are necessary in a democratic society, in the interests of national security, territorial integrity or public safety, for the prevention of disorder or crime, for the protection of health or morals, for the protection of the reputation or the rights of others, for preventing the disclosure of information received in confidence, or for maintaining the authority and impartiality of the judiciary."

Each country then had to alter their laws to confirm with this, where necessary. In 1998, the United Kingdom implemented the Human Rights Act which granted the judiciary power to apply these rights to cases, and a requirement for Parliament to check compatibility of new laws with the Convention rights. If a judge finds a law to be 'incompatible' with the given Convention rights, then the law must be amended to incorporate these protections.

European-wide cases have been heard in the European Court of Justice as well as the European Court of Human Rights to guarantee these privileges - and cases have tested the need for professional integrity (as a journalist or lawyer) and the compatibility of one with the Human Rights law. The Human Rights Court has also targeted the French laws on journalism as being incompatible.

Freedom of speech is guaranteed by article 5 of the German Grundgesetz ("basic Law"). There are, however, some restrictions, for example personal insults or hate speech (Volksverhetzung). The latter includes the propagation of neonazist ideas and the use of nazist symbols like the swastika, except for purposes of art, research or education. These restrictions are justified with the argument that they are necessary to protect the democratic constitution of Germany.

The constitutional provision that guarantees Freedom of expression in Canada is section 2(b) of the Canadian Charter of Rights and Freedoms. 2. Everyone has the following fundamental freedoms:... (b) freedom of thought, belief, opinion and expression, including freedom of the press and other media of communication

Due to section 1 of the Charter, the so-called limitation clause, Canada's freedom of expression differs from the provision guaranteeing freedom of speech in the United States of America in a fundamental manner. The section 1 of the Charter states: The Canadian Charter of Rights and Freedoms guarantees the rights and freedoms set out in it subject only to such reasonable limits prescribed by law as can be demonstrably justified in a free and democratic society.

This section is double edged. First it implies that a limitation on freedom of speech prescribed in law can be permitted if it can be justified as being a reasonable limit in a free and democratic society. Conversely, it implies that a restriction can be invalidated if it cannot be shown to be a reasonable limit in a free and democratic society.

Unlike most other nations that legally protect freedom of speech, Australia does not have a bill of rights. However, in 1992 the High Court of Australia judged in the case of Australian Capital Television et al. v. Commonwealth of Australia (Adban) that the Australian Constitution, by providing for a democratic system of government, implied the protection of freedom of speech as an essential element of that system.

The majority of African constitutions provide legal protection for freedom of speech. However, these rights are exercised inconsistently in practice. The replacement of authoritarian regimes in Kenya and Ghana has substantially improved the situation in those countries. On the other hand, Eritrea allows no independent media and uses draft evasion as a pretext to crack down on any dissent, spoken or otherwise. Sudan, Libya, and Equatorial Guinea also have repressive laws and practices. In addition, many state radio stations (which are the primary source of news for illiterate people) are under tight control and programs, especially talk shows providing a forum to complain about the government, are often censored. Freedom of speech is increasing in oil-producing countries (such as Equatorial Guinea, Chad, Cameroon, and Gabon), because it gives the oil companies a good impression.

Internet and Free Speech

The development of the Internet opened new possibilities for achieving freedom of speech using methods that do not depend on legal measures. Pseudonymity and data havens (such as Freenet) allow free speech, as the technology guarantees that material cannot be removed (censored).

A small minority has questioned whether involuntary commitment laws, when the diagnosis of mental illness leading, in whole or in part, to the commitment, was made to some degree on the basis of the speech or writings of the committed individual, violate the right of freedom of speech of that individuals, in jurisdictions where that is relevant.

Freedom of expression on the internet poses a wide range of problems and different legal practices prevail in different parts of the world. Policies towards sites - notably those that spread messages of hate, or promote terrorism or crime, or those that represent a perceived threat to national security - vary from country to country. Access can also be restricted by technical or infrastructural obstacles which thus constitute limitations to freedom of expression. UNESCO believes that the information and communication technologies should be made available to all:

Inadequate infrastructure in some regions makes it difficult, almost impossible, for large populations to benefit from the potential of the information and communication technologies. Thus, 1,000 people in sub-Saharan Africa have access to just 0.2 computers connected to the Web, as opposed to 120 connected computers per 1,000 inhabitants in the wealthiest OECD countries. Some languages are barely present on the internet making it difficult for people of some cultures to benefit from the information that is available. Thus, English is estimated to account for 52% of content on the world wide web; German 6.97%; Spanish 5.48%; French, 4.43%; Italian 3.06%; Portuguese 2.70%; Korean, Dutch, Russian and the four Scandinavian languages total between 8 and 10%.

Press Freedom

Press freedom (or Freedom of the press) is the guarantee by a government of free public speech often through a state constitution for its citizens, and associations of individuals extended to members of news gathering organizations, and their published reporting. It also extends to news gathering, and processes involved in obtaining information for the public consumption. With respect to governmental information a government distinguishes which materials are public or protected from disclosure to the public based on classification of information as sensitive, classified or secret and being otherwise protected from disclosure due to relevance of the information to protecting the national interest. Many governments are also subject to sunshine laws or Freedom of Information Acts that are used to define the ambit of national interest. Every year, Reporters Without Borders establishes a ranking of every country about freedom of the press.

The freedom of the press is considered to be the most important right which must be protected in a democratic society. This freedom can only be available in a society where there is a right to free speech and expression. Similarly, the freedom of information can be enjoyed only if there are sources from which information can flow. These sources, again, would be available where there is a right to speech and expression. The freedom of expression and the freedom to receive and impart information are corollary of one another. In fact, there is an overlap between the freedom of expression and the freedom to receive or impart information.

The freedom to impart information can be considered as an expression of an opinion, of the informant or of a third person. The seeking of information, on the other hand, precedes the formation of an opinion by the person who seeks the information, and consequently also its expression. But with regard to the press, freedom of expression and information run parallel to each other. While the press might be the medium of expression, someone else might possess the information. Until and unless these two freedoms be exercised together both would be useless.

In the case of information the only one who has the right of free distribution of that information is the party who is the author, originator or otherwise the intellectual owner of the information in question. In case of the press, however, the press can express opinions of others also, of course, held in good faith and believed to be true. It is incumbent on the press, with regard to the print media as well as audio-visual media, to impart information and ideas which the public has the right to receive. Otherwise, the press would not be able to play its role of 'public watch dog'. Thus for exercising the freedom of expression one must have the freedom of information. In this regard, the approval of the Freedom of Information Bill, 2000 (Information Bill) by Indian Parliament would be a welcome move.

Media and Human Rights

Until a decade ago, the word 'media' was synonymous with the word 'the press', which in turn was synonymous with newspapers. However, the Iraqi invasion of Kuwait in 1991, which led to the first Gulf War between America and Iraq, gave birth to the cable television network, and became a springboard for the Cable News Network (CNN) founded by Ted Turner of the Media Corporation. This was followed with the advent of the Internet, which has virtually revolutionized the scope and the reach of the media across the globe.

In India, the Press played a crucial role during the freedom struggle. The role played by great statesmen like Bal Gangadhar Tilak, Mahatama Gandhi and Pandit Jawaharlal Nehru is unparalleled, thanks to the zeal with which they devoted to their respective newspapers - Kesari,

Harijan and National Herald. They succeeded despite the repeated efforts made by the British regime to curb their writings by charging and then sentencing them in one sedition case after another.

The imposition of an eighteen-month emergency in the mid-eighties curtailed freedom of expression with censorship measures adopted by the then Union government. However, it was this emergency which led to the birth of various news magazines like India Today, Sunday, Onlooker, etc. and which in turn gave a stiff competition to the daily newspapers. They profited by printing analytical reports, based on first hand information gathered by their correspondents in the field.

Previously, many of the newspapers used to depend on the wire services like PTI, UNI, Samachar, etc. for culling the news due to the financial constraints and had limited access to the information. It would not be an exaggeration to say that the emergency turned out to be a blessing in disguise for the printed media in the country, as it definitely helped them to reshape the definition of 'investigative journalism' in the post emergency era.

In 1978, the then Government introduced 'The Press Council Act - 1978' to 'preserve the freedom of the press and also for maintaining and improving the standards of newspapers and news agencies in India'. This Act has to some extent helped the Press to be more transparent and also simultaneously be accountable. What is a little astonishing is the fact that even after the infusion of electronic media, i.e. cable channels and internet, the government has not made any effort to enlarge the scope of the Act, so as to include these two new modes of communications within its ambit. It would not be out of place to mention here that the Press Council has no punitive powers and therefore sometimes it is not taken seriously, as the strictures passed by it have little bearing on the editor, reporter, printer and publisher of the newspaper. One feels it is an exercise in futility.

In early eighties, a revelation made by Sunday magazine published by Anand Bazar Patrika from Kolkata with a front page story of the blinding of prisoners in Bhagalpur Jail had virtually rocked the entire nation when copies were waved in parliament. This was the first major case of human rights violations ever to have been reported in the media, and which threw light on the alarming state of affairs in the jail. Thereafter in mid eighties, Sheela Barse's investigative story on the condition of exploitation and abuse of female inmates of Arthur Road Jail in Mumbai, also in Sunday, resulted in an enquiry into the condition of prisons all over Maharashtra.

The printed media has played a significant role during the last twenty-five years or so in reporting the violation of human rights. However, of late the printed media has been receiving stiff competition from television with the advent of news channels such as Star News, Zee TV and Aaj Tak were thrown to air. This healthy competition between print and electronic media has compelled them to carve out a new kind of readership and/or viewership in other areas such as fashion, cuisine, health care, real estate, environment, sports etc. While defending the latest trends, the media say, "we cater for the demands of our readers and viewers".

Modernization of Media

But one fears that in the entire modernization and revolution process of the Indian media, human rights might take a back seat. This fear is further compounded due to the constant changes in the global economic pattern, which began with the introduction of the WTO six years ago. The recently concluded US-led war on Iraq is also going to change the financial and economic equations around the globe, in which 'human survival' might assume more importance than 'respect for the human rights'.

Although the concept of 'human rights' came into existence way back in 1948 with the UN's Universal Declaration to that effect, in India the National Human Rights Commission Came into existence forty-five years later, in 1993, with 'The Protection of Human Rights Act - 1993'. The State Human Rights Commission has came into existence barely two years ago and is still in the embryonic stage. One might wonder why the enactment of a nationwide law was delayed for 45 years? Well, no such necessity was felt as many of the Articles of the Universal Declaration of Human Rights have already found place in the Fundamental Rights enshrined in our Constitution.

The Indian Constitution is one of the classical documents of its kind and has been drafted in such a systematic and simplified manner that is easy to understand, even for a layman. This speaks the volumes for the vision and energy of Dr. Babasaheb Ambedkar whose efforts in the making of the Indian Constitution were quite gigantic. However, when it comes to the reporting of the human rights-related incidents, the newspapers devote very little space to them, unless the incidents it self is a very newsworthy and has national importance. Newspapers seldom make a serious effort to follow up such stories, which they report with a greater zeal in the beginning.

It is regrettable to note that in none of the educational institutes, colleges or universities in which journalism courses are conducted do topics like the Indian Constitution or human rights find any place. The apathy of these institutes towards these issues is to be deplored. A journalism student, aiming to become a reporter or a correspondent with a newspaper or a cable TV news network must know precisely that it is 'Freedom of Expression' under Article 19 of the Constitution of India which empowers him to express his views without any fear or favour according to his conscience.

Although the concept of fundamental rights under our constitution and human rights are quite synonymous, the reporting on the violation of human rights is a little difficult. A bare minimum knowledge of criminal justice system is essential to a reporter, if he or she wishes to report on human rights. At present, very few newspapers have reporters who are exclusively covering the legal beat. Frequently, the crime reporter who interacts with the police department is asked to cover the court reporting as well. Here again, there is a catch. Very few, indeed no, crime reporters are law graduates. Law graduates can earn more money by entering the legal profession.

It is a common belief that the violation of human rights takes place only at police stations or in prison. This is true to some extent. But there are other areas too, like railways, environment, health care, education, development, employment, etc., where the violation of human rights do take place but it is seldom reported.

The violation of human rights, no matter in which sphere of life they occur, essentially takes place because 'human values' are not recognized in the first place. The importance of the human rights needs to be taught from the primary level in schools, when children are the right age to absorb them. Police are often accused of violating human rights, but sadly, no effort is made by the home department to include the subject in the curriculum of police training academies. Here lies an opportunity to train policemen about the importance of respecting and observing human rights and the consequences of the breaching them.

The media can play a pivotal role by way of building up public opinion, and also by impressing on the government the need to incorporate the subject of human rights, both in schools and also in police training academies, and also in the training institutes for municipal councils, corporations and other revenue departments.

It is the duty of the government to provide its citizens with unpolluted air. But, if the local authority is going to give building construction permission in a 'green zone' or for the construction of a chemical plant in the area nearby to residential locality, then it would definitely be a violation of human rights. The de-reservation of plots for housing projects in metropolis is a huge scam, taking place with utter disregard to the human rights, but it is seldom reported in the media.

Ad-revenue

It is a common experience, at least in the big cities like Mumbai and Pune, that matters relating to de-reservation of plots by the builders, or the violation of environmental norms by the companies are rarely reported, as the reporting about their misdemeanors might deprive the newspapers of potential advertisements. The print media these days is undergoing lots of changes, thanks to the challenges thrown up by the electronic media. Time was when the editor was 'The Boss' of the newspaper and it was he who used to call the shots with the management. Now a newspaper is treated like any other manufacturing product, with the marketing (also known as 'Response') department at the helm of affairs. The editor is being reduced to a 'hired labourer', working purely on a contract basis.

Such a sea change in the attitude of the management of some of the newspapers means that they are unlikely to antagonize the government by reporting stories relating to the violation of human rights, lest these stories rob them of the advertisements issued by the Directorate of Audio and Visual Publicity (DAVP). This is a dangerous trend from the human rights activists' point of view.

Freedom of expression is enshrined in the Constitution of India as a fundamental right under Part III of the Constitution. Nevertheless, there has been a hierarchy of values and a gradation to these rights. The right to property, for instance is considered to be the weakest of these rights and is, at present, only a legal right- not a fundamental right. Even though freedom of expression is a fundamental right, with the passage of time, through several amendments a number of restrictions have been placed on the exercise of this right which have narrowed down their scope considerably.

Intimately associated with the freedom of expression is the idea of Human Rights - the basic right of every human being, irrespective of colour, race, gender or status, to live with dignity which means the right to food, clothing, shelter, primary health and education. It also means the right to practice (or not to) religion and the right to dissent. In recent years in India, dissenters have been persecuted and threatened, and in a few cases even physically eliminated. Dissenters who questioned beliefs, especially what were considered accepted practices, were the ones who faced the ire of the intolerant.

As in the case of the Hindus. In Hinduism there is flexibility at the philosophical level but not at the sociological level where one confronts the caste system. Even today, the caste system is so rigid that many who break caste rules are punished by what are known as the caste or jaati panchayats. At the religious level, we witness the re-emergence of the cultural police who have no hesitation in issuing fatwas against dissenters.

Despite freedom of expression being a fundamental right its unfettered exercise was scuttled even in the days of Jawaharlal Nehru. Even then there was always some form of censorship for the benefit of the rulers. For example, Mr. A. D. Gorwala's column in The Times of India written under the pseudonym "Vivek" was discontinued at Nehru's insistence for it was too critical of him. And no other newspaper was ready to publish Mr. Gorwala's column. This compelled Mr. Gorwala to start his own small weekly which he named Opinion to publicise his views and his right to free expression. The situation got worse over the years and during the (so-called) Emergency of 1975-1977 these freedoms were suspended.

A new phenomenon that has developed menacing proportions in recent years is what can be described as cultural policing not only by the party in power but by communal or non- secular parties who decide what is good or bad for our culture. Fortunately, the judiciary has been a source of protection of freedom of expression. In India, there has been only one case where the Supreme Court banned a book on the ground of obscenity and that was D. H. Lawerence's Lady Chatterly's Lover. In most cases pornographic books and movies, though they attract legal action under obscenity laws, generally die a natural death. A case in point is the blue films that were screened at a couple of theatres in Bombay. People got tired and ultimately the theatre had to stop screening such films not because of any legal or police action but simply because of the operation of the law of demand and supply.

The hurting of religious sensibilities is something that every group alleges when someone says or writes on a religious theme that is not to the liking of the religious group concerned. Unfortunately, those who claim their religious freedom has been affected generally take to the streets. This stifles freedom of expression. On the ground of protecting religious susceptibilities banning of books has become a passion with India's rulers of all hues. Books are banned without reading them, like the Satanic Verses. In fact, India has the dubious distinction of banning this book even before the Islamic countries did so.

Pradip Dalvi's play Godse was banned on the ground that it hurt the image of Mahatma Gandhi and justified his assassination. Such censorship is detrimental to the healthy growth of civil society. Even the Mahatma would himself have opposed the ban on the Godse play. The destruction of works of art (the most recent case being the paintings of M. F. Hussain) is also a clear sign of growing intolerance. In a democracy there are civilised ways of expressing one's dissent.

On the other hand, the sensible way in which certain Dalit writers like Namdeo Dhasal reacted to Mr. Arun Shourie's book on B. R. Ambedkar is a salutary example of democratic dissent. They opposed the banning of the book as it would go against their earlier stand when they opposed a demand made by caste Hindus for a ban on Dr. B. R. Ambedkar's Riddles of Hinduism. Riddles of Hinduism is a chapter in the Complete Works of Dr. Ambedkar published by the Government of Maharashtra. Liberals need to applaud the stand of the Dalit writers for their mature response to a provocative book by Mr. Arun Shourie.

The audio-visual media, especially television and the cinema are showing a growing number of films depicting violence some of which are extremely gory. Though it is not easy to establish a direct correlation between cinema, TV viewing and violence, there can be no denying that such depiction have had ill effects on the immature, adolescent, the unemployed or school dropouts. This has, for example, been responsible according to some for the "Shahrukh Khan phenomeno" where disappointed lovers kill girls who do not reciprocate their love, leaving an already marginalised group like women in a more dangerous public space. A film hero doing such things gets a sort of legitimacy among some sections of the public.

The writing of history books has been another major problem where the group, for the time being in power, seeks to inject its views, like under Congress rule, the Nehru-Gandhi dynasty sought to marginalise all other leaders including the Mahatma's role in the freedom movement. Even in the regional writings of history, the local heroes are exaggerated to look bigger and greater than they really were. This has led to the creation of sacred cows who cannot be touched. There is therefore need to draw the line between learned research and licence.

The recent spurt of celebrating festivals in public, disrupting traffic by erecting pandals on public thoroughfares has intruded into the freedom of expression of citizens who do not wish to participate in such festivals. This has led to the hardship of ordinary citizens who use these roads. But the politicisation of these festivals has led to greater problems. Initially it started, more as a weapon during the freedom movement, with a 10-day Ganpati festival. This festival was largely confined to Maharashtra. But in recent years it has spread to other cities and towns outside Maharashtra. Durga Puja, a 10-day festival in Bengal, equivalent of the Ganpati festival in Maharashtra is now assuming the same importance and duration in Bombay.

One would have understood it if this arose from religious fervour. But there is increasing evidence that these festivals are promoted by the politically powerful. For almost a month each year public thoroughfares are at their disposal, not to speak of a variety of gangsters and thugs who patronise these festivals who spend crores of rupees in building plaster of paris and thermocole replicas of well-known monuments and temples. The right to dissent here is not accepted and there is fear of physical retaliation for those who dare to protest; contributions are forced, film songs which are far removed from prayer not only rob the occasion of its solemnity but the loud music goes on round the clock taking the decibel level to an unbearable pitch. Thus the right of dissent is swept away by giving in to a false illusion of a majority that does not exist.

The national obsession with secrecy to hide uncomfortable facts is a blot on our democracy. In India this idea of the right to know is closely connected to the freedom of the Press which calls itself the "fourth estate". Till very recently the electronic media was controlled by the state and the newspapers were considered the only free agents. But are they really free? Are they not controlled by caste interests, joint families or joint stock companies. It is the print press that has unearthed a lot and has played the role of the opposition. But they do not have any more rights than ordinary citizens. There have been instances when this right has been misused as a weapon to intimidate the famous where it has degraded to licence and mudslinging. This is no freedom, for freedom entails responsibility which has to be exercised with self restraint and for a social purpose.

At the same time, this has led to public offices and institutions becoming more transparent and accountable to the public whose money they spend. Citizens groups in Rajasthan have organised protest against the reluctance of officials to part with information and have insisted that they have a right to know how much has been spent on building a bridge, for example. In fact, audit reports once placed on the floor of the House are public documents, but one sees a desperate bureaucracy trying to keep them away from public scrutiny. To begin with, at least all economic documents can be made public for there are no secrets in it that affect state security.

With the explosion of technology and the beginning of the information age, the concept of national sovereignty will soon become redundant because no country can control the flow of information on the internet. Then there is the Right to Privacy which should be harmoniously blended with the Right to Know. How justified was the media in prying into the private lives of Princess Diana and President Clinton? Wasn't the Starr Report a waste of public money where the private sexual exploits of two consenting adults disturbed the fabric of American society and almost wrecked the Presidency.

Freedom of Expression constitutes one of the central principles of liberalism. The Indian Constitution - largely liberal in spirit - recognised this inasmuch as "liberty of thought, expression, belief, faith and worship" figures in its admirable preamble. Freedom of Expression is also recognised universally as a Human Right - a basic right of every human being, irrespective of colour, race, gender or status. Since the promulgation of the Indian Constitution, the Right to Freedom of Expression has been under siege, both by the state and certain groups in our society. The First Amendment narrowed the ambit of this freedom. In the last fifty years, this freedom - which should have evolved into a larger one - has been more narrowly defined to reduce spaces where freedom can be exercised.

Further, in the last few years, greater, and perhaps even dangerous death threats have emanated from extreme groups or parties which have become self-appointed guardians of "morality" in the country. It is they who want to enforce what people can or cannot read, which film or play to be censored or which performer can or cannot appear on stage; or what an artist can portray. In a free society which boasts of democracy, it is the Constitution that should be the supreme law, not fatwas or edicts issued by cultural vigilantes.

The destruction of works of art or the banning or burning of books is a clear sign of growing intolerance. In a liberal democratic state, even while such acts should be curbed with an iron hand, there is need to educate people on forms of protest that are consonant with a liberal society. There is a genuine concern, with the growing trend in films made for the cinema and TV to depict violence and scenes of rape in a revolting manner. But even here, it is not for the State to interfere. It is the media itself which needs to institute self- regulatory mechanism to check this undesirable trend perhaps on the lines of the Press Council.

Threats to freedom of expression appear not only against the media or against widely known authors or artists. There are also growing threats to academic freedom and this is evident particularly in the writing of history. There is an increasing trend encouraged and promoted by fundamentalist and ideologically motivated groups to "invent" pasts which glorify exclusively and exaggeratedly their own specific traditions. This abuse of scholarship and distortion of history needs to be resisted.

Freedom of the press - a bastion of a liberal and democratic society - too has been under constant threats and pressures, not only from the State, but from extremists who do not hesitate even to use violence to silence journalists who do not share their beliefs. There is need to develop appropriate measures to protect the privacy of the individual particularly in the context of the intrusive powers of modern communications technology. There is need, further, to inquire into and modify laws relating to the privileges of legislators which have often tended to curb the freedom of the press to report and inform their readers.

In addition, the Courts too have not been always helpful, as they could be, in safeguarding the rights of the press. The frequent use of "stay orders" have tended to limit the freedom of the press to inform their readers. The Right to Know is a corollary to the Right to free expression. In a liberal state, citizens can exercise their Rights meaningfully only if they are also adequately informed. An informed citizenry is a pre-condition of responsible citizenship. The Right to Know, however, has acquired significance and relevance in our society, only recently. It is not unsurprising for governments - even the democratically elected ones - to hide uncomfortable facts from the people.

The need to safeguard the country's security interests is often the excuse advanced to withhold information. Under the blanket term "state security", numerous acts of omission and commission are hidden from public scrutiny. Liberals should support any legislation which seeks to empower citizens with the Right to Know, particularly in the areas where large financial outlays have been made. In a liberal society, acts of governments should be both transparent and accountable.

Censorship

Censorship is the use of state or group power to control freedom of expression. Censorship 'criminalizes' certain actions or the communication of such actions - or suggested communications of such actions. In a modern sense censorship consists of any attempt to suppress information, points of view, or method of expression such as art, or profanity. The purpose of censorship is to maintain the status quo, to control the development of a society, or to stifle political dissent among a subject people. For this reason, censorship is commonly used by social groups, organized religions, corporations and governments. However, there are also numerous groups which oppose censorship.

Types of censorship

Censorship can be explicit, as in laws passed to prevent information being published or propagated (as in Australia, China, or Saudi Arabia where certain Internet pages are not permitted entry), or it can be implicit, taking the form of intimidation by government or even by popular censure, where people are afraid to express or support certain opinions for fear of losing their lives, or their jobs, position in society, or in academia, their academic credibility. In this latter form it is similar to McCarthyism. These two forms (explicit and implicit) can be generalized to represent laws and government authority (explicit) and social forces or social persuasion (implicit).

State Secrets

Wartime censorship is carried out with the intention of preventing the release of information that might be advantageous to the enemy. Typically it involves obfuscation of times or locations, or delaying the release of information (e.g. the objective of an operation) until it is of no possible use to enemy forces. Mention of weapons and equipment (especially if newly introduced) is another favourite area for censorship. The moral issues here are somewhat different as release of the information carries a high risk of increased casualties among one's own forces and possibly loss of the overall conflict.

Implementation

Censorship is regarded as a typical feature of dictatorships and other authoritarian political systems. Democratic nations usually have far less institutionalized censorship, and instead tout the importance of freedom of speech. Some thinkers understand censorship to include other attempts to suppress points of view or ideas such as negative propaganda, media manipulation, spin, disinformation or "free speech zones" (ghettoizing or containing speech). These methods, collectively, tend to work by disseminating misleading information or by preventing other ideas from obtaining a receptive audience.

Others point out the suppression of access to the means of dissemination of ideas by governmental bodies such as the FCC in the United States of America, the CRTC in Canada, or by a newspaper that refuses to run commentary the publisher disagrees with, or a lecture hall that refuses to rent itself out to a particular speaker. Thinkers such as philosopher and novelist Ayn Rand consider this latter form of censorship to be an acceptable outcome of the defense of property rights. Contradictions of her position emerge from her disapproval of state backed monopoly license in the arena of radio and telecommunication broadcast and state funding of the arts.

Prevention and bypassing

Data havens and decentralized peer-to-peer file sharing systems such as Freenet can be used to prevent censorship. A recent phenomenom for avoiding censorship and speaking directly to members of society is Culture Jamming, where individuals or non-conforming groups use large-scale corporate techniques to attack implicit domination and censorship through trivial or deliberately irrelevant messages. More traditionally, mass protests are a method for resisting unwanted impositions.

2
Media and Social Responsibilities

In a single day the average human eye consumes hundreds of images and advertisments for various products. This overwheming amount of media in society cannot be ignored and has a large effect on those surrounded by it. The media can, in some ways, be seen as detremental to society due to the stereotypes it displays. Certain body images are favored in ads which are many times superimposed and not necessarily reachable, causing many people to attempt to fit a "norm" regulated that is simply false.

Though every piece of space in this city is dominated by images, companies using famous scantily-clad celebrities to sell their product which most of the time has nothing to do with the item itself. Media is increasingly becoming a sex-driven industry based on people's consumption of skin. There is an ever thinning line between media and pornography, in a few years people may be using ads in magazines to satisfy their sexual urges rather than Playboy. Media has proven that in society, sex does sell.

We do watch TV as well as walk down the streets of the city and therefore a consumer of the media. The media affects us largely because we see it as a reflection of a society which we are a part of. People are driven to act certain ways due to the media and while we make an effort not to conform to it there doesn't seem to be any alternatives other than gudging one's eyes out. An attempt towards the rectification of the rot that has set in the social and national life of the country is being made, with great enthusiasm, through judicial activism. However judicial activism alone does not suffice for the rectification of this all-pervading malaise. What is urgently needed is the support of other social agencies/institutions. A very important role in this matter can be played by media activism, the topic under discussion today.

It is undoubtedly true that the position of media or journalism is not that of a mission but of a commercial industry. The truth of the matter, however, is that our present journalism is used to presenting only half side of the picture. This is the root cause of all our problems. In view of the present circumstances media activism would amount to present a balanced reporting of the situation abandoning the present policy of selective reporting. The principle of modern journalism can be understood from this saying:"When a dog bites a an it is no news, but when a man bites a dog, it is news".

One practical example of this method is provided by our present journalism which is constantly engaged in giving maximum coverage to any hot news created by an unruly section of Muslims. If the percentage of hot news forms only one percent the percentage of soft news is not less than 99 percent. But the reader of the newspapers are totally in the dark about this 99 percent of the picture. Whereas the one percent is being repeated again and again. Similarly if an extremist Hindu creates a hot news, this will find a place in all the newspapers the next day. Whereas even in the Hindu world there is 99 per cent soft news while hot news forms not more than one percent.

As a result of this one sided study unreal opinion is formed by both the communities regarding one another. Taking extreme forms this unreal opinion at times turns into communal riots. The selective reporting of this nature remains a permanent obstacle to the path of national integration. For the rectification of this state of affairs a powerful journalists organization-as we already have formed for our rights-based on the principles of social responsibilities is required for the rectification of this state of affairs.

Globalization and Media

The "clash of civilizations" seems to have been exacerbated in the aftermath of the September 11, 2001 and more recently, the March 11, 2004 tragedies. New flare-ups of conflict and atrocities in Iraq and the Middle East also seem to demonstrate that divisiveness among peoples with different religions, cultures and political systems has become more pronounced. At the same time, we have seen evidence that globalization has boosted the forces of cohesion in many parts of the world and fields of endeavors. For example, the dramatic expansion of the European Union has proven that people from disparate cultures and traditions do yearn for universal values out of the belief that the well-being and ideals of a tightly-knit community of nations can be enhanced through a "win win" formula of measured, meaningful integration - and not necessarily at the expense of diversity.

It is too early to say that advances in the media and mass communication in the age of the Internet will help in accentuating the positive, centripetal aspects of globalization. That the gory images of war and summary executions could spread across the globe in nano-seconds could serve to more speedily and efficiently instigate hatred and extremism. However, it is the shared responsibility of media professionals in different parts of the world to use their ever-more powerful tools to inculcate the values of tolerance and empathy - and to render unacceptable bigotry and ultra-radical solutions to cultural and historical contradictions.

In helping to cement global values, the media could perhaps begin in fields that do not have a direct bearing on ideology. These include the fight against trans-national crime such as drug trafficking and the smuggling of human beings; child labor and degrading workplace conditions; AIDS, SARS and other epidemics hitting both rich and poor countries; and environmental, conservation and energy issues such as global warming and the worldwide shortage of resources from petroleum to drinking water. Seeing is believing. While government departments and institutions may be prevented by ingrained traditions and bureaucratic inertia from seeing and thinking out of the box, the ubiquitous and seemingly unstoppable reach of the Net - and global TV networks and news agencies - is having a strong impact on the behavior of ordinary people.

With the growing importance of the civil society particularly in Asian countries - and the fast-expanding clout of international and local-level NGOs - the media has a big role to play in spotlighting conflicts and malaises all over the world. Less constrained by the ideology and national-security calculations of their respective governments, people-level organizations including NGOs are in a position to bridge the East-West gap - in addition to taking part in relief work regarding global hunger, AIDS, water shortage, and other scourges. The media, however, has to show the way by providing unbiased coverage and well-balanced analyses.

In the past year, major media in the U.S. have been criticized for giving too much benefit of the doubt to the White House's justification for invading Iraq. The controversy over the "pro-government bias" of important American networks, websites and newspapers has been highlighted by the fact that these media units have a global reach unparalleled to any time in history. Many small towns and villages in Asia and Africa - at least those with electricity supply - get thhcv5eir news, particularly foreign news, primarily from Western TV and news agencies. And it is incumbent upon these transnational media behemoths - which more often than not take Western or American values as the autonomic global standard - to ensure objectivity and multiplicity of perspectives.

Otherwise, charges of "media imperialism" - which are at time justified - may impede the benevolent role that a globalized media could play in a deeply polarized world. Coverage of the global anti-terrorist movement - particularly the wars in Afghanistan and Iraq, which are destined to be defining moments of the 21 st century - has been enlivened and in a sense improved by a number of media upstarts in the Arab world. The emergence of Al Jazeera and other Arab media has done much to provide alternative voices and balanced coverage regarding a plethora of convoluted, multi-faceted cultural and military confrontations.

But bankrolling a new TV station, newspaper or news agency is a horrendous business proposition. The start-up of a regional or multinational media company - which must maintain expensive bureaus in at least several cities - is contingent upon huge investments from entrepreneurs with a globalized vision. This is true even in First World countries such as the U.S. The humble and somewhat haphazard beginnings of CNN showed the immensity of problems of finance, advertising and distribution. Since the early 1990s, various attempts to set up a "Chinese CNN" in the Greater China region have proven unsuccessful. This is despite the perception that there should to be enough potential in terms of advertising and subscription fees in China's 1.3 billion people market alone.

Moreover, China-towns all over the world are hungry for Chinese-angled but otherwise unbiased news coverage. On the other hand, modest successes have been achieved by quite a number of news services and agencies based in countries and cities including China, Hong Kong, India, Japan, and Russia that have user-friendly English versions. It is hoped that English-speaking countries in other parts of the world would use more of these news purveyors to help lay the groundwork for a multi-polar global media order.

The worldwide successes that have been scored by the Asian movie industry - whether it be Bollywood and South Korean dramas, Chinese kung-fu, Hong Kong action flicks or Japanese art-house and samurai offerings - show that the gap between East and West can somehow be bridged at specific junctures. Despite the tendency by many professionals to mix information with entertainment, however, the news media is a distinctly different, and more difficult-to-popularize genre. Yet perhaps more than film and other art forms, the cross-pollination of Asian and Western news services, values and operations could have a salient impact on the future of globalization, particularly the fostering of universal humanitarian values.

Shared Responsibilities

Electronic and print media around the world have a shared

responsibility to introduce to their respective audiences news and viewpoints that dovetail with the ethos of openness and affirmation of diversity. In this age of information and globalization, old norms such as censorship and bigotry are out of sync with an increasingly well-educated and discerning public. However, many Asian nations, including those that have acceded to the World Trade Organization (WTO), still put up formidable obstacles to foreign news media entering their markets.

In the name of banning pornography and political infiltration, quite a few governments have employed thousand upon thousand of Cyber-cops to police the information superhighway. While such market and political barriers may in the short term help to protect local industry and indigenous culture, visionary leaders at the relevant ministries of information, media and culture should take the long-term view: that only when their fellow countrymen have uninhibited access to information and perspectives on a globalized setting can they develop into mature, tolerant, and intellectually sophisticated world citizens.

Take China as an example. The new administration of President Hu Jintao and Premier Wen Jiabao has sent encouraging signals about their commitment to transparency of governance, media openness and even the "media supervision of the government." While most electronic and print media are still run by or affiliated with the authorities, there has been a welcome proliferation of angles and viewpoints. In line with China's WTO obligations, party and government officials are slowly but surely opening the door to joint venture and even wholly foreign-owned media and cultural corporations particularly in the areas of marketing and distribution. While Beijing needs to consider more thorough-going reforms such as scaling back censorship and allowing joint-venture news operations, the limited but positive developments in the globalization of the Chinese media have already helped produce a new generation of professionals and entrepreneurs with an international, forward-looking outlook.

In other large Asian countries such as India, the influx of foreign capital and know-how in the field of news media and information dissemination has also produced more good than harm, both for economic development and the nurturing of a new generation of world citizens. It is hoped that with more East-West cross-fertilizations - particularly Asian TV networks, websites and newspapers finding niches and audiences in the Western world - the goal of a globalized media fostering common values of symbiotic growth and mutual tolerance may be realized close to the first-quarter mark of the new century.

Journalism, Business and Ethics

Although the individual journalist is an essential unit of ethical agency, he or she doesn't operate in a vacuum. Most journalists are employees and, increasingly, employees of large companies or corporations the primary aim of which is to maximise the return to shareholders. While journalists are ultimately responsible as individuals, it is as individuals in a setting where their powers and duties are at least in part defined by their role in the corporate organisation, and many, perhaps most, of the ethical dilemmas journalists face begin with the inherent conflict between the individual's role as a journalist and his or her employer's quest for profit.

In its crudest form this conflict manifests itself in a desperate quest for ratings and circulation on the part of particular media organisations, and in this form the effects are often apparent to even the most casual observer because of the excessive zeal frequently displayed by reporters in the pursuit of news and current affairs, with all that this entails for ethical deliberation and sensitivity. In journalism generally, however, the pressures provoked by this conflict usually work in more subtle ways. Thus editors and reporters may come under pressure from senior management to be more 'reader friendly' in order to maximise ratings and circulation by, for example, taking steps to:

> increase advertising and subscription rates, to introduce cosmetic alterations of page design and makeup to give the impression of modernity, and to quietly reduce the amount of serious news.

Such pressures are generally at their most intense following corporate takeovers. When such takeovers occur, it is not unusual for journalists to be faced with retrenchments and for there to be declining support for more expensive approaches to news-gathering such as investigative reporting, greater use of material from 'sister' outlets, a proliferation of lighter stories about lifestyle, entertainment, celebrities and so on, and a greater preparedness to use material provided through public and corporate relations.

Corporate takeovers generally have major ethical implications for journalism, not least because they challenge the underlying ethical justification for journalism. These implications, which have been traced elsewhere are no less real in Australian journalism than elsewhere. As has been widely noted, the level of concentration of ownership of Australia's media is higher than in most other countries. As a result, many would argue, the corporate pressures on Australian journalists are correspondingly higher than in most other countries. And as a result of this most Australian journalists are employed in situations in which, as prominent journalist and former editor Michelle Grattan has observed:

> The bottom line has become hungrier and hungrier, and more and more the imperative by which performance, including the performance of editors, is judged.

Symptomatic of this is the recent observation by a senior media executive in Sydney that:

> In terms of content, there is no doubt that the consumer is more promiscuous than ever before, and that the only way to ensure that your relationship with him or her is more than a one night stand is to make the experience compelling. If all we do is report the news fairly and accurately, we haven't got a chance.

It is hardly surprising, then, that in recent years Australian journalism has been marked by the rise of what The Australian newspaper's Paul Kelly has called 'the international show business trend'. Indeed, a national study by the Australian Broadcasting Authority in 2001 found, in part, that the responses of news producers were dominated by the pressure of ratings and circulation, 'reflecting the commercial imperative of modern news production', and that many news producers were 'eager to give audiences what market research tells them they want'.

The ethical implications arising from this situation are considerable. They begin with what prominent Australian editor and journalist Max Walsh has called 'the perennial journalistic weakness of self-censorship...which suggests that red-blooded, socially aware, concerned young men [sic] who join newspapers quickly learn to survive, but in order to survive they must toe the editorial line'. In Australia:

> The dearth of alternative employers, the propensity to rationalise one's actions when preservation demands, and the excessive zeal of lieutenants are a combination potent enough to ensure plenty of self-censorship by journalists.

This effect strongly encourages journalists to internalise the values of the news organisation which employs them, and to become conditioned into particular institutional conventions. The result can be a form of timidity, meaning that certain issues or views or situations that rest uneasily with the corporate line will not be reported or exposed or aired. At the same time, many news outlets are encouraged by their corporate owners to give the greatest priority to finding and holding audiences which possess the qualities considered most desirable by advertisers in terms of levels of disposable income, education, occupation, age and spending habits.

While this might be entirely justifiable in terms of business practice and the need to maximise profit, it is much more difficult to defend on ethical grounds because there are obvious losers from such an approach - the less well-off sections of society whose information needs and desires become understated or ignored altogether. In this competitive corporate world, additional pressures on media outlets - and, through them, individual journalists - arise because the demand for news appears to be waning in major markets around the world. For the individual journalist, the net effect is that pressure to be 'first with the news' and to get the story with the greatest audience impact is greater than ever. The ethical consequences of this situation can be considerable, for there is no shortage of evidence to demonstrate that:

> the fiercer the battle for circulation the greater the commercial pressures on editors to erode journalistic standards on matters of truth, accuracy and ethical acceptability.

The corporatisation of the newsroom and the corresponding extension of influence of corporate pressures on journalists raise other ethical questions. Media companies have often demanded special favours because of their power over public information, and there can also arise considerable pressure for using a corporation's media outlets to promote, or at least cover in a positive light, the operations of other sections within the corporation.

Underlying such issues is the fundamental question of how media organisations can provide information and analysis of the forces of corporatism when they are themselves an integral part of those forces. There appears to be an inherent conflict of interest involved, yet there is no acknowledgment of it, no reference to it, in any of the journalistic codes of ethics or practice. Indeed, most codes emphasise individual responsibility and in so doing consistently fail to acknowledge the existence of this conflict. For example, many codes call on journalists to resist pressures from advertisers, thereby making the individual journalist responsible for withstanding such pressures when, generally, most of the power to stand up to advertisers lies with senior management.

In ethical terms, it is the audience which is the real loser from this situation. Most newspapers and broadcast news and current affairs programs claim to tell their readers, viewers and listeners 'what is going on' and, indeed, news and current affairs are one of the major external sources of information and opinion formation for most people. These people are ethically entitled to be able to rely on the accuracy and fairness of this information. Yet the forces of corporatism outlined above are working to erode the validity of such expectations. Further, these corporations are quite prepared to use the rhetoric of press freedom and the Fourth Estate as a bulwark against attempts at regulation, even when those attempts are grounded in the notion of accountability.

Australian media organisations have achieved a certain notoriety by calling for accountability and transparency from others while at the same time failing to be accountable and transparent themselves. Through such behaviour, the forces of corporatism are eroding journalism's claims, advanced under the umbrella of social responsibility theory, to service the political system by providing information, discussion and debate on public affairs; enlighten the public so as to make it capable of self-government; and safeguard the rights of the individual by serving as a watchdog against government.

At a theoretical level, one of the major weaknesses in many analyses of journalism ethics is the failure to accommodate the realities of corporatism. While many acknowledge that there are problems arising from management and ownership pressures, much of the literature places the onus for ethical behaviour squarely on the shoulders of the individual journalist and takes it no further. What appears to be needed is a coherent theoretical framework which facilitates incisive analysis of the interface between the practitioners in the field and the corporate forces which affect so many of them.

In order to develop such a theoretical approach, we could do worse than consider the offerings from other fields. One possibility is military ethics. After all, it could be argued that the central ethical dilemma of the individual journalist caught at the boundary of corporate responsibility is analogous to the individual soldier caught at the boundary of the evil military act. There are many differences between the positions of journalist and soldier. The journalist's role and the justifications for this role are substantially different from the role and justifications for soldiering, even - perhaps especially - in times of war. Journalism's chains of command are less structured; and most journalists have far more autonomy in given ethical situations than the individual soldier.

A more appropriate field for investigation appears to be that of management in general and business ethics in particular. Admittedly, this is a somewhat disparate field - what one observer has described as 'an uneasy hybrid of science, mathematics, psychology, social history and economics'. Even the so-called father of management thinking, Peter Drucker, has stated that management is a liberal art rather than a science, and that: One problem is that it is afflicted by too many fads. We have been saying for many years that we are using the word 'guru' only because 'charlatan' is too long to fit into a headline.

One of these 'fads' is business ethics, a subject which has been taken increasingly seriously in recent years, partly because of the widespread view that, in the words of Australian business ethicist: Business is the most powerful influence in most people's lives, therefore we need to understand business ethics.

This area has yielded many useful concepts and some of these appear to have considerable relevance to journalism. One is the notion that, at any given moment in most major corporations, one can find a vast array of vocabularies of motive and accounts to explain, or excuse or justify,.expedient action. This is also the case in journalism, where the much-vaunted public right to know is only the best-known public justification. Another useful concept when considering journalism ethics in a corporate setting is the notion of corporate culture, which has been defined as: the sum of all the values within the organisation...arising from that organisation's history that ensures it has its own distinctive personality different to any other organisation.

A further concept from business and management which appears to be directly applicable to the news media is the notion of stakeholders, meaning individuals or groups of individuals affected by or able to affect the achievement of an organisation's objectives. Stakeholders commonly identified include shareholders, management, employees, customers, suppliers, communities and, sometimes, the environment. The notion of stakeholders provides an alternative model to the stockholder view of business, summarised in Milton Friedman's much-quoted statement that 'the business of business is business'. The stockholder view is, briefly, that returns to shareholders have absolute priority over all other considerations, with all that this implies for ethical standards.

In contrast, the stakeholder view accepts that others have interests and rights of comparable weight. While it is important to acknowledge the conceptual limits of stakeholder theory -there is, for example, a growing chorus that it is too blurred a concept to be of sufficient analytical use-the notion of stakeholders continues to be useful for identifying and organising the multitude of obligations that corporations have to different groups. For this reason, it appears to be useful in journalism. In media organisations the stakeholders include shareholders, management, employees (including journalists), readers, listeners and viewers, and also the wider community, although there is a considerable debate about what a 'community' is or might be and accordingly it remains a somewhat confused and confusing notion.

While the stakeholder view has the advantage of extending ethical consideration to all of those affected by a corporation's internal and external activities, it also raises a fundamental dilemma - how to balance the conflicting interests of different stakeholders? This dilemma is not less acute in journalism than elsewhere, because many if not most journalists are caught between conflicting allegiances to their proprietor, their newsroom managers, their colleagues, their sources, their audiences and those whose activities they are reporting. Most journalistic attempts to resolve this dilemma take into account the assumptions underlying social responsibility theory, itself echoed in the notion of corporate social responsibility.

The latter involves corporations accepting responsibilities that go beyond the purely economic and legal responsibilities of business firms and involves an acceptance of 'a commitment to the public good that outweighs short-term individual self-interests'. Corporate social responsibility means, in effect, that corporate leaders take steps to bring corporate behaviour up to a level 'where it is congruent with the prevailing social norms, values, and expectations of performance'. The debates which have taken place over the validity of the notion of social responsibility in journalism are echoed in business. For example, there appears to be some conflict and, indeed, confusion in the literature between descriptive and prescriptive interpretations of corporate social responsibility - the descriptive thesis suggests that as a matter of fact managers and corporations generally act in socially responsible ways while the prescriptive thesis claims that regardless of the reality, they ought to act in socially responsible ways.

Some sections of the Australian corporate world appear to have accepted that they have corporate social responsibilities and, indeed, there is a growing literature suggesting that 'good ethics is good for business' and that corporations which pursue an ethical approach can improve 'the bottom line', win the approval of shareholders, and defuse the potentially negative effects of the growing movement towards ethical investment. The converse of this is that poor ethics can be bad for business and there is considerable evidence to support this view. In Australia, an increased focus on corporate ethics has developed against a background of disquiet over the behaviour of public figures and institutions, from the corporate controversies of the 1980s to more recent scandals over, for example, the collapse of major insurance and dot.com companies.

Within the Australian media, the acknowledgement of corporate social responsibility and the acceptance of what it entails remain problematic. Indeed, sections of our media have been accused of being 'the last people to understand ethical obligations and the worst to deal with in terms of setting ethical standards'. Many other questions which have been raised in business ethics echo those which have been raised in journalism. Thus the complicated web of issues falling under the umbrella of "conflict of interest" and covering such matters as manager and employee relationships with clients and customers parallels the ethical issues which bedevil journalistic relations with sources.

Most journalists, for example, need to cultivate key informants to use as sources and, at times, come under pressure to present or not present their reports in certain ways in order to maintain a useful relationship with those informants. How they should manage those relationships - and how those relationships might be analysed - may well be assisted by examining the ways in which business ethicists have advised managers how to deal with particular categories of client and customer.

Then there are the issues which have been raised around the notion of obligation. According to Provis, managers encounter different sources of obligation and these different sources "pull us in different directions". Journalists and their editors also face many conflicting pressures, and journalism may well have something to learn from considering how others have analysed their obligations and attempted to manage them in an ethical manner. Yet another focus of business ethics which has obvious relevance to journalism is the range of ethical dilemmas associated with the forces of corruption and bribery, especially - but not only - in non-Western countries.

In management this tends to focus on such matters as the awarding of contracts and doing business generally, but in the world of journalism foreign correspondents and their editors, in particular, ask many similar questions. Then there is the issue of trust, which has emerged as a key issue in business and is surely just as central to the world of journalism. After all, how can journalists have credibility with audiences without their trust? Indeed, why should anyone trust the news media in the first place? One of the contradictions of our era is the way in which a widespread lack of trust of traditional institutions - including business and the media - seems to go hand in hand with a remarkable level of naïve trust in fringe cults, religions, get-rich-quick schemes and so on.

Journalism is at the centre of this contradiction, and we might well benefit from considering how others have approached it. For example, business ethicists appear to have some useful insights into such issues as the conditions which need to be met before one party will or should trust another; whether trust is static or dynamic; and whether trust can be repaired once it has been broken or betrayed. The underlying point is that, because issues of trust are as inextricably intertwined with contemporary journalism as they are with modern business, we appear to have something to learn from each other.

Finally, it is worth reminding ourselves that the underlying force which drives business ethics is the same basic question which underlies journalism ethics - why be ethical? Indeed, given that journalism is increasingly operating in a context which straddles both environments, the case for doing so appears to have become overwhelming.

3

Changing Role of the Press

In recent decades, we have moved through historic ages defined by advances in communication technology-from electronic to satellite to digital. These systems of mass communication have transformed the conduct of politics, business and human relations, although journalism media have adapted to technology at varying speeds. At the same time, journalism practice adjusts to the demands of different kinds of political systems. Democratization has changed the political landscape in different parts of the world, but it is not yet a universal reality.

Despite the uneven technological pace and the different political systems in which it operates, it is instructive to try and understand what these changes imply for the future of the press. One way of examining the issue is through the public's prism. Sometime in the last century, technology evolved a mass audience for news. Mass media opened up for the public unprecedented levels of access to information. Newer technology has also empowered ordinary people to seek and to search out the knowledge and information that they need.

As the mass audience has splintered into groups according to diverse needs and interests, information literate communities revise the importance of journalism in their lives. A public that can source its own information and news decentralizes the flow of communication. This raises questions about the role of the press in society as the primary source of information and knowledge and as the collective forum of public debate and discussion.

Functions of Press

Let's examine the functions of the press as exhibited through the history of democracy. An autonomous system of shared information has always been part of democracy. The direct democracy in Athens generated a direct form of journalism in the marketplace. This created a common reference for the different members of its free society. In Rome, the accounts of the Senate and other public and social events were posted in public places. In authoritarian societies, such communication disappeared, replaced by proclamations issued by monarchs and nobles who were in power. The American Founding Fathers saw the value of the newspapers of the day as a way by which members of society exchanged views and sustained a continuing dialogue about shared concerns.

The First Amendment in the Bill of Rights was designed to protect a small press of partisan newspapers. The founders of American democracy saw the exchange of opposing ideas as essential to their desired system of government. Thus, the American Constitution enshrined the protection of freedom of expression and press freedom from laws that would abridge such autonomy. James Carey describes journalism as reflecting an ongoing and continuing conversation, as "reflected speech" which connects disparate communities. The earliest publications arose from the talk in public places where transients and local people gathered," the coffee houses in England, or in pubs, or 'publick houses,' in America" where" bar owners, called publicans, hosted spirited conversations about information from travellers who often recorded what they had seen and heard in log books kept at the end of the bar."

As public conversation, dialogue or forum, the press provided an essential element for a free society to function, that common reference of ideas, insights, images, and information that allows its members to participate in public life, enabling them to be part of their own governance. Studies trace the beginning of modern journalism to the 1830s when the daily newspapers gained mass circulation, supported by commercial advertising and operated for profit by their owners. These papers addressed themselves to human curiosity, the need to know and to reach out to the vast horizon of human realities beyond their own experience. The 'penny press' sold on the streets relied on stories which stood out of the ordinary even as these relied on a staple of sources, mostly about people who were already known and events or incidents that were presumed to be interesting. These demonstrated the press' bias for conflict and for bad news, which are possessed of obvious popular appeal.

The first publications included political debates and arguments, tidbits of gossip and other useful information such as shipping news. Even in these earliest forms, the journalistic package was a mixed one, designed perhaps to appeal to different kinds of people and to address diverse needs. But its political character and importance was ingrained in the practice remained. The 'news of the day' summed up the most significant events and developments, the issues of importance as well as selected stories of wide interest. In this way, the press educated the public as citizens, people with the freedom and capacity to establish the rules and principles that governed public life. The editorial decisions about what news to put out placed the press in a critical role of 'gatekeeper,' determining for the rest the information and news of the day.

The press' political dimension finds dramatic expression in the role of 'watchdog,' referring to the way journalism monitors the conduct of the rich and powerful, checking the exercise of power for possible betrayals of public trust. The press is referred to as the Fourth Estate to government's executive, legislative and judicial branches. But while the press has power in terms of its reach and influence, Michael Janeway says: "It is not the press' natural role to exercise power, but rather to call for or oppose its exercise by others, to investigate it, to witness it." In fact, this investigative impulse was developed only recently.

It was only in 1964 that the Pulitzer Prize included investigative reporting as a new category. The award recognized journalism which uncovered hidden scandal and corruption in high places. The decision emphasized the importance of the role of the press as "activist, reformer, and exposer" and "as an independent monitor of power." The press can discharge these functions in the most recent media of the Internet, but with a difference. The Internet also allows not just the press but ordinary people to become their own information and news provider.

Importance of Communication Technology, Press, and Politics

The global trend toward democratization continues to place the institution of the press at the heart of critical social and political concerns. Democracy highlights the importance of information in a society and continued learning and education as a feature of public life. The press has been ideally positioned to provide information that citizens need to know in order to participate in public affairs. The news media are instruments of open debate and discussion in society, engaging citizens in a continuing exchange of ideas about the issues of the times. Quite simply, a free press expands freedom and strengthens democracy.

In different parts of the world, technology has eased the political shift toward democratization. Indonesia opened up its society to satellite technology and the availability of news and programs from all over the world was slowly changing the public mind set in the country, even before the breakdown of Suharto's authoritarian regime. Later, the Internet quickened the pace of information dissemination among activists who challenged Suharto's long-standing rule. In the Philippines, the SMS or text-message system through cell phones enhanced the mobilization of mass rallies protesting the corruption of the Estrada government.

Communication technology has also dramatically recast the character of politics. In the US, studies have shown how television has changed the style of political campaigns and the manner by which the voter makes an electoral choice. The visual media in America politics has made possible a greater degree of manipulation of candidates' images. In a study of the impact of television on American presidential elections, Grossman notes that television allows people direct access to political figures and events. But it also emphasizes "personality, visual image and emotion rather than on ideas, issues, and reason."

In less developed democracies like the Philippines, television has pressed political parties to field candidates from show business or the media. In these two different environments, the use of television media has less to do with journalism than with the manufacture of media images and impressions. On another level, Grossman notes the development of the "electronic republic" forming in America: "a democratic system that is vastly increasing the people's day-to-day influence on the decisions of the state." The growth of telecommunications media involves citizens more directly in their own governance. This is true even in developing societies.

In the Philippines, instant polls conducted by TV or radio programs engage their viewers by asking them to text or call in their votes on questions related to controversial policy issues. There is little point to such communication without an educated and engaged citizenry. However, it can also be said that such communication makes it possible to form and sustain such a public. Otherwise, technology only facilitates the tyranny of the ignorant majority. Compared to developing democracies, relatively higher levels of information literacy may be found in the mainstream population of industrial societies. Citizens in these countries may have more education in general to make worthy interventions. However, where there is less development and less resources, the public may remain as the misguided and misdirected mass. By providing the means for continuing public information and education, the press helps society to achieve its goals.

Commercialization of the Press

Embedded in all democratic theory is the principle of the free market. Underlying the development of free press enterprise is the commercial drive that operates all kinds of business. In search of a media audience, the press has been driven by the profit issue and the need to make money. In this new age of communication, the practice and business of journalism involves the pursuit of an audience. News organizations and news outlets need to claim an audience share to attract advertisers. Advertising revenue provides media profits.

Commercialization has shaped the news product, imposing certain criteria based on popular appeal. Although the concept of 'news-worthiness' has always included relevance and significance, the press often excludes important and compelling news. Applied in different newsrooms, these values evolve news packages that are as different from each other in style and substance-the tabloids co-exist with high-minded broadsheets, the info-tainment segments hold their time against serious newscasting. But they all still adhere to certain traditional criteria of what makes 'news.' As such, news may become limited in scope and in subject and limited by space and time, conditions that in a way impose a certain predictability to the news.

How often have we heard people say that they are tired of reading about the same things? After a while, the scandals, the celebrities and controversies all seem the same, echoing elements from similar incidents in the past. Was it Thoreau who said he had no need to know about yet another fire, murder or accident? These days, can we also say that we have not yet seen all there is to know about scandal and scalawags, celebrities and the lives of the rich and famous? The mandate of the mass markets has evolved a news culture more likely to entertain than educate, to distract rather than instruct the public. In highly productive economies in the West, popular demand for more and more entertainment and recreation presses on editorial policies.

In the political field, political campaigns have made use of entertainment vehicles and advertising formats to get their message across or to attract the electorate. In the US, studies have shown the impact of commerce on people's perceptions about candidates. A study of the role of political advertising and televised news showed that people responded more to the stimulus of advertising messages that they did to the message in the news. In emerging democracies as in established democracies, news organizations have adjusted to the reality and merged entertainment and information goals. Cases have shown how commercialization has marginalized news and information that is relevant to political discourse.

The situation confronts the press with a critical challenge to revise and reinvent news practice to address change. Its failure to address the challenge of change wastes historic opportunity and the unique resources unleashed in the information age to create a learning society. The same failure can lead to a press diminished in significance and relevance.

Information Revolution and Literacy

Toward the end of the 20 century, as technology revolutionized communication, the mass audience was also breaking up into special interest groups or market segments. Alvin Toffler saw the "crack-up of the industrial mass society" and the split of the "mass market" into "ever-multiplying, ever changing sets of mini-markets that demand a continually expanding range of options, models, types, sizes, colours and customizations." The new communications media saw the rise of special publications; some taking the form of newsletters sent out to far-flung communities, catering to small groups bound by common issues and interests.

When video recorders enabled on-demand programs and movies, television networks lost their power to dictate and synchronize viewing hours. Cable increased program choices for the viewing audience and citizen band radio promoted greater interaction among listeners. The computer allowed communication and information flows to cut through time zones and to undermine geography as an indicator of one's location or address. The Internet has carried any material carried in traditional communication formats while creating original cyber news channels.

These advances have required the development of new skills and prodded the rise of a new form of literacy in the field of communication-knowing where to find what kind of information. As the sources of information have proliferated, access has involved special skills that the public has had to learn. These skills enable the individual to become his own gatekeeper of the news, seeking information as the need arises. All of the above have wrenched primary control over the flow of news from the elite news organizations that have for so long determined the course of newsgathering and dissemination.

Much has been said about the decline of the news audience in the US. In 1980, Toffler traced the statistics showing the circulation losses of leading newspapers across the nation. "Between 1970 and 1977, despite a 14 million rise in US population, the combined aggregate circulation of the remaining top twenty-five magazines dropped by 4 million. The decline in newspaper readership was matched by growth in radio and cable television, media that have traditionally rooted its function and purpose in entertainment. Neil Postman listed the elements of television news-"the good looks and amiability of the cast, their pleasant banter, the exciting music that opens and closes the show, the vivid film footage, the attractive commercials", rendering news as a diversion and distraction, as what has been called 'info-tainment.'

The decline of newspapers may be linked to the diminished public engagement and public interest in politics. William Greider noted the decrease of voting in presidential elections in the US since 1960, the narrow base of votes for representatives, and the minority votes that have decided election outcomes in the US Congress. Polls have also shown that after 1990, three in four Americans expressed dissatisfaction with the outcomes in congressional elections, even when their candidates won.

The world pictured in much of the news suggests that citizen engagement won't make a difference in improving the state of things. At the same time, in many developed societies of the West, populations are becoming more educated than their predecessors, who presume post-graduate degrees as a requirement for most careers. This public constitutes a more discerning market and more critical users of the news. It is not surprising then that individuals choose to connect with the outside world on their own, creating conversing communities as they enter chat rooms and click onto Web sites.

Through the Internet and the global transmission of live television, the news comes to them real-time, enjoying virtually the same access available to experts, government leaders and journalists. Some consumers of news possess so much more expertise about a range of subjects-a background that equips them to analyse events and issues for themselves. These people exist side by side the uncritical mass that are satisfied with pap and pulp in the media. The dual audience expects and demands opposing values in the news.

Re-Orienting Journalism

What should make the news? What should journalism

provide? What is journalism for? While it is difficult to generalize, complaints against journalism question the long-standing premise that journalism must popularize, make accessible to the greater numbers the important developments of the day. With the growth of competition, popularization has also resulted in a news style designed to attract more people, to pander to the public taste for the sensational and exciting. The tabloid culture has dominated and eroded news values. Editorial decisions so often ignore what is significant and relevant because these are more difficult to make interesting and appealing.

The greatest human stories are processes which aren't reported well. The narrow focus on events has allowed the process of environmental deterioration to go unreported. Not until the event of an environmental disaster does it make it as news, and by then it is too late. Events reporting can lead reporters to miss the context, the connections that make reality more understandable. People complain that staple of bad news can be disheartening, building up a sense of helplessness that may disable a community from doing anything to address their problems. The press may exaggerate its adversarial stance in reporting on government, concentrating on failures and excluding the successes. This could engender continuing public frustration. This kind of outlook does not foster the community spirit that feeds democracy.

Journalism serves citizens. Journalism must draw citizen attention to that which is significant and meaningful, to information that they need to know, although they may not necessarily be conscious of the need. It has been easier to give the public what is easy for them to appreciate, such as distracting and entertaining news. It is much more difficult to hold their attention with the accounts that try to make sense of developments affecting their lives.

Role of Press

Given a measure of information literacy for the greater numbers, the press must help this public find meaning in the mass of information that is at hand. The Internet allows the public direct access to so much government information. The public finds out, as they did during the investigation of the Clinton-Lewinsky case, about previously confidential material at the very same time that other government officials and other policymakers do. Lord thinks that direct access should not be the only form of communication but should be supplemented with the journalistic perspective and analysis. Still on direct access, Roger C. Smith wrote: The reason that journalists are necessary is that people do not have the time to sort through all the directly accessible info and extract what is meaningful to them. Even though the Internet will make it easier to get the information, the public will still face the same daunting challenge of sorting through it.

He pointed out that the advent of the Internet does not change this, although it will necessarily modify how it does the job. Another role that journalists will play with added importance and that is as "conversation starters and moderators." While this is related to the old description of journalism as reflected conversation, the new technology and an information literate society draws journalists directly into the flow of conversation. He added with insight into learning possible on both sides, "This could be just the thing to help people understand why we ask these nasty questions, and help us understand what questions they really need us to ask."

The need for adjustment on the part of journalists if the press is to remain as the dominant source of news and information. Journalists need to be as literate in technology but at the same time, they must safeguard its strengths, retain their ability to get to the sources and to evaluate the information they are given, and maintain the facility to connect different kinds of knowledge so these can make larger sense for those who only see part of it. Finally, journalists must continue to do what they have always done for the public, providing interesting accounts of the day's events, explaining and synthesizing different developments of significance, while observing the requirements of fairness and ethics.

Inherent in journalism-online or on traditional media-is the purpose of community; meaning a community of free men and women who have sovereign will. They need to be connected with a shared fund of information that serves for them a common reference with which to think on the issues of the day and to weigh their options as citizens. Returning to the roots of journalism, the advocates of public or civic journalism urge the restoration of the community of citizens in the centre of press concerns. The public dialogue and civic involvement of members a community forms "the civic capital" that is the basis of press enterprise. Without it, there is no real point to journalism. Journalism should replenish these civic resources and build up more public life.

A public is something more than a market for information, an audience for spectacle, or a pollster's random sample. Publics are formed when we turn from our private and separate affairs to face common problems, and to face each other in dialogue and discussion. Information technology could draw away community members from the public forum, making them feel self-sufficient in their cocoons of selected news and information. Journalists need to understand how these trends can be inimical to democratic society and craft practice that will rebuild their connections with the community and to strengthen public life.

Digital Divide in Journalism

The new technologies of information and communications (NTIC) have revolutionised the day-to-day work of journalists and they provide new opportunities for journalists to work better, more efficiently and more professionally. Reporters and media professionals should play a key role in the development of the information society. If the information society is truly about providing the knowledge, skills and services that will enrich peoples' lives and bolster democratic participation at large, then journalists must have access to new technologies that will strengthen their professional capacity to ensure reliable, quality, and accurate information for public consumption - whatever the mode of its dissemination. But will this happen?

In spite of great optimism fostered a decade ago when information change began to drive the process of globalisation, the reality for journalists in many parts of the world is that they are among those most affected by the digital divide. As the International Federation of Journalists states in its submission to the World Summit on the Information Society: Above all, the information society provides an unprecedented opportunity to expand the media landscape and to strengthen democratic pluralism through rapid citizens' access to new areas of quality journalism with the capacity to influence policymaking at local, national and regional level. Although the information society has the potential to improve the quality of people's lives, this will not happen unless the right choices are made to frame policy to suit society's needs for social inclusion, cultural diversity and equality.

Public confidence will not grow unless more is done to guarantee people's rights and to engage them in the debate over the consequences of change. Unable to tune in and log on to the advantages of the information revolution, journalists in developing countries face enormous challenges in their social and professional lives. Their technologically deprived conditions make them the second and third class citizens of the world of journalism and their mission to inform, particularly in the least developed countries, suffers as a result.

Global Challenge for Quality Journalism

Journalism should be about a professional responsibility to deliver quality content. To do that journalists need social and professional conditions that will stimulate high standards of work. They also need the most modern tools for the job. These are often what are missing in the daily lives of journalists. Where journalists are engaged in the use of new technologies they have seen enormous changes in working methods and the relations of the professionals with their environment. The information society facilitates investigations, access to information and the diffusion and promotion of media products, enhances networking and dialogue and offers additional tools for self-development, quality journalism and professionalism. But it also encourages editorial laziness, Internet-dependent journalism and a culture of immediacy that challenges ethical standards.

Too often journalists use the Internet without properly checking the reliability of sources. There is also an increasing problem of plagiarism. Journalists are increasingly desk-bound and have fewer opportunities to meet face to face with contacts and sources. Having said that, these are problems not faced by journalists in the least developed countries who are often excluded from the positive benefits of Internet services. The validation process of engagement in the Internet is an important issue for sources of information from least developed countries.

In order, for example, for opinions, ideas and basic information to be credible from these countries, it is necessary to have it available in on-line form. This discrepancy adds to the isolation of media and journalists within these regions. It is imperative to develop ways of raising the profile of information sources from these countries. This is not just a matter of improving the diversity and plurality of global information services, it is also about creating a process whereby journalists and media in poorer regions can themselves resist political and other pressures that they currently face. The IFJ is particularly conscious of the wider global implications of a new information infrastructure.

The Internet at its best is a force for pluralism and democracy. It also helps to break the barriers of state control - as the independent Radio B92 in Belgrade showed during the Milosevic years when the Serbian government tried, and failed, to silence its media critics, who used the Internet and satellite technologies to get their message out. Access to information is indeed a key advantage of the digital age. The information society must be developed within a framework that ensures easy and free access to communication and information. However, as the IFJ quotes in its recommendations, fair access for all, regardless of geography, and an operational framework which provides access for all groups is indeed essential.

Taken as a whole the development of the information society represents a watershed for the profession for journalism worldwide, but it is not a fair society. Participation in the information society presupposes a number of assets in terms of infrastructure, connectivity (availability and proximity of the equipment, quality of available information), knowledge (basic NTIC and computer literacy) and working methods. The challenge to media is also to establish a framework whereby the traditional role of journalism in providing a professional "filtering" process is extended to the gathering, storing and dissemination of all electronic information. This will require new initiatives in the field of journalism training, particularly targeted at freelance journalists and those working in the online environment.

The need for quality content is inevitably linked to the key role played by journalists in providing valuable content. An important step towards quality content lies in the recognition of journalists as authors of their work. Economics and moral intellectual property rights are essential in order to provide the best quality of media, thus encouraging creativity. Awareness should be raised on the positive effects of authors' rights recognition amongst both freelancers and staff journalists.

The digital divide is experienced bitterly by media professionals in the least developed countries who lack the abilities or do not have access to these facilities. It worsens de facto the existing disparities between the journalists of the north and their colleagues in the south. Freelances, the fastest growing community of journalists worldwide, are particularly victims of these inequalities. Their access to communication infrastructures and capacity to check their sources is often very limited. At the same time the capacity of journalists to develop their skills is impeded by lack of training facilities. The strengthening and creation of strong, independent and representative professional organisations and networks suffer as a result of the technology gap.

In 2002 Zambia has 8 telephones lines for 1000 inhabitants, Nepal has 12, Haiti and Togo, 9. The figure would be over 400 in any European country. 72% of Internet users live in high-income OECD countries, with 14% of the world's population. This appraisal of the situation is also a challenge for the near future: the more than 500 million Internet users today are expected to grow to nearly 1 billion by 2005. Journalists in the least developed countries are ill equipped in as far as carrying out their professional responsibilities. Although at the end of the day, they will have submitted their work to their editors, the manner in which they establish themselves leaves sometimes much to be desired.

In Zambia, for instance, the majority of journalists (print and electronic) are found at Government-owned institutions where the working conditions, in some cases, are pathetic. Communication facilities are almost non-existent and it is difficult for the journalists to get to their sources. At the Zambian National Broadcasting Corporation (ZNBC), journalists find it difficult to reach sources by phone because of the limited lines. Most of the telephone lines at the headquarters in Lusaka and the regional office in Kitwe, some 350 kilometres away, have been disconnected. Journalists would only be allowed to phone their sources sparingly and only when the issue is important, in management's judgement.

The journalists from the Zambia Daily Mail and Sunday Times, in certain cases, have to go out to Internet cafes to download stories for the newspaper companies.

This happens when telephone lines have been disconnected and the Internet facility (dial up) is off. Journalists have often complained that they do not have easy access to Internet facilities and depend on other means of communicating and researching. In Togo, most of the journalists do not know how to use the new technologies of information and the high telecommunication costs limit their capacities to check their sources. Most of the newspapers do not have their own newsroom but instead rely on the local capacities of photocomposition enterprises.

In Haiti low incomes restricts journalists' access to one hour or even half an hour of Internet connection (the equivalent of US$ 1 or 2). Access to the new technologies is very limited in the press houses. Few of the media are connected. Only a very small percentage of journalists actually use a computer as a working tool. In Nepal, a majority of journalists also lacks adequate computer Knowledge. English language training (written and spoken) is also necessary for Nepalese journalists, as 90% journalists work in Nepali Language media. Access to the English language is perceived as a gateway to the information society. The new technology trends and globally accepted norms will not easily be learnt if this is not ensured.

Safety training is also a critical point for Nepalese journalists, who are seriously affected by insurgency and terror. Journalists have been threatened both by security personnel and rebels. Nepalese journalists need balanced political reporting training. Professional standards of ethics, Human rights reporting and safety training need to be conveyed to the local professionals. Full access to information is a political challenge. The highly polarized and deteriorating political tensions in Haiti and the limited press freedom require that there should be full access to information for local journalists.

A press centre has been set up in Port-aux-Princes but access fees are too high for the majority of the profession. In Togo, a press centre has also been developed with the support of the IFJ Media for Democracy programme. However, the press centre is not supported by the government and its very existence is at stake, in a very difficult political context. The new media services should reflect the free expression of common and public interest.

Access to infrastructures and technological facilities on their own do not imply arrival in the digital age. The quality, relevance and ownership of media content, the accessibility to local news and analyses are key elements in the definition of the information society. In this sense, open access to networks, with network operators being required to offer access on equal and non-discriminatory terms to all service providers, is a pre-requisite. The IFJ contribution to the World Summit stresses this point: The information society must encourage local content on global networks. There should be direct participation of people from all regions in the production of local news and information services to ensure fair distribution of and access to information for all.

Global networks remain distant from the production and diffusion of local information services from the developing world. The populations from the least developed countries, which lack access to local news, are thus particularly penalised. The development of local contents and news networks would therefore be an essential initiative in the targeted countries.

4

Conscience of the Journalist

Ownerships and Profits

The overarching theme of ownership and profits came up time and time again. There was a strong feeling that editors place pressure on journalists, forcing them to compromise between what their editors demand and the path they would ideally like to follow. However, it was also recognised that editors are under equal pressure from the owners; a private owner has total power and this is a real problem. It seems that proprietors are the ones lacking in conscience, their only motivation being the profit that is achieved by appealing to the bottom line. With the influx of corporate owners onto newspapers (and into newsrooms), everything has been diluted with business tactics.

The drive for profit has turned "journalists into little more than content providers" and news is seen as a simple commodity in this market place. In this respect, it was noted that the broadsheets were seen as little different from the tabloids. It was commented that, "a newspaper may have to be a non-profit to be reputable. It may be impossible to have private ownership, profits and ethics all at the same time".

A further significant aspect was the awareness that short-term contracts, which journalists are being forced to sign if they wish to remain in the profession, contributed greatly to a general feeling of insecurity. It was thought that if people were more secure in their jobs, they would be able to turn down stories that they felt uncomfortable about. This was one of the factors that inspired the sentiment that noble desires are beaten out of people while they are young.

A Moral Profession

At best journalism is a moral profession; "it is a job where you have to make people care about things". Furthermore, the role of an editor can be defined as "to find out what people need to know, and then to make them want to know it". In this way it was felt that journalism could serve a profound educational role in society. It was noted that although journalists are seen very much as storytellers, not all journalists are good at it. This in turn can lead to poor journalists who chase controversial stories in order to cause outrage and achieve a public profile. However, this could also be seen as journalists performing a social function, by finding out the truth, which in turn keeps democracy in check.

It was largely felt that there was "too much lazy journalism". The tabloids can be accused of ignoring the actual moral climate, and digging up old-fashioned attitudes. The papers can, and quite often do, appeal to the majority view by fuelling pre-existing fears. In this sense newspapers are reactionary and play to the gallery. It was commented that journalists would do better to report on stories that challenge and engage the reader rather than simply inciting the majority against the minority.

Ethics and language

By its very nature, ethics is a reflective activity. This means that it is easier to be moralistic as you get older and you are no longer subject to the same pressures as the younger generation. It was noted that we in the developed world have the time to reflect on such matters, a luxury which many others do not have as their concerns are about meeting the basic needs for survival. Journalists need to move away from the language of economics and politics, which they are the most comfortable using, to comment on society. There is an uneasiness about using the language of ethics, of values and of what is right and wrong behaviour. However, this is the language that most people use in their homes and everyday life. These are not alien concepts, but journalists shy away from this type of language as being far too prescriptive and emotive.

The public feels that all journalists lie and go along with government spin. It was commented that there is a general assumption among the public that the media cannot be trusted or relied upon to be truthful, an assumption which is slowly eroding public expectations of the media. The public are not receiving the media they deserve, leading to a creation of a 'them-us' culture between the media and the public. This was reinforced with the idea that the public is not fully appreciative of what is involved in getting the truth. A member of the BBC commented that uncovering the truth often involves "trampling on certain individuals or groups".

Further it was felt (inside the BBC) that the public are not particularly concerned with ethics, and prefer entertainment programmes such as 'docu-soaps'. There was concern that the public needs to be able to express outrage, without bringing in tight regulations. Furthermore, it was asked by a participant, "what can...people do about ethics and integrity?" The two routes that were suggested as being open to the public were writing letters to the editor, and by appealing to the Press Complaints Commission. Editors created the PCC in 1990, after the NUJ Code of Ethics failed, and the broadsheets have largely used the commission to bring the tabloids to heel. A panellist commented that letters to the editor confirm the idea that journalism has to be a conversation, a give and take with the audience.

The ever-increasing pace of the development of technology has resulted in a higher level of competition. With the advent of digital cameras, satellites and the internet, reports can be made and filmed by a single person in one of the remotest areas of the world and be broadcast almost instantaneously over the web. The competition is stiffer than ever - to break the story first, to show the first pictures - in such an environment "the capacity for deliberate judgement goes". The 24-hour news stations have continuously to search out stories to fill their time, and this creates further problems. It is not unknown for newsrooms to "make any story at all stand-up as they have so much time to fill". It was noted by a participant that the conscience of the journalist is engaged when they can find no story, but they are still expected to pro duce one by their employers, a situation common to all those working within the media.

It could be said that if the media is seen as a microcosm of society, the increasing focus on technology and profits over values and integrity is apparent in the media, as in society at large. Have we expected too much by asking the media to be free from the trends that affect the rest of society? If the media wish to retain their credibility as producing real social comment that challenges society's complacency, an d if journalists want to be known on the strength of their writing and for the clarity and integrity of their thinking, then further debate needs to take place on the role of ethics and responsibility within the media.

Conflict Sensitive Journalism

Professional news reporters, whether being aware of it or not, re specialists in conflict. For reporters, change is news. And when there is change, there often is disagreement or conflict. There is conflict among those who like the change and those who do not, or those who want more change and those whos oppose change. So journalists deal with conflict very often in their work. But many journalists know little about the idea of conflict. They do not know the root causes of conflict, or how conflicts end. They do not know the different kinds of conflict.

For more than 50 years diplomats, negotiators and social scientists have studied conflict and developed a sophisticated understanding of it, just like medicine, business or music. But few journalists have any training in the theory of conflict. Most journalists merely report on the conflict as it happens. By comparison, medical reporters do not just report on a person's illness. They also report on what caused the illness and what may cure it. News reporters can have the same skill when it comes to reporting conflict. Having the skills to analyze conflict will enable a reporter to be a more effective professional journalist and a more aware individual. This is called Conflict Sensitive Journalism.

What is Conflict?

Conflict is a situation where two or more individuals or groups try to pursue goals or ambitions which they believe they cannot share. Not all conflict is violent. Conflict is normal when there is change. Some people want change, but others disagree. If their disagreement or their conflict is managed peacefully, it can be a positive process. But when conflict is not managed properly, it becomes violent. In violent conflict, people fear for their safety and survival. When we say conflict, we are usually referring to violent conflict.

Almost world-wide, it is predictable that conflict will arise where:

— Resources are scarce and not shared fairly, as in food, housing, jobs or land.

— There is little or no communication between the two groups.

— The groups have incorrect ideas and beliefs about each other.

— Unresolved grievances exist from the past.

— Power is unevenly distributed.

Consider the likely sources of conflict in your country. Consider what caused the conflict to become violent.

Violent physical conflict is easily identified and described by journalists. Individuals or groups in conflict try to hurt or kill each other and there are victims. But there can be other kinds of violence which do great harm in society and these are more difficult for reporters to see and to explain. Cultural violence can be the way a group has been thinking about another group for many years. It can include talk, images or beliefs which glorify physical violence. These include:

— *Hate speech* : Different ethnic or cultural groups openly speak badly of each other. One group blames the other for difficulties or problems it is suffering. Violence is encouraged to eliminate the blamed group.

— *Xenophobia* : A people 's or a country 's hatred or fear of another country creates misperceptions and encourages policies which promote conflict with that country.

— *Myths and legends of war heroes* : A society whose popular songs and history books glorify one side 's ancient victories can build hatred for the other side.

— *Religious justifications for war* : Extreme intolerance of other beliefs promotes conflict.

— *Gender discrimination* : To allow practices and laws against women that are not accepted against men is a form of violence.

Structural violence is harm which is built into the laws and traditional behaviour of a group or society. Harm is permitted or ignored. It can include:

— *Institutionalized racism or sexism* : Laws and practices which allow unequal treatment based on race or sex.

— *Colonialism* : A country 's lack of self-determination. A foreign authority forcibly assumes control over all important decision-making processes.

— *Extreme exploitation* : Such as slavery.

— *Poverty* : The world 's leading cause of violent conflict.

— *Corruption and nepotism* : Govenrnmental decisions are influenced or decided by bribery, favourtism and family or tribal connections.

— *Structural segregation* : Laws which force people to live in separate groups or places against their will.

These kinds of violence are extremely important to identify when reporting and analyzing conflict. Often they are the real cause of direct physical violence. Ending the physical violence will not be enough. It will happen again if the cultural and structural violence is ignored. Consider your country:is there cultural and structural violence?Is it reported in the media?Do the victims have a voice in the news?

Journalism and Conflict

Almost all societies have developed ways to regulate conflict without violence. Usually, a fair-minded person -a village elder or a judge or an international tribunal -is given authority by the community to decide how to resolve the conflict. The decision is respected by everyone. If the decisions seem unfair and are not accepted, the conflict may become violent. Many professionals, such as counselors, community leaders, diplomats, negotiators and scholars, have been thinking deeply about what it takes to end a violent conflict. These professionals have discovered that in any conflict -whether it is within a family, between neighbours, among groups within a country or across borders -certain things must occur for the conflict to end. Conflict does not end by itself.

One of the most important things to take place is communication. For two sides in conflict to move towards non-violent resolution, they must first talk. This is where good journalism comes in.

Journalism 's unconscious roles

Professional journalists do not set out to reduce conflict. They seek to present accurate and impartial news. But it is often through good reporting that conflict is reduced. These are several elements of conflict resolution that good journalism can deliver, automatically, as part of its daily work:

1. *Channeling communication*: The news media is often the most important channel of communication that exists between sides in a conflict. Sometimes the media is used by one side to broadcast intimidating messages. But other times, the parties speak to each other through the media or through specific journalists.

2. *Educating*: Each side needs to know about the other side's difficulty in moving towards reconciliation. Journalism which explores each side 's particular difficulties, such as its politics or powerful interests can help educate the other side to avoid demands for simplistic and immediate solutions.

3. *Confidence-building*: Lack of trust is a major factor contributing to conflict. The media can reduce suspicion by digging into hot issues and revealing them so there are no secrets to fear. Good journalism can also present news that shows resolution is possible by giving examples from other places and by explaining local efforts at reconciliation.

4. *Correcting misperceptions*: By examining and reporting on the two sides 'misperceptions of each other, the media encourages disputing sides to revise their views and move closer to reducing conflict.

5. *Making them human*: Getting to know the other side, giving them names and faces, is an essential step. This is why negotiators put the two sides in the same room. Good journalism also does this by putting real people in the story and describing how the issue affects them.

6. *Identifying underlying interests*: In a conflict both sides need to understand the bottom-line interests of the other. Good reporting does this by asking tough questions and seeking out the real meaning of what leaders say. Good reporting also looks beyond the leaders 'interests and seeks the larger groups 'interest.

7. *Emotional outlet*: In conflict resolution, there must be outlets for each side to express their grievances or anger or they will explode in frustration and make things worse. The media can provide important outlets by allowing both sides to speak. Many disputes can be fought out in the media, instead of in the streets, and the conflict can be addressed before it turns violent.

8. *Framing the conflict*: In a conflict, describing the problem in a different way can reduce tension and launch negotiations. In good journalism, editors and reporters are always looking for a different angle, an alternative view, a new insight which will still attract an audience to the same story. Good journalism can help reframe conflicts for the two sides.

9. *Face-saving, consensus-building*: When two parties try to resolve a conflict they must calm the fears of their supporters. By reporting what they say, the media allows leaders in conflict to conduct face-saving and consensus-building, even reaching to refugees and exiles in far-away places.

10. *Solution-building*: In conflict, both sides must eventually present specific proposals to respond to grievances. On a daily basis, good reporting does this by asking the dis-puting parties for their solutions instead of just repeating their rhetoric of grievances. Good journalism is a constant process of seeking solutions.

11. *Encouraging a balance of power*: Conflicting groups, regardless of inequalities, have to believe they will be given attention if they meet the other side in negotiations. Good journalism encourages negotiation because the reporting is impartial and balanced. It gives attention to ll sides. It encourages balance of power for the purpose of hearing grievances and seeking solutions.

These 11 activities are only part of what goes on in reducing conflict between persons or groups. Journalism does these things, as part of its normal good reporting. But when we understand the effect of what we do, we can better appreciate how important our role is in a conflict. We must get our facts right and choose our words carefully. It also helps us as reporters to be aware that these activities are going on in many closed-door negotiations or peace talks. Knowing this, we can report what we learn about the negotiations with greater understanding. In Sri Lanka, when negotiations first began, the negotiators were concerned that the media did not understand the process and would create mispercep-tions and destroy confidence.

One way of achieving more alternatives in a dispute is by bringing more people into the conflict. It produces more ideas for seeing the conflict differently. It helps discover different solutions to be shared. When two sides are dead-locked, other members of the community, such as religious leaders, the business community, the civil society, a friendly neighboring country, or inter-national organisations, can bring different visions and alternative solutions. Conflict resolution can be highly complicated. After 30 years of war, the conflict between two groups in Mozambique was resolved in 1992.

— Fourteen different parties, six countries and six non-governmental organizations were involved.

- There were so many parties and ideas that it became difficult for either group to walk away.
- In the Mozambique peace talks, there were groups inside and outside the negotiations, helping the two sides communicate, prepare ideas and respond.
- Everyone started by finding a small agreement. Then they worked on bigger agreements.

What does conflict analysis mean for journalists?

- Journalists should seek out other parties and other points of view. They should not only repeat old grievances by the old elites.
- Journalists should examine what the parties are seeking and the possibility for withdrawal, compromise or transcendence. Journalists should write about these possibilities.
- With conflict analysis, journalists can understand what diplomats and negotiators are trying to do, and can report it more reliably.
- With conflict analysis, journalists can identify more sources to go to for information.

For citizens in a conflict to make well-informed decisions and perhaps resolve their conflict, they must have good journalism. Around the world, professional journalists have developed principals and basic standards by which they try to achieve good journalism. Unfortunately there are many places where journalists have to work under different rules imposed by governments or by powerful interests. But wherever professional journalists come together to freely consider what they do, and to guide themselves, they refer to these professional standards. There are more than 50 professional journalists 'associations around the world with similar codes of conduct or standards.

A good journalism should not do;

— *Defamatory*: Good journalism does not tell lies and twist the truth about people.

— *Derivative*: Good journalism does not simply repeat what has been reported somewhere else. Copying others 'news may repeat false information.

— *Malicious*: Journalism is powerful. News reports can ruin reputations, put people in danger, or cause public panic. Good journalism is not used to intentionally harm other persons.

— *Corrupt*: Good journalism does not accept bribes. It does no special favours for anyone. Good journalism is not for sale.

Good journalism should include:

1. *Accuracy*: Getting the correct information is most important of all. Everything which is reported must be described accurately -the spelling of names, the facts as they happened, and the real meaning of what was said. Before they report it, good journalists seek the evidence and accurate facts. A good journalist will rush to get the news first. But first, the journalist must get it right. People will not talk to journalists if they fear journalists will not repeat their words accurately, or will not describe things as they really are.

2. *Impartiality* (balance): Almost every code of good journalism puts importance on impartiality, on not taking sides. To do this, a good journalist will seek to produce a report which is balanced. To be balanced is to include both sides. There are always two sides in any story involving conflict. Citizens need to know what the other side says, and how it will affect them.

Balance is as important in every story as accuracy. People will not talk to a journalist who only reports one side of the story. Impartiality also means that the professional journalist is not an active leader in any political group or movement. Impartial journalism is an important defence for reporters in a time of conflict. Journalists should be respected because they take no sides.

3. *Responsibility*: Journalists have obligations to the people they report about, and to the society to whom they report the news. Journalists have a responsibility to protect their sources. Many people will not tell journalists important news if they fear they will be revealed. Good journalists also use only honest methods to obtain the news, which means they do not break the law.

These are the basic standards that produce journalism which the people can trust. It is called reliable journalism. All reliable reporting should be accurate, impartial and responsible. It applies to every aspect of the job - ssigning stories, editing copy or sound bites, writing headlines, directing, producing, or managing newsrooms. At any time, good reporters ask themselves: does my work meet the test of reliable journalism? Does my report have accuracy, impartiality and responsibility in it?

Reliable journalism and democracy

It is reliable reporting which earns journalism a privileged place in many countries 'constitutions and laws. Through the media, the people can exercise their right to free speech guaranteed in Article 19 of the International Declaration of Human Rights. Where there is free speech and reliable journalism, citizens can make well-informed decisions in their own best interest. That is an essential element of democracy.

Reliable, diverse and independent

But for democracy to properly flourish and bloom, the media must not only be reliable but also diverse. No single media outlet can do enough. It takes many media outlets to ensure that competing points of view and different reports are brought to the public 's attention. The reliable and diverse media must be independent. The media must be free of government or powerful interference that blocks the reporting of other voices and other interests. An independent media must be supported by laws and courts and independent regulators, who protect the media from interference. An independent media must also discipline itself, and submit to laws and regulators which are honest and non-partisan.

Some journalists say it is not our job to take responsibility for what happens when we report the news. We just report the conflict the same way we report on a soccer match -we just describe it. But this is not enough for conflict sensitive journalism. Many journalists today recognize that we are more than just professional spectators and distributors of the facts. We are aware that other people know how to create facts for us to report. They have a media strategy. They choose certain facts to tell the media, to use the media to influence the public 's view of the conflict.

Good journalists know there are no bare facts. If we only report the bare facts about violent conflict, citizens will only understand the conflict in those terms. But if we search for news beyond the bare facts, and present more information to citizens, including possible solutions, they may see the conflict in different terms. If a car bomb went off yesterday we should not just report it and repeat what the usual leaders say about it. We should also report how it affected ordinary people 's lives and seek their opinions about the conflict. We should also report on new attempts to end the conflict and provide information which exposes the bare facts.

The news we report can be destructive for a community, by promoting fear and violence. Or our news reports can be constructive, by making citizens better informed, and possibly safer, by also reporting on efforts to promote conflict reduction. This is conflict sensitive journalism. A conflict sensitive journalist applies conflict analysis and searches for new voices and new ideas about the conflict. He or she reports on who is trying to resolve the conflict, looks closely at all sides, and reports on how other conflicts were resolved. A conflict sensitive journalist takes no sides, but is engaged in the search for solutions. Conflict sensitive journalists choose their words carefully.

Checklist for conflict sensitive journalism

— Avoid reporting a conflict as consisting of two opposing sides. Find other affected interests and include their stories, opinions and goals. Interview merchants affected by the general strike, workers who are unable to work, refugees from the countryside who want an end to violence etc.

— Avoid defining the conflict by always quoting the leaders who make familiar demands. Go beyond the elites. Report the words of ordinary people who may voice the opinions shared by many.

— Avoid only reporting what divides the sides in conflict. Ask the opposing sides questions which may reveal common ground. Report on interests or goals which they may share.

— Avoid always focusing on the suffering and fear of only one side. Treat all sides 'suffering as equally newsworthy.

— Avoid words like devastated, tragedy and terrorized to describe what has been done to one group. These kinds of words put the reporter on one side. Do not use them yourself. Only quote someone else who uses these words.

— Avoid emotional and imprecise words. Assassination is the murder of head of state and no-one else. Massacre is the deliberate killing of inno-cent, unarmed civilians. Soldiers and policemen are not massacred. Genocide means killing an entire people. Do not minimize suffering, but use strong language carefully.

— Avoid words like terrorist, extremist or fanatic. These words take sides, make the other side seem impossible to negotiate with. Call people what they call themselves.

— Avoid making an opinion into a fact. If someone claims something, state their name, so it is their opinion and not your fact.

— Avoid waiting for leaders on one side to offer solutions. Explore peace ideas wherever they come from. Put these ideas to the leaders and report their response.

As journalists, our most powerful tools are the words we use. And the pictures and sounds. We can use our tools to build understanding instead of fears and myths.

PEACE JOURNALISM

There is a pervasive belief, especially in English-speaking

countries in the West, that journalists "just report the facts." The problem with this belief has become steadily more obvious in a media-savvy world: many people know how to create and tailor facts for journalists to report. Indeed, most governments think of their actions and statements as part of a "media strategy" which cannot be separated from the business of running their country's affairs. What this means is that the facts do not crop up innocently, waiting for journalists to discover and report them. The reporting, and a calculation about its effects - on public opinion, for instance — is usually already built into the facts. And governments rely on this reporting to help bolster their own images and attack their opponents.

But, how does a government know what facts to create, or how to present these facts so that reporting is done the way that those players would like? Only from their experience of reading, watching and listening to stories in the past. This means that every time a journalist reports on an issue, that story adds another layer to the collective understanding of how journalists are likely to respond in similar situations. In this way journalists influence the kind of facts likely to be provided for them to report in the future - the future behaviour of, say, parties to a conflict. Journalists, their sources and their audiences are counterparts in a feedback loop of cause and effect.

So the claim that journalists "just report the facts" gives an incomplete, and in some cases, inaccurate account of the journalist's role. All journalism is an intervention between the story originator - in this case the government - and the audience - the public. And journalists make choices about the ethics of each intervention. Peace Journalism seeks to minimize the rift between opposed parties by not repeating "facts" that demonize or set the stage for conflict. Therefore, the basic question a Peace Journalist would ask before crafting any story would be "what can I do with my intervention to enhance the prospects for peace?"

In a phrase, Peace Journalism is a broader, fairer and more accurate way of framing stories, drawing on the insights of conflict analysis and transformation. The Peace Journalism approach provides a new road map for tracing the connections between journalists, their sources, the stories they cover and the consequences of their reporting — the ethics of journalistic intervention. It opens up a literacy of non-violence and creativity as applied to the practical job of everyday reporting. It follows that Peace Journalism holds the greatest appeal for journalists working in situations where it is impossible to avoid thinking about their responsibility for the consequences of their reporting. Much pioneering work was done by the Media Peace Centre in Cape Town, South Africa, through the transition from Apartheid.

Journalists in Indonesia have collaborated with the present authors in training dialogues about Peace Journalism and in a recent field trip to Poso, in Central Sulawesi. The area has been riven by conflict and periodic outbreaks of violence for the last two years of Indonesia's shaky transition from the New Order of President Suharto. Participants produced Peace Journalism treatments for eight national publications as well as TV and radio.

Peace Journalist would strive to do the following things

1. avoid portraying a conflict as consisting of only two parties contesting one goal. The logical outcome is for one to win and the other to lose.

   — instead a Peace Journalist would disaggregate the two parties into many smaller groups, pursuing many goals, opening up more creative potential for a range of outcomes.

2. avoid accepting stark distinctions between self and other. These can be used to build the sense that another party is a threat or "beyond the pale" of civilised behaviour: both key justifications for violence.

   — instead seek the "other" in the "self " and vice versa. If a party is presenting itself as "the goodies", ask questions about how different its behaviour really is to that it ascribes to "the baddies" - isn't it ashamed of itself?

3. avoid treating a conflict as if it is only going on in the place and at the time that violence is occurring.

   — instead try to trace the links and consequences for people in other places now and in the future. Ask:

   a. Who are all the people with a stake in the outcome?

   b. What will happen if...?

   c. What lessons will people draw from watching these events unfold as part of a global audience?

   d. How will they enter the calculations of parties to future conflicts near and far?

4. avoid assessing the merits of a violent action or policy of violence in terms of its visible effects only.

   — instead try to find ways of reporting on the invisible effects. For example, the long-term consequences of psychological damage and trauma, perhaps increasing the likelihood that those affected will be violent in future, either against other people or, as a group, against other groups or other countries.

5. avoid letting parties define themselves by simply quoting their leaders' restatement of familiar demands or positions.

   — instead enquire deeper into goals:

   a. How are people on the ground affected by the conflict in everyday life?

   b. What do they want changed?

   c. Is the position stated by their leaders the only way or the best way to achieve the changes they want?

   This may help to empower parties to articulate their goals and make creative outcomes more likely.

6. avoid concentrating always on what divides the parties and the differences between what they say they want.

   instead try asking questions which may reveal areas of common ground. Lead your report with answers which suggest some goals maybe shared or at least compatible.

7. avoid only reporting the violent acts and describing "the horror." If you exclude everything else, you suggest that the only explanation for violence is previous violence (revenge); the only remedy, more violence (coercion/ punishment).

   — instead show how people have been blocked and frustrated or deprived in everyday life as a way of explaining the violence.

8. avoid blaming someone for "starting it."

   instead try looking at how shared problems and issues are leading to consequences which all the parties say they never intended.

9. avoid focusing exclusively on the suffering, fears and grievances of only one party. This divides the parties into villains and victims and suggests that coercing or punishing the villains represents a solution.

   — instead treat as equally newsworthy the suffering, fears and grievance of all sides.

10. avoid victimizing language like destitute, devastated, defenceless, pathetic and tragedy which only tells us what has been done to and could be done for a group of people. This disempowers them and limits the options for change.

    — instead report on what has been done and could be done by the people. Don't just ask them how they feel, also ask them how they are coping and what they think. Can they suggest any solutions?

11. avoid imprecise use of emotive words to describe what has happened to people.

    a. "Genocide" means the wiping-out of an entire people.

    b. "Decimated" (of a population) means reducing it by a tenth of its former size.

    c. "Tragedy" is a form of drama, originally Greek, in which someone's fault or weakness proves his or her undoing.

    d. "Assassination" is the murder of a head of state.

    e. "Massacre" is the deliberate killing of people known to be unarmed and defenceless. (Are we sure? Or might these people have died in battle?)

    f. "Systematic" (for example, raping, or forcing people from their homes) means the actions have been organised in a deliberate pattern. (Is this the actual case or have there been a number of unrelated, albeit extremely nasty incidents?)

— instead always be precise about what we know. Do not minimise suffering but reserve the strongest language for the gravest situations or you will beggar the language and help to justify disproportionate responses which escalate the violence.

12. avoid demonising adjectives like vicious, cruel, brutal and barbaric. These always describe one party's view of what another party has done. To use them puts the journalist on that side and helps to justify an escalation of violence.

— instead report what you know about the wrongdoing and give as much information as you can about the reliability of other people's reports or descriptions of it.

13. avoid demonising labels like terrorist, extremist, fanatic or fundamentalist. These are always given by us to them. No one ever uses them to describe himself or herself and so for a journalist to use them is always to take sides. They mean the person is unreasonable, therefore it seems to make less sense to reason (negotiate) with them.

— instead try calling people by the names they give themselves. Or be more precise in your descriptions.

14. avoid focusing exclusively on the human rights abuses, misdemeanours and wrongdoings of only one side.

— instead try to name ALL wrongdoers and treat as equally serious the allegations made by all sides in a conflict. Treating seriously does not mean taking at face value, but instead making equal efforts to establish whether any evidence exists to back them up, treating the victims with equal respect and the chances of finding and punishing the wrongdoers as being of equal importance.

15. avoid making an opinion or claim seem like an established fact. ("Eurico Guterres, said to be responsible for a massacre in East Timor....")

    — instead tell your readers or your audience who said what. ("Eurico Gutteres, accused by a top UN official of ordering a massacre in East Timor....") That way you avoid signing yourself and your news service up to the allegations made by one party in the conflict against another.

16. avoid greeting the signing of documents by leaders, which bring about military victory or ceasefire, as necessarily creating peace.

    — instead try to report on the issues which remain and which may still lead people to commit further acts of violence in the future. Ask, What is being done to strengthen means on the ground to handle and resolve conflict non-violently, to address development or structural needs in the society and to create a culture of peace?

17. avoid waiting for leaders on "our" side to suggest or offer solutions.

    — instead pick up and explore peace initiatives wherever they come from. Ask questions to ministers, for example, about ideas put forward by grassroots organisations. Assess peace perspectives against what you know about the issues that the parties are really trying to address. Do not ignore proposed solutions because they do not coincide with established positions.

Role of Media to Reduce Conflict

The good news is that the media can be highly effective in reducing conflict in strife-ridden societies. International agencies and non-government organizations (NGOs) are increasingly convinced that an unbiased and diverse media ranks almost as high as emergency relief in countries facing or active in war. Reliable information - such as where to get food, when is it safe to return, what common ground exists among all sides - is an essential element of stabilizing a society. In countries moving towards democratic government, a free and accountable media, one that monitors rights abuses and promotes divergent opinions, helps deter a return to violence. A biased or hate-mongering media can sabotage almost any other peacebuilding effort.

But the role of media in conflict resolution is still evolving and is deceivingly complex. The definition of media, the Western traditions of journalistic neutrality and commercial imperatives, the distinction between peace programming and propaganda, all need clarification. And the potential - consider the reach of a single transmitter - deserves far greater recognition in the field of conflict resolution. One useful tool for mapping out the potential is to view the media as several stages in a continuum of intervention. The continuum can help NGOs determine how to approach and effectively use the media. It is also useful to conventional journalists in examining their work and the potential impact of that work, beyond traditional limitations.

5
Media Accountability

The fate of mankind lies in the hands of the media. That is a dramatic way of putting a simple chain of thought: mankind is in danger unless democracy reigns everywhere. There is no democracy without informed citizens. The media are the instruments in mass society that inform people. The late Soviet Union provides evidence: huge tracts of land have been terminally polluted; hundreds of thousands of ancient books and works of art were destroyed; 20 to 60 million people were massacred between 1917 and the mid-eighties. All that would not have happened if the Soviet media had been free, and willing, to report and protest.

Even in industrialised democracies, everybody agrees that media need improvement: owners, media professionals, consumers. One should not forget that, contrary to a common complaint, the media are much better now than they used to be. But they are not good enough. There is a need for what? Accuracy? Decency? Credibility? Let us say a need for quality. Media quality means good service to the various groups in the population. There are two traditional policies to insure good service: using the law and trusting the market, both negative. The law aims at abuse by business. It is certainly needed but fascists and communists have demonstrated how dangerous the law, i.e. the courts, i.e. the State, i.e. the government can be for freedom of expression.

On the other hand, the market is supposed to counter abuse by the State, but the garbage produced by many of the commercial media, their efforts at manipulation, the big failures even of the elite media - prove that the market cannot, by itself, insure quality. So, maybe a third solution must be tried, more positive, less dangerous - like media ethics. It could contribute to solving a fundamental dilemma in mass communication: on the one hand, wherever free enterprise disappears, press freedom goes too; on the other hand, the media cannot be truly free to serve society if their management sets profit as its number one goal. A distinction between three concepts.

— *Ethics involves each individual*: it is a matter for parents, schools, churches and peer groups to teach.

— *Media ethics is internal to the profession*: it has been much debated and variously codified. And then, there is 'quality control'. It does not smell of morality, which irritates some people; besides, a corporation, as such, cannot have a moral sense.

— *'Quality control' has positive connotations*: it has meant big prestige and profits for Japanese manufacturers. Lastly, it implies action, not talk. Quality control can be done by the three groups of protagonists, owners, professionals and users in many different ways, either separately or together in various combinations - using 'media accountability systems' or MAS.

There is no need to evaluate 'ethics'. It is like motherhood and apple-pie: no one objects to it. So when media misbehave and public hostility or governmental threats become too loud, you observe a multiplication of workshops, seminars, conferences, articles, books, broadcasts. Merely talking about ethics does raise consciousness. But usually after a few months the talking recedes and fades away. If not, then the first practical initiative people usually take is to write a code. Nearly all nations in the world have at least one code of media ethics, most have several. It is the only MAS to have multiplied and to be so widespread.

Criticism of Codes of Ethics

In the US, lawyers say a newspaper or broadcasting station should not adopt a code which could be used in court against them—a risk confirmed to me by an Australian lawyer specialised in libel suits, who told me he uses codes as weapons. However, a code generally induces jury members to believe in the good faith of the medium. And big media groups have little to fear from law suits: they can afford to prolong the process until the plaintiff gives up.

Others say that codes, mere pieces of paper, threaten press freedom: governments could turn them into law. This, of course, can be a ploy to insure that no restriction, even a moral one, will limit the freedom to make money . More seriously, codes are said to be lists of vague prohibitions and noble exhortations, detached from reality: the best illustration would be the press codes of the Soviet Union - or the old code of the National Association of Broadcasters in the US, neither of which had any relationship with media reality.

Certainly a journalist should not publish unchecked information, not libel, not invade privacy, not cause unnecessary distress, not kill a story in exchange for a favour, not show racism or sexism etc. But it seems more important to stress that he/she should do a number of things, like acquiring competence in his/her field of activity (and not remain a general assignment reporter); like focusing on important news (as opposed to spicy or spine-tingling items); like separating news and entertainment; like giving news from every field (including from abroad); like making the news interesting for, and understandable by, ordinary people; like labelling pseudo-news as news fabricated by whoever can profit from it; like seeking new ideas, instead of avoiding them.

An MAS is any kind of non-governmental means used to insure that media are 'socially responsible'. They come in more than thirty different shapes. The concept of MAS is global, hence nebulous, as it includes:

— individuals (like ombudsmen or in-house critics)

— groups of people (like contents evaluation commissions)

— regular meetings (like local press councils)

— single documents (like codes of ethics)

— small media (like journalism reviews)

— a particular operation (like an ethical audit) or

— a long process (like a university education or in-depth research).

MAS have several immediate purposes:

— criticism, the oldest, the easiest and most common method to improve the media

— monitoring, needed now because media products are so numerous and short-lived - and because media sin more often by omission than by commission.

— access to the media, both in the sense that everyone should be able to use a wide range of media - and in the sense that every group in the population must be able to broadcast information.

— training, the long term solution to most media problems: both the education of professionals and the sensitisation of citizens.

Some MAS consist in a text or a broadcast programme of:

— very visible correction boxes.

— pro-and-con opinions presented on all important public issues.

— Letters-to-the-Editor and Open Forums.

— online message boards and forums for immediate feedback.

— accuracy and fairness questionnaires, mailed to persons mentioned in the news or published for all readers to answer.

Some MAS consist of:

— codes of ethics which media professionals have discussed and agreed upon - with, preferably, input by the public.

— regular media sections in newspapers and newsmagazines - or programmes on radio and television.

— journalism reviews, local or national, devoted principally to media criticism (e.g. the American JR).

— books written by professionals or by expert observers to expose media failings and recommend improvements.

— movies and television series dealing with media, sometimes critically, like WKRP in Cincinnati or Murphy Brown. Or a satirical program like the daily Les Guignols on Canal Plus.

Some MAS consist of individuals or groups:

— in house critics, 'staff review groups' or 'contents evaluation commissions' (like those established by the Japanese dailies as early as the twenties) to scrutinise their own newspaper for possible violations of ethics.

— media reporters who keep a critical eye on a whole sector of the media industry and report on it to the public; and when the occasion warrants it, courageous whistle-blowers.

— press ombudsmen, paid by a newspaper or broadcast station to deal with complaints from customers; and an ethics coach operating in the newsroom.

— liaison committees set up by media and some group with which they may occasionally clash, e.g. the legal profession or the police.

— citizens appointed to the editorial board .

— local press councils, regular meetings of professionals from the local media and representative members of the community.

— regional and national media councils (composed of representatives of media owners, professionals and citizens), created by the media both to adjudicate complaints by media users and to defend press freedom against governmental threats.

— special 'quality control' projects by media-related groups, like labour unions, professional associations, NGOs.

— consumer associations, especially associations of media users, using awareness sessions, mail campaigns, opinion polls, evaluations, lobbying even boycotts.

— the 'société de rédacteurs', an association of newspeople, which usually owns shares in the company they work for, hence has a voice in the setting of editorial policy . Similarly, the employers who own their medium .

— the, even rarer, 'société de lecteurs', an association of readers which buys shares in the capital of a medium and demands to have a say, even very small, in the general policy of the company.

Lastly, some MAS are processes:

— the crucial MAS: higher education.

— the further education of working journalists, through one-day workshops, one week seminars, six-month or one-year fellowships at universities.

— internal awareness programmes to increase the attention of media workers to the needs of citizens.

— regular opinion surveys; and, better, surveys of panels of citizens after they have been briefed by experts and have debated a given issue.

— the regular encounter of newspeople with citizens in some kind of press club or on the occasion of town meetings.

— non commercial research, done mainly by academics, often in 'media observatories' or foundation-funded think-tanks, on such topics as the perception of media messages by the public or the content of media or the absence of content.

Obstacles to MAS

No more than other human beings do media people like change. So, strong pressure is needed for them to accept reform. It can be a crisis like the one that followed the Gulf War - or a series of sex scandals in Britain. More efficiently, it is the threat of governmental action, or that of the market. In no profession do people like innovations, especially when they threaten positions of prestige or power - but that is not the whole story. At both extremes of the political spectrum, there is opposition to press freedom. Ethics and MAS are seen as inventions of native democrats. The only way to make the media serve either 'the nation' or 'the people' is either to apply force or to own them all.

Left of centre, social-democrats tend to look upon MAS as a PR ploy to avoid regulation. They claim that any effort on the part of media to be ethical can only be cosmetic: media controllers pretend to be concerned about public service while they remain obsessed by maximum profit or propaganda. Right of centre, ultra-liberals present ethics and MAS as a communist plot against freedom of speech and free enterprise. They denounce codes as belonging to the same despicable species as laws and regulations. Especially in the US, you find people who fear that self-control mechanism will be exploited by the government to restrict freedom of expression. That fear has never been justified even in India where the Press Council was set up by law.

Cynics say ethics and MAS are useless. 'Good' media know what is right anyway - and the 'bad' media do not give a damn, which is obvious in Great Britain. Actually most journalists are neither good nor bad: they can do with guidelines and the external moral pressure of peers. Realists find reality too complex and diverse for a three page code to be helpful and journalists are in too much of a hurry to go and dig in a code. As for the enforcement of rules, media people are too concerned with personal matters such as keeping their job, getting promoted, obtaining influence and fame - while media users are ignorant, unorganised and unaware of their power.

As for the owner, his first responsibility is to run his company profitably. He often thinks the law is enough and an MAS is a violation of his right of property. If the citizen does not like what he is served, let him stop consuming. Maybe the owner also feels (rightly) that MAS are the sign of a slow revolution in the media world: a movement towards participation of both producers and consumers, journalists and public in the running of media. However, some proprietors do feel a responsibility towards the public, while others have realised that quality control was profitable. There are also objective obstacles to the setting up of MAS. One is the status of the journalist, an employee who can be displaced, demoted, fired if he does not obey orders. He/she could only refuse if protected by a law, a union or the public.

Another obstacle is the ego of journalists, which seems often to be quite fragile. Though they have been elected by no one, nor had their competence tested by entrance examinations, many journalists feel endowed with superior grace. The priests of information find it very hard to acknowledge their mistakes. Media people, some of whom spend their time exposing decision-makers for various sins, find it very hard to take criticism themselves.

The code of the International Federation of Journalists contains a last clause claiming that "a journalist will accept only the judgement of his peers to the exclusion of any other". Thus solidarity turns into complicity: rarely are offenders reported to disciplinary committees, any more than to management or the public. Even the criticism of peers is not easily tolerated. The main opposition to ombudsmen comes from the newsroom. So, in France for instance, journalism is the only profession without self-control mechanisms.

Two further obstacles to the development of MAS cannot be expected to yield to training, negotiation or experience. For one thing, many MAS are expensive, if they are to do their job well, i.e. fast and visibly. An ombudsman, for instance, needs to be an experienced, respected journalist, obviously well paid. A Press Council can only operate properly, fast, and carry out all its tasks (like media monitoring) if it has a comfortable budget. But journalists have no money to spare. There are few foundations outside of the US. And it is considered better not to ask the State (although it is done in Finland and Germany).

MAS are a good investment to improve both the quality of a medium and the image of a firm in the eyes of government, courts and public. But some owners do not want to help: why should they pay to yield power and be criticised? Others cannot afford to: they cannot, for instance, forbid freebies and junkets simply because they are unable to pay for those expenses. Last but not least. what may be the worst obstacle is time. Quality control uses up time which, in the media world, is always in short supply. And many MAS take a long time to bear fruit (like education), or simply to get known.

None of the MAS is perfect, but their drawbacks may seem almost insignificant compared to what appears to me as a basic flaw of media ethics as it is conceived nowadays: it creates the notion that the newsperson is wholly responsible for what is good or bad in the media ; that if only he/she behaved ethically, media would be cured of their many ills. The journalist is turned into a scapegoat. When reading codes or attending seminars on ethics, the impression one gets is that some of the most serious failings of US journalism consists in moonlighting, plagiarising, accepting gifts and favours, using unnamed sources, uttering 'politically incorrect' epithets or being rude to grieving relatives.

We are led to believe that newspeople make the major decisions: allocate resources and shape editorial policy. But was it because journalists were unethical that media, from the twenties to the sixties, ignored reports on the dangers of tobacco? Is it because journalists are unethical that there is so little coverage of the outside world? Admittedly, it is wrong not to check one's facts or to distort the meaning of a speech by inaccurate quotes or to be rude to grieving relatives (issues much debated in seminars and workshops). That type of misdeed is highly visible to media consumers and the amount of them adds up to a considerable volume. But in bad service to the public does it honestly compare with the misdeeds of media firms, like omitting news that might irritate advertisers, not giving reporters the means to do their job properly?

Ethics have played a role in the evolution, in a slow, subtle way. And their part is bound to increase exponentially, as is clear in new democracies, in Eastern Europe, Latin America and black Africa. However, expecting too much from ethics is just as dangerous as ignoring ethics. Nowadays, the major threat to media freedom, hence to their quality, is in a wild exploitation of communication channels by giant companies, such as Time-Warner or News International. Ethics cannot by themselves make market forces serve mankind. Even if MAS developed everywhere at all levels and linked into a network, which does not seem likely in the near future - even then it would still not be enough. There would always be a need for laws and regulations.

So it is not a matter of either/or. What is needed is combination Law + Market + Ethics. People have heard about the Law and also about the Market. They have heard much less about Ethics and almost nothing about MAS. Media ethics should be looked upon as one means of preserving and improving media freedom and quality, on which the survival of human society is predicated. Ethics are not only a direct means to obtain quality media, but indirectly a means for the professionals to obtain the trust, hence the support of the public.

Professionals are not numerous and are financially dependent on media owners. Since they cannot count on politicians or businessmen to volunteer assistance, they can only turn to voters/consumers, who are legion and can exert powerful pressure on decision-makers. In other words, ethics should not be merely a concern for the professionals: the public needs to be involved.

Regulation and Self-regulation

Even though the media in democratic societies ostensibly enjoy freedom, they are in fact in all countries subject to quite a number of laws and regulations. Instruments for their regulation are constitutions, penal codes and general laws, in some cases special press laws or international declarations and conventions. Concerning constitutions and laws one can say that constitutions tend to grant rights to journalists and restrict the power of the government in this field, whereas laws can be both rights granting and rights restricting for journalists. It is usually constitutions that grant Press Freedom and Freedom of Expression as well as prohibit censorship. Exceptions for this are the UK with the marked absence of a constitution, and France where Press Freedom is instead granted through the adoption of the Declaration of Human Rights in 1789 and the European Convention on Human Rights in 1950.

A study of the situation in the 12 European Union member states from before the enlargement of 1995 shows that special laws on the press exist in Italy (rights and duties of journalists), Luxembourg (very restrictive and negative), Portugal (collides with other laws), in Denmark and France. Most press laws tend to be restrictive rather than rights granting to journalists, the exception being the Swedish press law which is oriented towards protecting the press from undue influence of the government and other interest groups.

Restrictions of Press Freedom have been cited in most countries' studies (except Italy) and usually consist of restrictions caused by laws in cases of privacy violation (UK, France, Spain), libel, defamation and slander (Belgium), criminal offences (Denmark), court proceedings, protection concerning minors (UK, Spain, Germany), the naming of suicide victims (Denmark) and the denial of the holocaust (the Netherlands). The biggest group of restrictions concern state secrets or national or public security (Spain, UK, Germany, Greece and Ireland), and this is also the area which is most often abused by governments in attempts to muzzle the press. Complaints of massive press freedom infringe-ments through the legal situation come from Portugal, UK, Belgium, Ireland, Luxembourg and Greece. This is an indication of how fragile the relationship between democracies and their press is.

In general the following elements are regulated in a legal form: press freedom, freedom of expression, privacy, libel/defamation/slander, right to reply, access to public information, discrimination, precondemnation and court proceedings, responsibility of the publication, censorship, source protection, and minors. Privacy is protected in a number of countries through laws rather than the constitution. Protected are in general private persons and especially their right to their own image.

Privacy protection is often restricted, when a public interest in the story about a person can be determined. Persons of public interest like rock and film stars, royalty but also politicians usually enjoy a lesser degree of protection of privacy. In other words, in most countries it is assumed that persons who have public functions and responsibilities are by definition 'of public interest' and can therefore not claim special protection. Protection of privacy is one of those areas that depend not only on the legal situation but also on the cultural context. It is for example only occasionally a problem area in Germany where it is not subject of major legal prescriptions, but a huge problem area in the UK where legal prescriptions are also missing. It is therefore an area that depends on the interest the press is taking.

The other side of the protection of privacy is represented by the regulations of libel, defamation and slander. This covers the area where a person's honour or reputation is damaged by publication of untrue, inaccurate and false information, rumours, assumptions and allegations. The difficult area in this matter is the question whether an allegation or information can be proven accurate or confirmed. In a number of countries the laws on this matter are used frequently against the media, for example in Greece, Ireland, Luxembourg and the UK.

Special situations exist in Belgium and Luxembourg where libel-laws on attacks against the king, civil servants or officials respectively exist and can be used against journalists. Compared to this the situation in present Russia is also questionable, where politicians enjoy special protection of their right to privacy instead of losing their privilege to their public function. The right of reply is not granted in Ireland, Portugal, and the UK. In the Netherlands it is not legally granted but can be invoked by court order. No information was available on the situation in France, and Greece. All other countries studied gave their citizens a right to have a reply published on a matter that concerned them and about which the press had written.

Access to public information is guaranteed for everybody in Germany, Denmark, the Netherlands, Portugal, since 1986 in Greece and implicitly through the adoption of the Human Rights Convention in Italy. It is specially granted to journalists in Portugal, where it can be challenged by the Act about State Secrets from 1993. It is not granted in Ireland and the UK, and in Luxembourg it is dealt with by the Code of Ethics, not by any law. It is not regulated in Spain and the situation in France remains unclear.

Discrimination of ethnic minorities and discrimination in general is prohibited by law in Germany, Belgium, Denmark, France, Portugal, and the UK, by the Constitution in the Netherlands and Spain, and by the Code of Conduct or Code of Ethics in Ireland, the UK and Italy. No information was available on the situation in Greece and Luxembourg. Precondemnation is constitutionally prohibited in Spain, legally in the UK and Denmark, by the Code of Conduct or Ethics in Italy, and with reference to the European Human Rights Convention in Germany and France. No information was available on the situation in

Greece, Belgium, Luxembourg, the Netherlands and Portugal. It is however one of the prerequisites of modern democracies that any person is considered not guilty until proven otherwise and the media in all democratic countries are asked to respect this democratic principle or else face prosecution.

In most countries it is the journalist who is held accountable for the publication. In some countries the law asks for the designation of a responsible editor (Germany, France). In general however journalists prefer to be held responsible for their own products. Press Freedom and Press Regulation (or nowadays rather Media Regulation) are two fundamentally contradictory principles in modern democracies. Media Freedom has been fought for and has been instituted because the press is seen as an important player in the control of the government in particular and the political and economic system in general. But controlling the powers leads again to the creation of power which needs control - and that is where media regulation comes into play.

When we look at media regulation we look at a very delicate system of checks and balances. The state of the constitution or the legal system tells us little about how this delicate system of opposing powers really interacts. Press freedom, freedom of expression, the prohibition of censorship may be granted in the constitution, but in reality they may be continuously under siege, through subtle or unsubtle means of pressure: by placing partisan people into influential functions in the mass media management, by controlling printing or distribution systems, or by invoking laws that protect the state security, journalists are hindered and prevented from fulfilling their tasks: to inform the public and to provide chances for the control of power of authorities and interest groups.

On the other hand, the media may abuse their influence on the public by being partisan, abusive, slanderous or negligent. There is a part of the media that has made it its task to feed the public with sensations rather than information, because sex, crime and violence sell. This part of the media does so with good economic reasoning, but in justification of this action often argues that this is what the public wants, while deliberately underestimating that it may simply be what is more easily consumed by the public as a reflex rather than as a rational intent. The media may easily be instrumental in ruining a person's reputation, career and life. It may even bring down a government. And it is this power that provokes governments to regulate the media by restricting it, claiming to protect the individual and often doing that.

Yet, the temptation is great to use the measures to protect the individual into instruments of control over the media. And that is a dangerous development for the democratic system. Journalists all over the world have answered this challenge by organising what is called self-regulation of the press. Self-regulation of the press finds its most concrete expression in the numerous Codes of Ethics or Practice that journalists have accepted as their own professional guidelines. The codes are most frequently adopted by journalists only, but in some countries (Belgium, Greece, Norway, Poland and Sweden) journalists and publishers have joined in the adoption of the codes, even though tension areas between publishers and journalists may exist in a number of fields, for example when dealing with the separation of editorial content and advertising or when dealing with stories that might trigger off economic repercussions.

A recent study of 31 national codes has found no less than 57 principles journalists vow to adhere to in the various countries, and the ten principles that were found most often in the various codes are : truthfulness, honesty, accuracy of information; correction of errors; prohibition of discrimination on the basis of race/ ethnicity/ religion etc.; respect for privacy; prohibition to accept bribes or any other benefits; fair means in information collection; prohibition to allow any outsider to have influence on the journalistic work; prohibition of discrimination on the basis of sex/ social class etc.; freedom of expression, speech, comment, criticism; professional secrecy. Comparing these principles, we find that there is quite some correspondence with the above list of elements that are generally subject to media regulation.

Elements regulated in legal form:	Ten principles most often found in national Codes of Ethics or Practice:
Press Freedom	Freedom of expression, speech, comment, criticism
Freedom of Expression	Respect for Privacy
Censorship	Professional secrecy
Privacy	Truthfulness, honesty, accuracy of information
Right to Reply	Correction of errors
Access to Public Information	Fair means in information collection
Source Protection	Prohibition of discrimination on the basis of race/ethnicity /religion etc.
Libel/Defamation/ Slander	Prohibition of discrimination on the basis of sex/social class etc.
Discrimination	Prohibition to allow any outsider to have influence on the journalistic work
Precondemnation and court proceedings	Prohibition to accept bribes or any other benefits
Minors	
Responsibility for the publication	

In fact, all except the right to reply and access to information can be found in more than half of the codes and the only point not specifically mentioned in the codes is special protection of minors even though in practice their protection is frequently covered under more general principles and very often minors are given special consideration in journalistic practice. It is therefore interesting to note that regulation and self-regulation of the media are in fact dealing with the same issues: it is just the perspective that differs and the question of who deals with the transgressions: the legal system or the profession.

6

Gender Equality in Media

Women are still the missing story in today's media. After more than a decade of research indicating that women are dissatisfied with their media portrayal the industry has done little to change its practices. Women are grossly under-represented and where they do feature, they are still portrayed in a narrow range of stereotyped roles. But not only women are unhappy. Generally, the contemporary journalism scene reflects an accumulated mistrust of media organisations, a widespread scepticism of journalists' ethics and resentment of the growing power of the media.

Political and public debate, both at national and international level, indicate that there is an increasing demand for new rules and regulations aimed at making media more socially responsible. Gender issues may not be the driving force behind this movement, but media failure in this area adds to public anxiety. Journalists and media organisations may, with varying degrees of success, disavow responsibility for the non- and misrepresentation of women, but there is little doubt that media professionals, whether they own the newspapers and broadcast media or whether they are employed to gather, edit and disseminate information have an urgent need to articulate principles of performance and to make themselves ethically accountable in a transparent and public manner.

Governments around the world have tried to justify restrictive media laws with ethical considerations, arguing that the press will only be responsible if the government forces it to be. It is not, therefore, an auspicious background in which to make a positive evaluation of self-regulation as it affects treatment of women. And it is not just a matter of making public complaints systems more efficient and more effective, it is also a question of trying to win the argument within the media industry that inequalities in portrayal of women are poisonous to the good health of a fair and harmonious society.

Self-Regulatory Mechanisms

Most countries have laws prohibiting discrimination on the basis of sex but there are few cases where these are tested in confronting the invisibility or unfair portrayal of women in the media. Apart from libel, privacy and other laws defining the limits of press freedom vis-à-vis the individual citizen, questions of ethics are normally left to the press itself or to self-regulatory bodies including members from outside the profession. In some countries the government intervenes directly, establishing a license system with codes of conduct incorporated into the media law or by setting up a commission with government representation to determine who can work as a journalist. While ethical issues are covered in many of these measures, no case is known where a license was revoked or a journalist's accreditation withdrawn because of unethical conduct involving gender issues.

On a world-wide scale self-regulatory bodies, such as press councils, are in the minority. They exist in several of the industrialised western countries, their establishment is being discussed in several countries of central and eastern Europe and the former Soviet Union, but there are few press councils in Asia, Africa or Latin America. Press councils, where they do exist, normally consist of representatives from journalists', editors' and publishers' organisations. Often the chairperson is a media lawyer. Individuals have the right to complain to the press council if they feel they have been mistreated by the media. The press council evaluates the complaints and if it judges them justified, reprimands the paper.

In Germany, for instance, the press council monitors press behaviour in relation to the Press Code which embraces 16 principles designed to preserve professional ethics but do not constitute grounds for legal liability. The Council comprises two bodies, the Council Plenum and a Complaints Committee, which issues rulings on complaints. Both bodies are made up of journalists and publishers. There are no provisions that women have to be represented. The Swedish press council provides a system free to complainants and fully supported by the press. All newspapers have bound themselves by contract to submit to the council's ruling. Appropriate retractions, replies or reprimands are usually published within a few days.

Press councils adopt charters which define ethical principles. Most of these charters denounce discrimination on the basis of race, sex, national origin or religious belief, but a short survey of annual reports published by press councils in various countries (Sweden, Denmark, Germany, UK and Australia) shows that no complaints or cases have been taken up in the last year which confront the issue of gender equality directly. Most cases focus on violations of privacy or demand a right of reply. Where the press is state-owned, the government has the possibility to exercise control over ethical questions. But while this power is regularly used to intervene where questions of politics or the interests of state officials come into play, there are no cases where governments have reprimanded state-owned papers for unfair portrayal of women.

In some countries, such as Saudi Arabia or Iran, where religious laws govern media ethics, indecent portrayal of women can be prosecuted. But here religious leaders define what constitutes decent and fair portrayal on behalf of women without women being directly involved in discussions of media ethics. In Latin America, the "Colegios de periodistas" have established so called "tribunales de etica", which monitor adherence to the code of ethics. But there have been no cases where the "tribunal de etica" disciplined journalists for sexist reporting. While the colegios and also the journalists' unions have codes of ethics that denounce discrimination on the basis of sex, no special guidelines for reporting gender issues have been developed.

Journalists' organisations have adopted codes of conduct or practice defining ethics in journalism. Virtually all these codes include a clause calling on the professionals not to write or publish material that discriminates against persons on the basis of race, sex, religion or national origin.

The International Federation of Newspaper Publishers (FIEJ) has never adopted an international code of practice for publishers. While the IFJ code represents what is an accepted standards of ethics in journalism worldwide, national codes often define journalists' ethics in more detail and in some cases provide for sanctions if the code is violated. In Australia, for instance, any member of the Australian Journalists' Association (AJA) may charge another with a breach of the code. The complaint is then considered by an independent judiciary committee. About

150 complaints are received each year. So far, these have not been recorded in a systematic way, but the General Secretary of the AJA reported that there have been no successful complaints against journalists breaching the code's paragraph on sexist reporting.

Some journalists organisations have developed guidelines for journalists or how to avoid sexist reporting. These try to make members more aware of gender issues, without providing for sanctions or disciplinary procedures. Reporting guidelines further approach the subject in a positive manner and, instead of aiming to impose correct behaviour on journalists, these initiatives aim at changing journalists' attitudes to women when selecting and presenting news. Generally, the issue of portrayal of women in the press is barely addressed in any of the industry-based self-regulatory bodies.

There have been no cases where press councils have reprimanded papers for sexist reporting in spite of the fact that women, as numerous studies have shown, are dissatisfied with the way they are portrayed in the media. This is largely due to the fact that most women do not use the systems of complaint. They feel that the question of non- and misrepresentation of women cannot sufficiently be addressed and solved in bodies that focus on individual cases. A violation of privacy is easier to prove and a right of reply correcting factual mistakes is easier to obtain than trying to prove that articles in the press only show half the picture or that the positions and role of women in society are misrepresented.

Considering that women, even though they make up more than half of the world's population, are grossly under represented in political parties, government posts, decision-making positions in private companies or in public life in general, the press might argue that newspapers do little more than mirror the current standards and priorities of civil society. But women's criticism of the press for not showing the advances women have made in recent years but instead opting for stereotyped portrayal remains valid. In many journalists organisations questions of portrayal have become an issue largely due to the growing number of female members, who call on the organisation to take a stand on gender issues. But most journalists' unions have been slow in addressing the issue and few have adopted equal opportunities policies or guidelines for non-sexist reporting.

Public Broadcasting

While the situation in commercial private broadcasting is similar to the one in the press (with few exceptions as for instance ITV stations in the UK and networks in the US) public service broadcasting is subject to broader and deeper regulation. The Canadian Broadcasting Act of 1991, for instance, states in Article 3 (iii): " through its programming and the employment opportunities arising out of its operations, serve the needs and interests, reflect the circumstances and aspirations, of Canadian men, women and children, including equal rights,...".

Even before the broadcasting act a rich body of policy and statutes provided for high journalistic standards and practice in portrayal of women, but two studies of the 1988 licence renewal hearings showed that the Canadian Radio and Television and Telecommunications Commission (CRTC) was reluctant to use its power to push broadcasters to respect and implement the guidelines. Applicants for licenses were hardly asked about gender stereotyping, it was not made clear to them that gender portrayal was governed by a conditions of license; and sanctions were not imposed in the case of applicants who ignored the guidelines.

The adoption of Article (iii) in the broadcasting act has given the issue more prominence and while no sweeping changes in broadcasting policy have been reported, the Canadian Association of Broadcasters (CAB) has addressed the issue of gender reporting more regularly and more seriously. In 1993 the CAB adopted a voluntary code regarding violence in television programming, which complements the CAB's code of ethics and which addresses the question of violence against women directly. The Canadian example makes a point in favour of regulation and generally, public service broadcasting companies have been more open to addressing the question of gender portrayal.

Most state-owned broadcasting stations in developing countries have special programmes for women as an integral part of their programming schedule. Zimbabwe Broadcasting Corporation, for instance, has an hour-long programme everyday offering advice to women on issues of child care, health etc. "But mainstream programming remains a male domain," concluded women journalists from Zimbabwe at a women's conference in Harare in August 1993.

In Japan, women journalists reproach the public service broadcasting station NHK for lagging behind on gender issues and state that promotion of fair portrayal of women does not figure highly on NHKs agenda. Not that they are surprised given that less than 10 per cent of the industry workforce is female. In Europe, two groups of countries can be identified. The first, a minority group, including the United Kingdom, Spain, the Netherlands and the Nordic countries, is a group where there is a vision of the need to protect and to promote standards in media as they affect women.

The second group, including France, Belgium, Italy and Germany, have laws which define general principles of equality and profit discrimination but do not have codes of practice by which media standards can be judged. Bodies such as the UK Broadcasting Standards Council and the Portrayal department of the Dutch public service NOS have shown a possible way forward. They not only issue guidelines, take up complaints, monitor programmes and publish reports, but they also developed strategies aimed at taking the issue to the newsroom and at involving the public in the debate.

Effect of Self-regulatory Mechanisms in Gender Equality

Looking at the world's media we see a shrug of indifference about the status of women in society. Apart from few initiatives in public broadcasting, some women's publications which aim at portraying women more accurately and equal opportunities programmes sponsored by a few journalists' organisations, mainstream media have not seriously addressed the issue of gender equality. Self-regulatory mechanisms in the press have not proven to be effective in promoting fair portrayal of women. Press councils, where they exist, have barely addressed the issue. Publishers' codes of practice have done little to change stereotyped portrayal of women and journalists' unions trying to implement codes of conduct through disciplinary procedures are paralysed the dilemma of attacking the individuals they exist to protect.

The reasons for the failure of self-regulatory mechanisms in promoting fair portrayal of women in mainstream media are many and various. In the industrialised countries, commercialisation of media has been identified as one of the factors keeping women from having more access to and fair portrayal in the media. In the United States, the notion of "tabloid television", with a diet of sex, violence and sensationalism in abundance, is fast becoming the mainstream force in programming. In an environment where economic considerations and profit maximisation largely determine media content, non-populist issues such as gender equality will not make the headlines and journalists' ethics are difficult to enforce against the overriding forces of the market.

Another reason is the general lack of awareness of publishers and journalists alike. Codes of conduct have two major setbacks in trying to change journalists' attitudes on gender portrayal. First, they are difficult to enforce without co-operation of publishers and tend to put pressure on the individual journalist who may not be in the position to change his or her company's editorial policy. Secondly, they address the issue of gender portrayal in a negative and combative manner. Journalists are called upon to avoid discrimination but they are not given advice on how to do this or how to effectively promote equality in their newsrooms. In countries where regulation has succeeded in promoting gender equality it is always accompanied by supplementary initiatives aimed at changing attitudes of programme makers.

While press councils and codes of ethics can serve as a point of reference, particularly in the areas of monitoring, training and strengthening professional organisations a more comprehensive approach is needed to promote gender equality in media portrayal. More practical initiative has to be taken to put codes of conduct into practice.

Media monitoring

The failure of the press to take up gender issues is being watched formally and informally be a range of national and local monitoring organisations who examine media coverage and use the information gathered to promote a dialogue with media professionals. Such work is vital to understand the media landscape in which women live. Media monitoring studies provide useful material to raise awareness among media professionals about what constitutes fair portrayal of women in the media. They provide practical examples and could help make the discussion about journalists' ethics less theoretical and more linked to journalists' everyday working lives.

If self-regulation is to have any meaning at all it requires an understanding by journalists of the issues involved in the portrayal and representation of women in media. Training institutions play an important role in shaping the professional qualities of young journalists, but their contribution should be put in a broader perspective by 14 comparing the influence which various sources exercise on the development of ethical values.

Most apprentice journalists come from a social and cultural environment in which fundamental messages, received at home at school and in the framework of popular culture, have already formed an overall impression that the question of gender is a marginal one. The journalism training process does little to challenge these prejudices and, indeed, there is evidence that in some circumstances, it reinforces the notion that gender issues are not terribly important. In the field of media portrayal of women the performance of journalism schools in dramatically underplayed.

If journalism training institutions are unconvinced about the issue of how media portray women and sexism in general, it is not surprising that most journalists, men and women, starting out on a career in journalism, are vulnerable to early suggestions that gender is largely irrelevant and marginal to the business of ethical journalism.

Role of media women associations

Media women associations exist in a large number of countries and they have done a lot of work in monitoring media, publishing reports on portrayal of women and organising activities to promote gender equality and to access of women to the media. In terms of membership they often overlap with the national journalists' organisations having large number of female journalists as members. Therefore there is scope for more direct co-operation between women media associations and journalists' unions in organising joint activities or discussing reporting guidelines. At an international level the IFJ has involved regional media women associations in its "Media for Democracy programme".

In regional workshops portrayal of women in the media is being discussed among female journalists, women media associations and women's groups with the aim of developing a common strategy. Similar initiatives by international organisations of publishers have not been started so far. Media women associations need to be brought into the debate on journalists' ethics. With extensive experience in the area of gender portrayal they can usefully contribute ideas and strategies how to make self-regulatory mechanisms more effective.

Journalists organisations can do more to put codes of ethics into practice. Apart from making each member aware that the code exists and that it does address the question of gender portrayal, union meetings and seminars could be organised to focus on how journalists select and present news. Journalists' organisations can help to put the issue on the agenda of editorial conferences by supporting those journalists who try to promote fair portrayal in the newsroom. Initiatives of individual publishers, such as introducing women's pages that go beyond the usual fashion-children-gossip-approach need to be supported.

But co-operation of journalists', publishers' and broadcasters' organisations as representatives of the profession is crucial if one tries to make codes of conduct more effective. It is not sufficient that journalists' unions try to enforce the code of ethics within their membership. Co-operation of media owners and a joint approach to media ethics is needed to make self-regulation more effective.

7

Globalisation of Media and Young Generation

Approximately one-third of the world's population is made up of 2 billion young people under 18. They make up half the population in the least developed nations; less than a quarter in the most industrialized ones. Their challenges range from basic survival to discrimination and exploitation. Moreover, there are myriad differences in cultures, traditions and values. Nevertheless, children and youth everywhere share some universal traits: They are fundamentally more optimistic, more open and curious than their adult counterparts. Increasingly, children are enjoying unprecedented freedoms in many countries.

Unfortunately, others confront growing health and social problems, ranging from deepening poverty and ethnic strife to substance abuse and sexually transmitted diseases, political turmoil and warfare. Arguably, the proliferation and globalization of media are among the key factors that have shaped and defined the current generation of young people. In many countries, youth have access to a greater number of multimedia choices than ever before-conventional, satellite and cable TV channels; radio stations; newspapers and magazines; the internet and computer and video games.

In addition, many are exposed to the same programs, the same characters and the same marketed spin-off products. Today there is greater availability of foreign programming and media, and less official censorship and control in many parts of the world. Information, email and images flow around the world faster and more freely than ever. Indeed, mass media are making the world smaller, and culture and media are increasingly inextricable, especially for young people.

Television: A Dominant Medium for Young People

Television is the dominant medium for young people-and adults-around the world. From the mid-1980s to the mid-1990s, the number of television channels, household television sets and hours spent watching television more than doubled. There are now approximately 250 television sets per thousand inhabitants in the world-far more than the number of telephones. Satellite television reaches all continents, offering increasing numbers of channels targeting specific market segments, including young viewers. In the late 1990s, some 50 television channels directed specifically to children were launched, several of which have had enormous international success. However, this has caused national television services in many areas to cut back their own production of children's programs.

As the graphs illustrate, weekly television viewing far surpasses radio listening in nearly every region, and dwarfs newspaper and internet use. Average daily use of television among those school-age children around the world with access ranges from between 1.5 hours to more than four hours; many of these same children will rarely read a book. The prominence of television in young people's daily lives

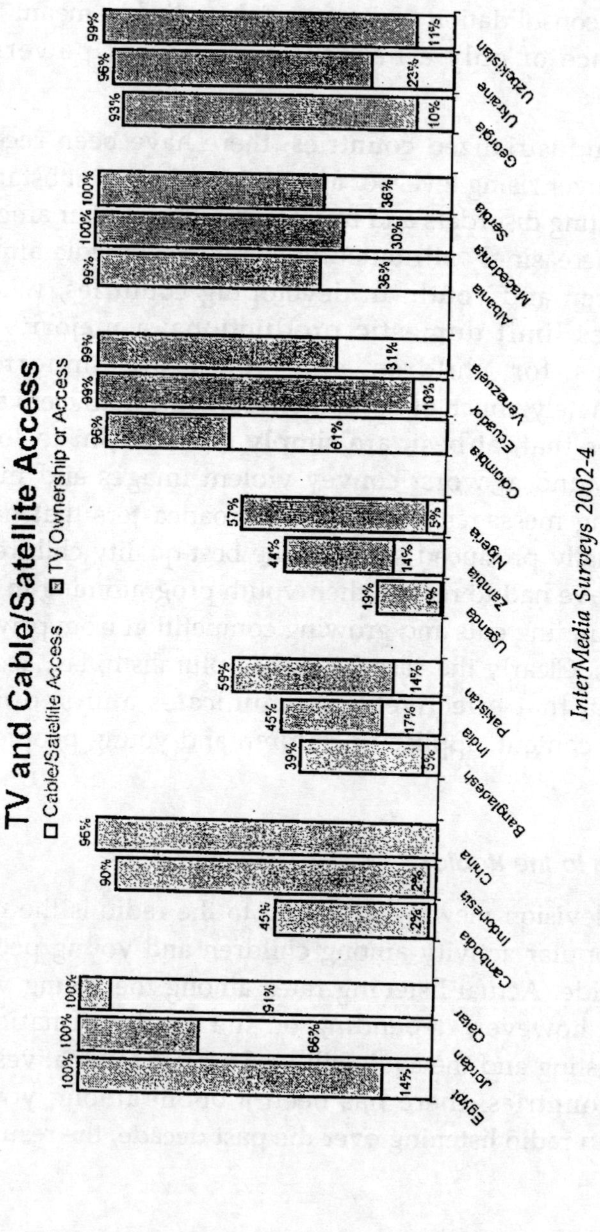
TV and Cable/Satellite Access
Cable/Satellite Access
TV Ownership or Access
Egypt
Jordan
Qatar
Cambodia
Indonesia
China
Bangladesh
India
Pakistan
Uganda
Zambia
Nigeria
Colombia
Ecuador
Venezuela
Albania
Macedonia
Serbia
Georgia
Ukraine
Uzbekistan
InterMedia Surveys 2002-4

makes it one of their major information sources about the world around them. The prevalence of television viewing among young people raises serious concerns about recent national and global trends in the television industry. The rampant consolidation of commercial media has meant the dominance of only a handful of large and powerful companies.

In industrialized countries, there have been recent outcries over rising levels of aggression, obesity, substance abuse, eating disorders and unsafe sexual behaviour among youth, increasingly attributed to commercial media aimed at children and youth. In developing countries, where resources limit domestic productions, a majority of programs for children and youth are imported. Unfortunately, much of the content contains characters and messages that, at best, are simply not relevant to local cultures, and at worst convey violent images and mass marketing messages. Plus, public broadcasters that have traditionally produced some of the best-quality children's media have had to reduce their youth programming in the face of funding cuts and growing competition from private channels. Clearly the case for media pluralism, i.e., access to media that effectively communicates and supplies relevant content, applies to children and young people as well.

Listening to the Radio

After television viewing, listening to the radio is the next most popular activity among children and young people worldwide. Actual listening rates among the young vary greatly, however, depending on the quality of national broadcasting and the availability of private alternatives. In many countries, there has been a boom among young people in radio listening over the past decade, the result of the emergence of dozens of private radio stations. This is particularly the case in Africa and the former Soviet bloc countries. Most young people tune in to the radio primarily for music and entertainment. However, some local radio stations have been very successful in attracting and informing more socially active segments of the population, young and old alike.

A good example is the ANEM network of independent radio stations in the former Yugoslavia. It has become a major source of diverse information and entertainment for youth interested in social life. In some countries, listening to the largely political fare of public international radio broadcasters-the BBC, VOA, Deutsche Welle and Radio France Internationale, among them-remains surprisingly high among young people. According to 2003 surveys, 16 percent of young people 15 to 19 listened to international radio in Albania, 12 percent in Bangladesh, 21 percent in Nigeria and 26 percent in urban Haiti. These relatively high listening rates testify to young people's interest in political and social events, and reflect the need for high-quality information, still lacking in many countries.

Use of Computers and Internet

The internet has been gaining popularity among young people, though at a much slower pace than television and radio. In spite of significant differences among the developed and developing world, the use of computers and the internet is rising steadily, fastest among young men. That there are so many more computer-literate young people than adults indicates the younger generation's greater interest in and aptitude for technological advances. Around the world, young users are increasingly turning to the internet as a source of information, communication, socializing and entertainment. At the same time, web access is the source of the greatest divide, both between countries (internet use in industrialized countries far outpaces use in the developing world), and within countries (internet use concentrated among wealthier and better-educated urban youth).

Nevertheless, even in countries where internet and computer use is low, young people actively seek access whenever possible, most often in internet cafes. Young people are enthusiastic about the internet because, more than any other medium, it helps them establish contact with the outside world and freely seek information. Perhaps it is 'free' access to information that also accounts for the higher levels of trust young people (and adults as well) often place in information on the web than in information from traditional media.

But, the openness of the web and young people's apparent inability to distinguish clearly between content and advertising worries parents and child advocates alike. Young people use the internet primarily for communicating (email and chat rooms); downloading (computer games, software and music); and obtaining information (about education, entertainment, sports, "taboo" topics not addressed by adults, and news that may be censored for political motives).

Print Media

In contrast to the steady rise of other media, in many countries print media have experienced a setback from the role they once played. Several recent developments have served to further decrease the numbers of young readers of print media. In part, this is a result of the improved quantity and quality of information available from television and radio. In industrialized countries, young people are distracted by numerous media choices and technologies. In poorer countries, few youth-oriented publications exist and those that do often have limited circulation or are too expensive for most youth to afford. In the former Soviet bloc countries, youth press once played a fairly vibrant role and received significant government backing.

Since the fall of the Berlin Wall, however, youth press has largely disappeared and has not been replaced by a regular alternative forum for young people. Starting in the early 1990s, newspaper readership levels declined sharply throughout the region, especially in those countries experiencing the greatest economic difficulties. Many publications folded without government subsidies and could not attract sufficient advertisers or subscribers. Those that did survive had to raise their prices, making them unaffordable for many. Lastly, the distribution system was so badly weakened in many countries that it is now common for newspapers and magazines to arrive in rural areas weeks and months late, if at all.

The publications in strongest demand among young people are those that appeal to their specialized interests-comic books and popular specialized magazines on computers, fashion, sports, science, business and music. Many are high quality, with slick and appealing content that cater to young people's interests, yet are often too costly for the average young person (or adult).

Informational Divide

In spite of improvements in quantity and quality of media for children and youth around the world over the last decade, there still exists an informational divide both between and within countries. The divide between better-educated, wealthier youth and less-educated, rural youth determines access to, use of and preferences for different types of media. The informational divide takes many different forms. In developing countries, highest overall media use most often occurs among urban, affluent young people. But in some countries, television viewing rates are just as high in rural as in urban areas because of community viewing habits and because of the lack of alternative media. In industrialized countries, in contrast, media use tends to be highest among lower socio-economic groups because television is inexpensive entertainment. While wealthier young people devote less time to television and video games, they spend more time using computers and print media.

Boys tend to access media more than girls, and use audio-visual and digital media more often as well. Yet, in some cultures, the opposite is true because restrictions on girls' activities often keep them at home. For the same reason, boys frequent outdoor places of entertainment more often, such as cinemas, internet cafes and video parlours. The vast majority of young people in the world do not have access to computers or the internet, mainly due to economic reasons. Buying a computer and securing a web connection are still big investments in many countries. In addition, poor infrastructure puts young people in smaller towns and villages at a disadvantage.

Technical problems also discourage wide internet use in some countries and do not allow young people to fully appreciate all the possibilities the web offers. Apart from economic considerations, there are also young people who shy away from the internet because of the prevalence of English-language content, or the absence of content in their own language. Others are simply not particularly interested or do not fully understand its uses and possibilities.

As media options for most children have grown in recent decades, so too have concerns about the quality of media aimed at children. Growing numbers of parents, educators, researchers and policy-makers around the world are alarmed about the lack of quality media for children and young people and the growing availability of low-quality entertainment featuring violence, sexual content, undesirable role models and lack of diversity. There are also serious questions about the short- and long-term effects of this material.

Numerous studies have been done on the effects of media-violence in media in particular-on children. Young people often speak of the power the media has on their lives, and any parent can attest to the impressionable, unquestioning and imitative nature of children. How much the mass media influence children and young people is somewhat debatable, but sociologists and researchers in different regions have observed some of the following adverse effects:

— growing influence of entertainment media on youth style and identity

— decreasing role of traditional sources of influence: family, school, community, religion, etc.

— appeal of individualism and personal, as opposed to collective or societal, achievement

— some confusion in values (misguided sense of right and wrong, of human relations)

— an increasingly blurred line between advertisements and program content

— distortion of reality and rising expectation gaps

— newfound culture of "glamour" and "celebrity"

— creation of harmful or unrealistic stereotypes; a promotion of intolerance or apathy

— emphasis on the banal and trivial; de-emphasis on education, creativity and culture

— tendency for young people to think less for themselves and to follow media-set agendas.

Children and youth advocates lament these negative effects because they recognize the enormous, potentially positive influences media can have on young audiences-namely broadening their world outlook and destroying stereotypes, increasing communication and access to diverse ideas, and promoting critical thinking and participation in social and political life. Fueling concerns is the decline of parental supervision over young people's media habits. In part, many parents are simply too busy to be closely involved in what their children are consuming.

Also, youth programming is sometimes not scheduled when most youth are actually watching, so they end up watching adult material. In addition, it is increasingly difficult for adults to know what young people are consuming. They can't keep up with the changing television fare, electronic games and websites, and they also cannot track where their children are consuming media-in their rooms, at school, at friends' houses, in internet cafes or even just hanging out. In Japan, for example, the majority of young people possess mobile phones and more than three-quarters of them access the internet via their phone.

Quality Media for Young People

There is no clear consensus on what comprises quality

media for children/young people. Producers, children's specialists, parents and children all have somewhat different notions, although criteria such as being credible, comprehensible and uplifting, and empowering youth to think for themselves are recognized as key ingredients. Indeed, it seems easier to agree on what quality media for young people is not: dull, boring, patronizing, overly commercial or violent, vulgar, disrespectful, biased, manipulative or corruptive.

While it is important to remember children and young people are as diverse in their tastes as adults, they tend to favour entertainment-oriented content, with lively and interesting characters, informal style and language, and dynamic and engaging presentation. They are also naturally drawn to subjects that interest them-music, sports, style, culture, celebrities, science and technology, etc.-and those that convey messages about how to have fun, be successful and look good. Yet young people are not interested solely in light entertainment fare. They are also eager to learn, and drawn to information that shapes their identities, builds their sense of social belonging and makes sense of the world. They are attracted to content that entertains them, and to that which presents children and young people similar to themselves, in situations that relate to their own lives.

Many young people also appreciate media content that deals credibly with topics they may find difficult to discuss with parents or adults, such as personal relationships, sexuality, AIDS, drugs, self-esteem, etc. They value factual information and advice provided by experts, as well as material prepared and presented by young people themselves. In focus groups InterMedia has conducted in different countries, youth say they believe only young journalists can really understand their problems. Similarly, young people feel adults either miss the point or present issues in ways that are too serious, pedantic or patronizing. In addition, youth in countries with widespread poverty, corruption, political turmoil and/or disease also seek realistic, relevant and meaningful content to help them understand and cope with hardships they face in their daily lives.

In reality, in spite of all the media options seemingly available to many young people, young audiences aren't really given a fair choice. There is a dearth of quality programming for youth and children across the board. There is even less choice in the majority of countries heavily dependent on foreign imports. A great deal of exported media for children and young people are produced with formats and content that can appeal to and be understood by as many cultures as possible. Thus, the prevalence of animated programming and media violence is generally driven not so much because it is what young audiences want, but largely because of competition and global marketing.

Young people in the industrialized world are not all as apathetic and tuned out as they are sometimes perceived to be, and are interested in content meaningful to their lives. Studies in Western Europe and the United States make a distinction between apathy and cynicism, i.e., young people's expression of disinterest in social and political life is often superficial and "part of the condition" of being young. For many adolescents, "cynical chic" is a way of dealing with their own sense of powerlessness and what they see as "inconsistency, complacency or hypocrisy on the part of adults." Thus, many young people will say discussion of serious issues is "boring," but they will often have interesting and informed opinions on these issues.

One of the largest problems regarding media rights for youth is simply lack of coverage of children and young people in the news. What little coverage there is too often portrays youth in the context of sensationalist issues, e.g., child abuse, exploitation and violence, with little respect for the dignity and privacy of the children and scant opportunity for young people to speak for themselves. Young people around the world feel excluded from or disserved by the media when they are portrayed simplistically as superficial, apathetic, poverty stricken or delinquent.

The 2001 UNICEF-sponsored study in Buenos Aires, Montevideo and Santiago on students' perceptions of urban security issues is a good example of the media's powerful role in setting agendas and shaping opinions and images of youth. The study showed young people in these cities felt the media do not portray youth realistically or sympathetically. Media-and television in particular-often present a negative and exaggerated picture of young people as juvenile delinquents. A majority of respondents perceived from the media that youth commit more crimes than adults, crimes of equal gravity to those of adults, and crimes at an earlier age than in previous years. This kind of inaccurate and inflammatory coverage tends to distort public and political debate in favour of repressive, rather than preventive, educational solutions to growing violence in many societies.

Participation of Children and Young People

Dozens of examples of young people's participation in the media attest to their interest in the world around them, especially if given the chance to meaningfully express themselves on issues affecting them. A growing number of interest groups and media organizations have become involved, creating numerous opportunities for young people to participate in media. Participation takes many forms-content development, production, professional skills training and media education-and applies to television, radio, the internet, print media, video, photography and CDs.

The most visible and successful youth participation programs are usually those that incorporate the ideals of "genuine and effective" participation, i.e., an environment in which young people are involved in every step of the process from planning to evaluation. Challenges to "genuine and effective" participation include: getting adults to let go; creating an environment at home or school where participation is serious and encouraged; overcoming cultural norms that children should be seen and not heard; and generating enough funds to sustain projects. Youth participation in media generates highly positive outcomes for the young people themselves, as synthesized by the UNESCO Clearinghouse's 2001 Yearbook Outlooks on Children and Media:

— A strengthened sense of pride, power and self-esteem as a result of feeling their voices are worth listening to, that they are part of their community, and that they have achieved an understanding of others and of their own culture.

— A wish to see their own everyday dreams and their own local, social and ethnic culture and reality portrayed in the media.

— Strengthened ability and curiosity, and increased media competence, i.e., their critical understanding of the media.

— Greater social justice engendered by allowing young people who do not manage well in traditional, print-based schools to take part in audio-visual media production.

— Greater interest and involvement in society on their own terms, which in turn inspires action to improve coverage of youth issues in the media and the situations in their own communities.

The UNESCO International Clearinghouse on Children, Youth and Media is a good source for information on specific projects and issues involving children, youth and media around the world. In addition, UNICEF has two useful websites. A few examples of the growing number of successful media projects and programs for and with children and young people:

ANDI - The Brazilian News Agency for Children's Rights monitors media coverage of children and youth, and trains and works closely with journalists in their reporting on children and youth-related issues. ANDI's efforts have led to greatly increased and improved coverage of children and youth issues in the Brazilian media and the model is now being applied in eight other Latin American countries.

TROC - The Young Reporter of Albania. Dozens of young people, from 13 to 18, from all over the country receive training on this weekly TV news magazine program. Students learn all aspects of video news production and are responsible for planning and producing the weekly program with limited adult guidance. The program is very popular in Albania and in neighbouring countries among young viewers who value TROC as the first socially responsive TV show that provides perspectives from all over the country.

Mukto Khobor (Free News) - The widely viewed weekly, 25-minute news and current affairs program in Bangladesh, is produced by youth 11 to 17. It focuses on children and child rights issues, and provides a forum for young people to express their views, empowers young journalists with specialized skills, inspires young viewers who see the success of their peers' work in the media, and shows young people have valuable input on current problems.

Children and Broadcasting Foundation for Africa - Created in 1995 to ensure the implementation of the Africa Charter on Children and Broadcasting, and to sensitize broadcasters and producers to the need for good-quality children's television. CBFA targets young people 9 to 16, media professionals and broadcasters, conducting workshops, production seminars, screenings and meetings, with a focus on the needs and rights of children in Africa.

Egypt's Video and the Community Dreams project expands the knowledge and experience of the Centre for Development and Population Activities' "New Horizons" program and empowers and strengthens the voices of young women and girls in Egyptian society. Teams of women from four different Egyptian communities gain confidence in their video production skills, and in their ability to address challenging or sensitive topics. Team members gain new visibility as spokespeople and leaders and have helped to break down stereotypes. The teams' tapes have been used to spark discussion and promote the search for local solutions in each community.

Media Advocacy

In the last two decades, media for children and youth have become more of a global issue. Numerous players have begun to realize children's rights through the media-whether to ensure young audiences have access to diversified and high-quality media content, create opportunities for young people's voices to be heard, push for ethical coverage of children and youth, and strive for (self-) regulation of the media and for quality media education.

A broad range of governmental and non-governmental initiatives and activities speak to the growing commitment to realize children's rights through the media. Numerous meetings, conferences and summits have taken place on the subject. Excellent guidelines have been written on how to report on children's issues as well as how to ensure effective youth participation in media. Many important studies have been done exploring young people's media habits and the effects of media on youth attitudes and behaviour. Broadcasters and advertisers have adopted voluntary codes to ensure inappropriate material isn't aired during hours when young people watch or listen. Legislation has been passed requiring television and radio stations to devote a percentage of airtime to quality children's programming.

Numerous media consumer and watchdog groups hold the media to account when they do not live up to minimum standards and their social responsibilities toward the public, including children. While these are surely encouraging signs, serious obstacles to advocating for children and youth through the media remain, among them the lack of funding and political will, cultural differences, and the need for far more training for youth and for those producing material about or for young audiences. Such efforts must continue to harness the enormous positive potential of the increasingly powerful global media to make a real difference in children's lives around the world by informing them, listening to them and ultimately empowering them.

Media, Ethics and Reporting of Commercial Sexual Exploitation

Child abuse and exploitation have figured prominently in the mainstream media in recent years, it has invariably been in the context of horrifying evidence from court proceedings, or better still, the involvement of some well-known (adult) public figure. American researchers have found that although children under 10 made up almost 20% of the US population, they represented only one in every 60 characters on primetime TV. Children's voices are not heard - especially not by the rest of the community. But then the world of television is not like the real world. Its demography reflects its purposes: to produce audiences for advertisers. Looking at it through the prism of age reveals a population curve that, unlike the real world, but much like the curve of consumer spending, bulges in the middle years of life. That makes children and the elderly relatively neglected.

This analysis of the impact of the free-market is one aspect of prevailing currents of control of media and information sources. Another is the tendency of some governments and state authorities to manipulate information, usually through tight state controls of broadcasting media, to meet political imperatives which often do not reflect the considered needs and rights of abused sections of the population. It is in this context that media coverage of the commercial sexual exploitation of children, like the other aspects of children's lives, takes place.

The media industry is either a commercial undertaking which exists to produce profit, never more so than today with the growth in media outlets, achieved through new technology, bringing ruthless competition for limited markets, or it may be subject to political and state controls. In either case, journalists and media workers struggle to maintain a professional centre of gravity. In reality, it is futile for them to ignore the economic and political conditions in which they work. Yet media are, unarguably, a major influence on cultural development throughout the world; with a responsibility, many believe, particularly in sectors like public broadcasting, to inform and to educate.

The challenge facing media professionals, whether they own newspapers or broadcast media or whether they are employed to gather, edit and disseminate information, is to define rules and regulations by which they work and to articulate principles of performance which are transparent and can be tested in a public manner. But how? The question, as this paper tries to consider, requires serious examination of the way media work, of how existing principles of accountability apply, and how media must be freed from reins of political and economic control which limit professionalism and undermine ethical standards.

The media's role in the evolution of commercial sexual exploitation is complex. On the one hand, they tell the stories of abused and abuser, through news reports, photographs, documentaries, and drama. But on the other, they can themselves become the exploiter, for instance by creating sexually provocative images of children in news or advertising, or, at worst, as the vehicle for child pornography, or sources of information for paedophile networks and sexual tourism.

Furthermore, the way the media portray children has a profound impact on society's attitude to children and childhood, which also affects the way adults behave. Even the images children themselves see, especially of sex and violence, influence their expectation of their role in life. This paper does not seek to provide easy answers to complex and difficult issues nor to ethical dilemmas. But there are standards to be set and guidelines which media can adopt themselves in addressing the need for a public information policy which provides people with extensive, reliable and ethical reportage about the way children are treated in society.

Although there is much that can be improved in media performance, the conclusions are not only intended to make media more accountable and journalists more responsive to systems of complaint and public scrutiny. It is also a question of encouraging debate within media about the portrayal of children and their exploitation. This is an issue which defines the good health of a just and decent society and is, therefore, a matter of profound professional concern for all who work in media.

Media, Children and International Law

The international legislative and regulatory framework relevant to the role of media and the commercial sexual exploitation of children is ample, but not specific. These clauses do not constitute an exhaustive list, but offer some important pointers on the role and responsibility of journalists, and the media in general. For example:

The United Nations Convention on the Rights of the Child enshrines children's right to freedom of expression (Article 13); to protection of privacy and against attacks on his/her honour and reputation (Article 16); and also calls on the mass media to disseminate information and material of social and cultural benefit to the child (Article 17). Articles 34 and 36 commit governments to protecting children from all forms of exploitation, including pornography.

The European Convention on the Exercise of Children's Rights also emphasises children's right to express their own views in decisions affecting them, and calls on national bodies to provide information on children's rights to the media.

The Council of Europe Recommendation 1286 on a European Strategy for Children introduces the call for a change in the way children are viewed in society. The media should promote children's right to a healthy and balanced development , and all professionals who come into contact with children should have special training on children's rights (Article 8). The publicising of children's rights is a first step to increase public awareness and promote change in the traditional view of the child, declared the Council of Europe's Parliamentary Assembly . It highlighted the negative effects of the media on children, and wanted to see more controls over new information and communications technologies.

The Council of Europe's Recommendation No.R (91)11, concerning Sexual Exploitation, Pornography and Prostitution of, and trafficking in, Children and Young Adults, is an important one. It highlights the media's role in reporting this issue by inviting them to contribute to a general awareness of the subject and to adopt appropriate rules of conduct. It also warns against the abuse of children's images and voices in an erotic context. On the matter of law, it judges that while the public should be informed about the conviction of child pornographers, the identity of victims and alleged offenders should be protected. And it demands an end to publicity for sex tourism.

The Council of Europe Recommendation No.R (85)11 on the Position of the Victim in the Framework of Criminal Law and Procedure draws attention to the interests of the victim, and the need to protect him/her from any publicity which will unduly affect his (sic) private life or dignity. And Recommendations No.R (92) 19 and No.R (89) 7 focus, inter alia, on the use of new information technologies for the distribution of pornography.

European Union legislation also refers to the issue in its 1989 Television without Frontiers Directive, (Article 22) which bans programmes which might seriously impair the physical, mental or moral development of minors, in particular those that involve pornography or gratuitous violence.Yet it provides a get-out for broadcasters who select broadcast times or use technical measures to ensure that minors would not normally have access to the programmes.

Raising Awareness

The important role which media can play in raising public awareness of the abuse of children and in combatting all forms of criminal and sexual exploitation is well understood. But the issue is not as clear cut as many would like; media coverage can shine the spotlight on those directly responsible, but the victims all too often are also caught in the glare of publicity.

In the report of the Council of Europe's Committee on Crime Problems , the experts emphasised the responsibility of the media and their potential contribution to any policy aimed at preventing the sexual exploitation of children and young adults. The term media denotes here any means of expression transmitting a message for individuals or groups. In its broad sense therefore, the term covers means used for conveying information, such as the printed press, books, radio, television, videograms and advertisements; it also includes the ihproducerslt who use such media (publishing firms, radio and television companies and advertising agencies etc).

The Committee of experts warned:

> Often the mass media function as a two-edged knife in this area of concern. The unravelling of sensational sex and crime cases involving children and young adults tends to overemphasise the issue and to blur the picture. Sometimes, though, it is the media which help to uncover cases of sexual exploitation and to raise awareness of the problem.
>
> But it is also the media that generally infiltrate the public with liberal and tolerant attitudes towards child pornography and prostitution or provide the ways and means (for example advertisements) by which this sex gratification may be achieved. Therefore, their co-operation and their orientation towards safeguarding the rights and the dignity of children and young adults is extremely important.

In February 1996, the Guardian newspaper printed a two-page article by the award-winning reporter Maggie O'Kane. It described the life, and death, of girl prostitutes on the streets of Bradford, in England. It was a sensitive, perhaps overly-emotive, yet gripping piece of writing; accompanied by a useful set of proposals for supporting the ,street kids'. Next to it, was a sizeable photograph of an anonymous 13-year-old prostitute, with her shirt open to her waist.

This was the angle which alarmed Eva Aurland, Youth Coordinator of the International Confederation of Free Trade Unions, which has launched a major campaign against child labour. She condemns the picture as sensationalist and unnecessary. Her view is shared by

Rachel O'Brien of the Children's Society in the UK, which helped with O'Kane's investigation. Child abuse victims in homes would not be photographed, their identity would be protected, she argues. Yet once on the streets, although they are-in the law's eyes — suffering assault every day, they are ,fair game'.

It cannot be denied that the media play a crucial role in bringing the horrors of child exploitation into the public arena, and can be extremely influential. American research reveals that 72% of the public obtained knowledge of child abuse from newspapers, 56% from radio and TV. In 1992, a Swiss journalist arranged a child sex-tour through a travel agent. He wrote such a devastating account of the agent's operation, that the subsequent public outcry forced the agent out of business. At the same time, media coverage of prosecutions under laws against sex tourism, now in operation in at least 12 countries, also helps to warn off men who might be tempted by the idea.

There can be dangers in saturating the public with too much exposure of the issue, thereby creating acceptance and indifference. Many observers have warned of the public's "famine fatigue" when exposed to persistent, harrowing images in television coverage of recent disasters in Africa. The same problem may arise if coverage of children remains singular in its focus on the plight of the victim or the salacious nature of the offences involved.

Media researcher Nancy Signorielli sees two sides to sensationalism:

> Although child advocates may argue that sensational coverage distorts and exploits a serious problem - perhaps doing more harm than good - sensationalism solves several editorial problems; that is, it can be the response

> of reporters and editors trying to fulfil the responsibility to cover serious social issues, while continuing to turn a profit. Sensationalism permits an important but unpleasant topic to be covered in such a way that it still captures the readers' attention - and sells magazines.

Eva Aurland would like to see the media place more emphasis on the role of the police, politicians, and other authorities in protecting the children, rather than the children themselves. Her colleague at the ICFTU Elsa Ramos agrees, urging more analysis of the social causes: the pimps, the drug culture, the parents in poverty who are proud to have sold their daughters for a sum which will enable them to support the rest of the family. iaMedia should not be so shy about putting the blame on the individuals responsible for the exploitation, and the governments who condone itld, she says. For example, newspapers which uncovered the activities of a Bolivian lawyer who, they alleged, paid kidnappers US$40 for a boy whom he sold to a Belgian couple for US$10,000.

But media organisations must invest more time and effort into investigating such stories, if they want to avoid falling foul of defamation laws. It is easier to interview the children, who are hardly likely to sue. In a time of down-sizing and falling editorial expenditure on training and investigative journalism generally, the outlook for more in-depth media coverage is bleak. Nevertheless, media need to broaden the scope of reportage. The story of child sexual exploitation in general and its commercial aspects in particular is not being told in full. To examine how this can change requires a look at the professional freedoms which journalists require to work effectively, a summary of the principles or guidelines journalists and programme-makers should follow, and the pressures-legal, financial, or cultural-which are standing in the way.

SETTING STANDARDS

The work of journalists, broadcasters, and medi organisations is regulated at four different levels:

1. *Codes of Conduct*: Most journalists usually have the own professional code of ethics, formulated by trac unions or professional associations. Usually a form self-regulation;
2. *Guidelines*: Media organisations themselves, especiall in the public service broadcasting sector, may draw u guidelines for professional conduct. Usually a form self-regulation;
3. *Structures for Regulation*: certain regulatory bodies, suc as press councils, may be established each wit different powers and responsibilities and which ma or may not, have the force of law to support them;
4. *Legislation*: the law may be used to underpin notion of professional journalism and the systems set ou above. The law may also support structures fo licensing journalists and regulations providin penalties for breach of ethical conduct.

Legislation circumscribing the media and commercial sexua exploitation of children includes laws for the protection c children, such as the withholding of information identifyin children in court cases, in care, or as victims; laws to protec children from moral corruption; laws restrictin pornography; and general laws on freedom of expression The Canadian Criminal Code, for instance, makes it a offence to publish anything that depicts a child performin a sexual act or assuming a sexually suggestive pose whil in a state of undress. In Norwegian law, on the other hand there is no general protection of public morals, except for ban on pornographic material.

With regard to codes of professional conduct, we have found no journalists' organisation which offers a specific code of good practice for covering the commercial sexual exploitation of children. It must be said that although journalists are conscious of a values-related system in which news and information is reported, many of them are ignorant of the form and exact content of the codes of conduct to which they work. There are no clearly established international standards, although the IFJ's International Code of Principles on the Conduct of Journalism, agreed in 1954 and now under review, contains the key elements of a journalist's ethical responsibility. Any code will reflect standards of journalism according to understood values within society. It will also deal with questions of enforcement and disclosure, often accepting that openness enhances accountability, credibility and, ultimately, freedom.

Inevitably, the role of codes of ethics in journalism, which begin with sweeping generalities, becomes important when resolving the ethical dilemmas which will arise in particular cases of reporting. In the area of reporting on children and commercial sexual exploitation, there are four closely-allied ethical dilemmas surrounding professional conduct and investigation of the subject:

— Confidentiality of sources;

— Undercover journalism and use of subterfuge to obtain information;

— Co-operating with, and making information available to law enforcement agencies; and intervening in events under observation;

— Identification of individuals.

Confidentiality of Sources

The right to safeguard the anonymity of sources of information is crucial to the journalist's ability to investigate. In Sweden and other Nordic countries, this right is enshrined in law. An Act passed in 1993 in France laid down that:

> Any journalist who appears as a witness concerning information gathered by him in the course of his journalistic activity is free not to disclose its source.

The law also controls searches of media premises, which must not obstruct journalists in their work. However, in most countries journalists have to fight to defend this right, often risking fines or imprisonment in the process. The Canadian Broadcasting Corporation in its Journalistic Standards and Practices, for instance, upholds the principle of freedom of information and considers the protection of a journalist's sources to be an important element of this principle, but it reminds journalists that ,protection of sources is not a legal right'. CBC says it will not advise employees to defy a court order, but will provide legal counsel. Lars Bruun, in his review of ethical codes, found that 42 journalists' organisations around the world made mention of professional secrecy. For instance the Nigerian Union of Journalists' Code of Conduct reads: It is against the ethics of the profession to divulge information received in confidence, no matter what the consequences.

This principle was given backing in law in 1981, when the High Court of Lagos State ruled that the Senate of the National Assembly had exceeded its authority in summoning a journalist to disclose the confidential sources of an article. Often, the court's decision as to whether a journalist may legally withhold the identity of sources depends on the circumstances surrounding the case. In Japan, for instance, the Sapporo District Court interpreted the Code of Civil Procedure as allowing journalists to treat sources as ,an occupational secret', unless the information was required to ensure a fair trial:

> A journalist alleged that parents were complaining about child abuse in a local nursery school. The owner of the school sued the journalist for erroneous and defamatory reporting. Under questioning, the journalist refused to identify his sources. The courts upheld his privilege on the ground that, when a fair trial is not at issue, compelling disclosure of confidential sources would improperly impair the reporter's pursuit of his profession.

Journalists recognise that betraying sources not only inhibits their own ability to investigate; it also makes it more difficult for every journalist to work, and may even put their lives at risk, as well as the safety of the informants. The exploitation of children is such a sensitive issue that many abuses would never be revealed unless the people who provide the information: children, prostitutes, carers, and many others, could be confident that their anonymity would be preserved. Strengthening the journalist's rights in this area should be an element in any strategy aimed at creating the best professional conditions in which to examine the process of commercial sexual exploitation of children.

Use of Ethics Codes

Ethics codes are useful and they work most of the time. But sometimes genuine conflicts arise between values, and ethical decision-making is required. This difficult skill is like other skills of journalism: it takes training, time and effort to become good at them. The classic conflict of values comes when a journalist believes it is necessary to abandon the rule of truth- telling, by telling lies or using subterfuge in order to obtain or confirm information, especially about illegal activities. In her review of 28 codes of ethics in 26 European Countries, Tiina Laitila found that 86% made reference to the use of fair means in information collection. However, the definition of ‚fair' is open to debate. Clause 5 of the Code of Conduct of the National Union of Journalists (UK and Ireland) states :

> A journalist shall obtain information, photographs and illustrations only by straight-forward means. The use of other means can be justified only by over-riding considerations of the public interest.

Deciding when the public interest becomes ‚over-riding', and what ‚other means' are permissible, is left up to the conscience of the journalist, or often to the employer. This clause affirms that journalists are entitled to exercise a personal conscientious objection to the use of such means. But the conditions in which "other means" apply need to be carefully monitored. It must be borne in mind that the pressure of commercial competition, and the consequent imperative to be first with sensational news, often contributes to a climate in which subterfuge and ‚cheque-book' journalism become standard practice, not for reasons of public interest but primarily for reasons of circulation and commercial advantage.

The challenge facing journalists and those who support high standards of journalism is to create the conditions for sound professional judgement. Sometimes decisions may coincide with commercial advantage, often they will not. Most ethical guides would acknowledge that it may be ethical to lie, but any journalist who faces such a dilemma must be convinced of the relevance and weight of the public interest, conscious of the harm it might do to credibility, and willing as soon as possible to face a "publicity test"-public scrutiny of the circumstances. Journalists investigating the commercial sexual exploitation of children, should consider carefully whether it is justifiable to lie to, or deceive, either the exploiters, or the victims, in order to uncover the facts.

In her analysis of honesty in investigative journalism, Jennifer Jackson calls for an 'emotional' allegiance to truthfulness: a hatred of lies.

> Yet our allegiance to truthfulness needs also to be in part rational; it needs to be reflective, judicious. While it will not normally even occur to people of honest disposition that the end they seek might justify telling a lie, such people can recognise that in quite exceptional circumstances, the end they have in view does justify their lying. They will, of course, reach such a decision reluctantly and with caution...

Journalists can apply the ,publicity test' in advance of an investigation by assessing whether the public would regard the deception as justified. But they should also ask themselves whether there is no alternative route to the story, which does not involve lying. It is unlikely that the public would object to the subterfuge employed by Dutch programme-maker Aart Zeeman who used a hidden camera in order to track down the makers and vendors of child pornography in Amsterdam. Jackson herself concludes:

> It may be suggested that investigative journalists who are prepared to lie to get their stories (and the editors who print their stories) are hypocrites, lying in the name of truth. Yet...lying in order to detect and expose lies is not necessarily hypocritical; sometimes it may be morally necessary or permissible for a journalist to lie, and then

> the journalist's lie will (when revealed) appear justified even to those who are really honest, who genuinely care about truthfulness.

Nevertheless, an assumption that media are always licensed to deceive in order to get a story, undermines the moral authority of journalistic ethics. In the context of the commercial sexual exploitation of children there are important distinctions to be drawn, particularly because it is not just the pimps and pornographers who are involved, but the children themselves.

There is an ethical line to be drawn between subterfuge required to uncover the largely illegal activities of exploiters, and investigation of the children themselves. This may not be easy, given that working 'undercover' generally means total secrecy. But the fact that so many of the children are eager to find someone they can trust and who will listen to them, underlines their vulnerability. Experience of deception will further damage their self-esteem, and their relationship with others.

Journalists and media organisations need to apply the highest possible standards of honesty and openness when dealing with exploited children. In practical terms, this means a greater emphasis on ethical questions in journalists' training, to encourage ,a more finely tuned moral sense' . This should focus on concrete examples of specific dilemmas, including the coverage of children's exploitation. It also requires a constructive and supportive debate within newsrooms about these issues, as well as a greater awareness and sensitivity within the media about public attitudes on child pornography and exploitation.

Co-operation with the Community

Just as journalists are committed to "truth-telling" they are, as citizens, called upon to respect notions of community. Should journalists work hand-in-hand with the authorities and law enforcement officers in reporting on child exploitation? It is a complicated question, on which little guidance is given by formal ethical codes. Aart Zeeman's team followed the Amsterdam police for a year while making their documentary. However, this can also be a dangerous strategy.

In Taiwan, one of the major television stations recently broadcast film of reporters accompanying police on raids of bars and brothels. It included scenes of young men and women being questioned, apparently without any special regard for minors, and with only token efforts to avoid filming their faces. It is vital that journalists do not become identified in the public mind with security forces, for exactly the same reasons which apply to the protection of sources. But does this mean that journalists who discover evidence of illegal trafficking or exploitation of children, for example, should not pass it on to the authorities?

Again, this is not an unusual dilemma, but it is one of the most difficult to resolve. Convincing arguments can usually be marshalled for and against almost every case. It is a dilemma which depends upon the circumstances, and the conscience of the individual journalist. Aart Zeeman believes the media should not behave as 'the third or fourth arm of the police', and would not want to pass on data outside that broadcast in the programme. His view is that anything which serves to link the media more closely with law enforcers, in the minds of those supplying information will make them more reluctant to talk to journalists in general.

The BBC's Chief Advisor on Editorial Policy James Boyle said the Corporation would allow supplementary material to be taken away only if it were clearly in the public interest, and that no danger to any member of staff would result. Brazilian journalist Roberto Mader judged that he would pass on information only to help the girl prostitutes he interviewed in Latin America. In general, media professionals agree that criminal investigation itself is the job of the police and should be clearly separated from the exercise of journalism. But in countries suffering first-hand from the effects of sex tourism and growing exploitation, it is perhaps natural that journalists' associations and media themselves should feel justified in taking a more proactive role.

The Vietnamese Journalists' Association, for instance, states that the media do cooperate with authorities such as police, drug agencies, and families, to prevent the commercial sexual exploitation of children; and that some offenders have been brought to trial as a result. In Taiwan, in 1990, a child prostitute in the Huahsi Street red light area left a note for passers-by appealing: 'please save me'. The China Times Weekly took up her case, and pressured the Wanhua District police into searching for ,Little Chen', as she signed herself. At that time, says Cheryl Lai of the Association of Taiwan Journalists, the authorities paid little attention to child prostitution. But because of the media publicity, the police finally tracked down 14-year-old 'Little Chen', and she was returned to school. This is one case where the police were forced to act by media intervention.

This example raises the question of the role of media in taking up child exploitation cases. Journalists see themselves as neutral observers, but there may be times when the offences they see being committed are so appalling that they must intervene. Again this is a question for individual conscience, bearing in mind all the factors referred to above, but it may be a legitimate role for media to play in certain circumstances. For instance, many journalists reporting the war in Bosnia have witnessed atrocities, but only two of them have agreed to take part as witnesses in the war crimes trials in the Hague: British journalists Martin Bell, and Ed Vulliamy. Bell recognises that he would be a Serbian target if he returned to Bosnia as a reporter. Both journalists accept that "Many colleagues think that to have given evidence is bad professional ethics." However, Vulliamy draws a distinction between ,objectivity' — a journalist's duty to report the facts-and ,neutrality :

> At a certain point, the perpetration of atrocity crosses a line, and breaches not only international law but the bases of civilisation.

Beyond this point, he argues, ,neutrality' becomes complicity. The same criteria can very well be applied to child exploitation. The International Federation of Journalists-although respecting the rights of conscience of individuals-notes that by taking sides, journalists not only endanger their own safety, they can put their colleagues at risk.

Reporting Truth

If journalists have a duty to the truth in their reporting and to independence in their work they also have a responsibility to minimise harm from their actions, particularly to people who are themselves the victims of injustice and abuse. The Guardian, which generally adheres to a high standard in its news coverage, is not alone by any means in publishing photographs of child prostitutes, even under arrest. This is particularly true of western media images of children in developing countries, although the technique of obscuring part of the face is now sometimes used. However, more often it is the adult-the suspected abuser-whose identity is hidden.

In Taiwan, however, there is now a law whereby the names and photographs of convicted pimps and clients of underage prostitutes, and the hotel where the violation occurred, "should be published" after conviction. Interpol confirms that many countries have legislation protecting the identity of children involved in court proceedings, children in care, or children who are subject to abuse, but laws vary according to who they protect, and under what circumstances. They generally apply to young people under the national age of majority. There is also some controversy about how energetically they are enforced. The Council of Europe's Committee of Experts emphasises this aspect:

> The disclosure, during administrative and judicial proceedings, of information which may serve to identify the victim, is a particularly important aspect of secondary victimisation. The psychological consequences of such disclosure may be particularly serious for the children and young adults concerned and are liable to deter the parents or those responsible for the young person from lodging a complaint.
>
> ...The dissemination of such information by prosecuting authorities, courts or administrative authorities may cause harm to the young victims of sexual exploitation. The Committee strongly emphasises that cases must be handled with due respect to the victim's privacy.

Despite widespread international understanding of this question, in South East Asia, a newspaper printed the names of two children who had given evidence in the prosecution of a foreign paedophile. Child protection agencies believe legislation should allow offenders to be prosecuted without children being required to testify against them, to avoid any risk of identification or publicity. In Norway, a similar law means women do not have to give evidence in cases of domestic violence.

Victims in general cannot be sure that their identity will not be made public. For instance, the Canadian Broadcasting Corporation guidelines recognise that: Broadcasting the identity of a crime victim most often only adds to the person's grief, anguish and trauma. The CBC tells staff not to broadcast the names of victims, especially of crimes against the person, such as sexual assault. Yet alleged victims of assaults that have not been proved in court are not offered the ,privilege of anonymity'. Child prostitutes are often afforded even less protection than other young abuse victims, creating an understandable reluctance to report their exploitation. This perception that once children are working on the streets, in bars, taking drugs, or otherwise participating in the world of adult vice, they forfeit the rights of ,innocent' children, is shared in some quarters of the media as well as the law enforcement agencies.

In a survey of five Taiwanese daily newspapers, Chi Hui-jung discovered a general hostility to young prostitutes. Out of 133 news items about arrests for offences involving underage prostitutes, 34.% used unsympathetic headlines, and 35% were unsympathetic in content, using language such as childish; selling herself, deflowered; doesn't study but sells her body; and slut. She concluded that crime reporters do not see the juveniles involved as minors, but use adult standards to judge and blame child prostitutes, and rarely see them as victims. On the other hand, the same reporters are very tolerant towards the clients. Only 4% of the headlines were negative about them, and 91% did not mention them at all, in common with 71% of the reports.

Such figures reflect a lack of recognition around the world that a crime is being perpetrated by an adult. It should never be the children who are cautioned or condemned. Most media reports on this issue originate in arrests and thus from the police, and are filed by reporters on crime beats, who are generally less likely to consider the interests of the children involved, or make serious efforts to protect their identities. Journalists covering disadvantaged groups in society who are generally sympathetic to the movement to abolish child prostitution, take greater care in their reporting not to add to the harm already suffered by the children.

Where children are not specifically protected by law, it is the journalist or editor who must take the decision on whether to identify them. There are some who are even prepared to flout the law for the sake of a ,sexy' or sensational story. This is particularly damaging in countries with strict contempt of court rules, where the media revelation of unauthorised details in advance of a court hearing can lead to the case collapsing. Even when children themselves are not named, details may be given which endanger them. One newspaper, for instance, which interviewed an 11-year-old boy, boxed out his face in the photograph, but went on to name his ,sugar-daddy' and the streets he worked.

The issue of identity is at the heart of journalistic endeavour. It is in the nature of journalism, from the first lesson in journalism school onwards, to provide facts, including personal details about whoever is involved in a story. The decision to suppress information has to be carefully considered, but the nature of commercial sexual exploitation of children should always encourage a journalist to respect, above all, the rights of the victim. Sometimes, this may not be easy. June Kane, UNICEF's Media Coordinator for the World Congress, calls on documentary makers to think twice before using footage of bar girls in Asia, for example, but will a producer working on a programme about bar girls, be able to alert viewers to the real tragedy of sex tourism, without picturing the girls at work, or telling individual children's stories?

Myths and Stereotypes

In the material provided for the World Congress there is a call to the media to avoid exploiting and victimising the children in their coverage, and to depict them in a way which maintains their dignity. It is a brave, but challenging call. To achieve this, media professionals need to re-examine their old habits. Peter Almond points out that a collection of myths ,contaminate' the public's, and the media's, perception of children. The media cling to these myths; they are familiar, convenient, easily adapted to conventional formats of news and entertainment. In short, myth is easier to report than the more subtle and complicated reality.

Such myths can lead journalists to mould exploited children into typecast roles as sinners or victims. Families in developing countries, people living in poverty, or victims of war and disaster lose their individuality and their humanity. Victims are portrayed as helpless sufferers, unable to act, think, or speak for themselves. Whole countries and communities become categorised under generalised headlines. In Thailand, the portrayal of girls from the north of the country drifting into prostitution has become so pervasive that a special project has been launched to protect some of those at risk.

In a survey of magazine coverage of child abuse in the United States, Nancy Signorielli found that victims were rarely reported to react to their abuse. Women's magazines covered the issue more frequently than news and business magazines, but in a more sensational way. As a result, men were less exposed to the problem. Gerbner also discovered that a high proportion of children on TV appeared as victims. Disproportionate preoccupation with even sympathetically presented or iraccidentalll victims in an underrepresented population, relative to exhibiting their own share of numbers and exercise of power, diminishes and degrades that group.

Fierce commercial competition is one factor leading the media to exploit victims, suggests Dr Michielsens. The exposure of emotions and sensationalisation of events attract audiences and sell news. Cash-conscious media organisations apply greater pressure on news teams for productivity. Journalists, therefore, sometimes take the ill-considered, easy route to news-gathering, perpetuating-whether consciously or unconsciously-the sorts of myth and stereotype identified by Peter Almond. In this process individuals and groups are not treated with respect and their needs and views are not properly appreciated.

Some media organisations are becoming aware of the danger of dehumanising victims in far-away places. James Boyle says the BBC now has clear rules, which apply even to dead bodies. "Human beings have the same dignity all over the world". There are a range of approaches being developed, to avoid stereotyping and victimising exploited children, while at the same time telling their story accurately and vividly. Roberto Mader felt that all the programmes he saw about children's exploitation in Latin America and other southern countries, while strongly denouncing important human rights abuses, left the impression that nothing could be done. All you feel at the end of the programme is depressed.

Language is another obstacle to the documentary format. Subtitles are expensive, and often unpopular with audiences. Broadcasting organisations tend to avoid them. ihIt's an excuse not to listen to people at all - you just have a voice-over soundbite. Yet people are amazed when they see ordinary people speakingl. Aart Zeeman traced children back to Hungary, the Czech Republic and the Philippines, but avoided identifying the former victims he interviewed. inI don't think it adds anything to show their faces, unless they are grown up now and choose to tell their story. Children don't understand the impact being on TV can have.

Altering the names of people and places is one obvious answer for newspaper journalists. But for the documentary maker, the dilemma between using images which will keep the audience's attention, and not endangering or victimising the children, cannot be easily resolved. For The Care Connection, programme makers ,invented' different ways of getting round the problem. Cameras were positioned at unusual angles — above interviewees' heads or by their ears-or shots were cut away to focus on the movements of their hands, which also registered the emotional impact of their words. The technique of "pixilating" — blurring a small portion of the screen-was rejected. "It's always associated with criminals, or somebody who deserves what they get", explained researcher Simon Cooper.

Other broadcasters have sought different, less controversial approaches to the topic, such as a dramatisation, followed by a studio debate. Belgian director Gil Verhaert proposed the fictional formula for a six-part series on La femme, l'enfant, et la prostitution, in Africa, Asia and Europe. "We have a lot of information, but we cannot feature the real people because they are all either afraid of the Mafia, or are involved in court casesle, he explained. "Audiences are interested in dramatic events. But it does not have to be sensational. If you keep to the truth, it's more than dramatic enough.

Many of the journalists reporting on commercial sexual exploitation of children are committed to uncovering what they regard as a profound social evil: "We have a role to play in increasing awarenessll, says Aart Zeeman. ieIt's such a disgusting thing". The work of such media professionals not only acts as a counter-weight to media indifference and lack of awareness, it adds to the resources available to campaigners. The material produced may be linked in with campaigns on the issue by local NGOs, or destined for educational use-as in the case of Gil Verhaert's project. He hoped his work might be used in the Philippines among families who sell their own children into prostitution. In Bangkok, a campaign has been launched to show parents the horrors their daughters would face in the sex trade.

Freedom of Expression and Challenge of Self-Regulation

Journalists tend to be wary of regulators. They have much evidence to support the view that intervention in the affairs of journalism inevitably leads to forms of censorship. However, it is a legitimate question whether media self-regulation is a sufficient answer to public concern over standards of journalism in and age when the changing media landscape, and particularly the growth of global media enterprises appears, in theory at least, to put media beyond the range of national public accountability. Effective self-regulation, by which the errors of media professionals are dealt with by their peers, may not be so convincing when media organisations appear to use professional codes to support their particular interests, which in a commercial system of mass communication by no means necessarily coincide with those of journalism or the public interest. There has been in the past criticism that self-regulation has been used to provide what might be called a iasocial alibila for the mass media industry, that is to prevent society from taking more definite (legal) measures.

This argument goes to the heart of the uncomfortable balance of interests which prevails in today's media — that ethical standards are being sacrificed in defence of commercial interests. One of the principle problems lies in the implementation and enforcement of rules. Very often even regulatory bodies lack the power to enforce sanctions which bite. In Canada in 1990, the CBC's Equity Task Force found that, with regard to equitable employment and portrayal, self-regulation and incentive measures have failed to accomplish desired and anticipated results. Some professional codes aspire to the very highest moral standards, as in Chile, Journalism and journalists must be in the service of truth, social justice, human rights and the ideals of the improvement of society and of peace among peoples.

And there is no doubt that many individuals, like those quoted above, are committed to exposing and condemning sexual exploitation. Sadly, many more choose to reflect the commercial or political interests of advertisers, proprietors, or political parties. This control seldom takes the form of direct intervention or censorship, but far more often of self-censorship by the media professionals themselves - who may not even be aware that they are exercising it. In an Indiana University School of Journalism study in the 1980s,

88% of the journalists questioned said they acquired their ethical values from the newsroom itself.

Aidan White identifies several extra factors which encourage "the tendency towards self-censorship and self-denial of social responsibility" among media professionals, including: the growth of new technologies, which threaten to overwhelm existing regulatory structures, or the unaccountable nature of transnational media corporations which evade terrestrial control of media standards, or the increasingly insecure working environment in which journalists work. Journalists' unions who have tried to enforce their own ethical standards through disciplinary proceedings, have found themselves in the tricky if not impossible position of attacking individual workers they exist to support. Despite all this, codes and guidelines still have a crucial role to play, in raising awareness and providing a model of good practice.

In Spain, in 1993, for example, regional and national broadcasting organisations joined with the national and regional Education Ministries in agreeing Self-regulation Principles for Television Channels concerning the specific content of their programmes with regard to protecting children and young people. The document recognises ,the significant role which television plays in Spanish society and its influence on society, particularly children and young people'. Specific guidelines on reporting child abuse could be drawn up by professional associations to accompany their general ethical codes, along the lines of guidelines for reporting AIDS published by the NUJ (UK and Ireland).

The support of media employers and regulators is crucial to improving newsroom values as highlighted by Cheryl Lai: Much of the biased or sensationalist coverage, especially headlines, is created by editors, and it will be difficult to gain improvements given Taiwan's patriarchal society unless high-level media editors and managers implement such a policy from the top down. Attitudes to censorship and freedom of expression vary widely from country to country and culture to culture. In all countries, broadcasting tends to be more highly regulated than newspapers and magazines.

The importance of the right to freedom of expression cannot be under-estimated, yet it is not without boundaries. Both the UN Universal Declaration of Human Rights and the European Convention for the Protection of Human Rights and Fundamental Freedoms draw attention to the responsibilities accompanying this right, including ,respect for the rights or reputations of others'. The question of freedom of expression is relevant in particular to child pornography. Amy Adler argues that the US Supreme Court, in its anxiety to protect children, has thrown out ,important speech- protective features of the law', including ,the traditional protection afforded to artistic expression'.

But American lawyer Andrew Vachss, a specialist in child abuse cases, believes that the controversy over art is a red herring thrown up by the paedophile community. The issue of rights to freedom of expression cannot be ignored, but should be turned around to focus first on the rights of the child to freedom from fear and exploitation. As June Kane points out, 'Journalists should, as always, look at the facts, and have at their fingertips the medical and other evidence to prove that the commercial sexual exploitation of children cannot be justified.

Media in the World Today

There is increasing alarm in a number of countries that the

way children are portrayed by the media today may increase the risks they face. Controversy continues internationally about how far children's behaviour is influenced by what they see on television - particularly with regard to violence. The loudest recent public controversy about the portrayal of children has focused recently on the American film Kids, directed by Larry Clark. Some critics condemned the film as voyeuristic, and expressed disbelief that the young actors, mostly amateur, who enacted the film's brutal sexual encounters, were themselves above the age of consent. The film raised worrying questions both about the exploitation of increasingly youthful actors, and about the impact on young audiences who might regard the characters as role-models.

In some countries, the film was barred to under-18s. The crucial question is whether adults themselves are encouraging children to become prematurely sexually active, or to seem to be so. This question is particularly relevant to pop music and modelling which are two of the most influential industries among young people today. The recent revelation that a 12-year-old schoolgirl had been signed up by an adult modelling agency in the UK, with the approval of her parents, caused widespread soul-searching in the media. Was it a harmless bit of fun, or the symptom of a dangerous trend? The commentators disagreed, but most expressed alarm. Even the girl's mother admitted that there was a ,sexual angle'; expanded upon by psychologist Dorothy Rowe:

> There is something intriguing about the young girl who is just discovering life and is beginning to wonder what it's all about. It is the kind of titillation in which a virginal girl intrigues a man. In areas of sexuality intended to intrigue, it is especially dangerous because the child is

> being presented with issues that they are not really ready to deal with, no matter how precocious they look.

British Member of Parliament Ann Winterton judged it to be a ietrend almost verging on the paedophilicl.. The fear must be that, the more grown-up women are persuaded to aspire to having a childlike body, the more the distinction between adults and children, also with respect to sexuality, will become blurred. Then, in May, the watch-manufacturer Omega announced that it planned to withdraw advertising fron. a major fashion magazine, Vogue, in protest at the use of waif-like models. Within a couple of weeks, Omega had obtained more publicity - all of it free and much of it highly complimentary - than a year's worth of advertising in magazines. Ironically, the threat was withdrawn on the instructions of the chairman Nicolas Hayek, ostensibly in the interest of press freedom.

The impact of public pressure on the media, on this issue as any other, should not be underestimated. Parents and educators in France, for instance, have been urged to react when TV stations show material lacking in respect for children, whether or not it is intended for young viewers. In Australia, a national campaign to improve the portrayal of women in the media included the distribution of information packs telling audiences how to complain about what they heard or saw.

Jennifer Rowe, former editor of the Australian Women's Weekly, commented: In the end, all media are driven by their ratings or their readership, and if they can see that they are losing that, by persisting in an attitude that is outmoded, they will change. The most fascinating aspect of the model controversy is how it was handled by the newspapers themselves. The girl's first appearance, according to Alexander Chancellor, was on the front page of the Daily Telegraph.

> The next day she was taken up by the tabloids. She was pouting and smouldering in the photographs in an alarmingly grown-up way. The tabloids were thrilled of course, but also censorious.

Indeed, its professed outrage did not stop the Daily Mail from reprinting a full-length picture of the girl in her ‚smouldering' modelling pose, under the heading ieWho on earth would allow a child of 12 to pose like this?lg It might have queried, more relevantly, who on earth would publish a picture of her doing it. And as if to reinforce the sexual message, the feature was placed next to a small beauty item giving advice on how to achieve ‚a perfect pout'. The morally self-righteous stance adopted by some sections of the media is directly contradicted when it come to stories and images that make money.

For the popular music industry, international TV channels like MTV, where pop videos make up a large proportion of output, are a very significant means of reaching young people and children - even those too young to attend concerts or buy CDs. Professor Monique Remy analysed the images of young people in these videos. She found: "stereotyped masculine and feminine images, sado-masochistic scenes, Asian exoticism, fetishist female garments, women as bloodsuckers and trouble-makers, both men and women grotesquely made-up, with an element of androgeny".

Women appeared as child-like, asexual yet provocative, dangerous, yet also victimised. In their analysis of 166 videos broadcast by MTV, WTBS and NBC in 1984, Barry Sherman and Joseph Dominick drew attention to the provocative style of dress, and the portrayal of young women as either aggressors or victims. The Council of Europe's experts also warned of the ,insidious' exploitation of children's and young people's bodies in show business and the media, and the use of children's pictures or voices to create an erotic atmosphere. Certainly some media commentators have perceived this as evidence of a ,widespread phenomenon.. ..of confusion over the boundary between adults and children', in which parents have colluded in the sexual exploitation of their children.

Little wonder then, the argument goes, that if the media consistently present young and old audiences alike with images of children in a sexual context, some adults will believe that children are ready and able to participate in sexual activity. Rachel O'Brien believes it is dangerous to view these developments as ,armageddon' - a catastrophic loss of innocence about which nothing can be done. But she does perceive a widespread confusion about what childhood means, and points out that the definition of childhood itself differs from community to community, and age to age. Children are aware of their bodies, and do need to explore and learn about sex. But this should be done gradually, in a tolerant, safe environment; through natural contact with other children, and with the support of parents.

On the one hand, many children are denied sex education, while on the other there is a glorification of children in provocative poses. It seems that either we want our children to be totally innocent, or to be prostitutes. And the whole question of their rights as individuals gets left out." All this makes the notion of a ,youth oriented society' into a slogan of little substance, concludes George Gerbner. The media are oriented towards ,markets and power' rather than youth. Advertisers focus on consumers and potential consumers - and we will look at advertising specifically later in this paper. But in television output children have no power. They "take on the characteristics of a social minority with less than their share of attention, values, and resources, and consequently diminished life chances."

The solution may be simple to see, but not so easy to achieve. That is, to give a voice in the media to children themselves, to listen to their views and aspirations. And to educate them to be knowledgeable and critical about how the media work. International conventions and recommendations already emphasise the right of children to have a say in decisions affecting them, and call for a change in the way children are regarded . The Draft Declaration from this Congress also emphasises that children have a right to express their views on matters affecting their lives, and calls for children's participation in action (Article 6). Why should children not also have more say in the media? Dr Ulla Bjornberg proposes documentary programmes on young people's lives in different countries, with the aim of giving children aged from 7 to 18 - including poor and migrant children - an opportunity to air their opinions.

Children are not regarded as sources because they are not trusted to distinguish accurately between fact and fiction-a belief that also applied to children giving evidence in court until recently. New means of giving children access to the media as sources should be investigated, perhaps through the mediation of child helplines, with reassurance that information offered would be strictly confidential. Wilkinson point out that: child abuse does not fall squarely into a specific area of reporting. Is it part of the police beat, medicine, sociology, or government? The Post doesn't have a child abuse reporter per se, and I doubt that any major newspaper does.

The British Home Office also decided to produce a ,good practice' video for judges and lawyers. Governments or NGOs might consider making good practice videos for editors and journalists. Another measure to assist journalists in covering children's issues seriously and accurately would be for NGOs in each country to compile a directory of reliable experts on different topics, which could be available on every news desk. International bodies have called for more information to be given to children - both through the media and at school - about the dangers and risks of sexual exploitation, and how to defend themselves. But children, from primary school upwards, also need media literacy training, to help them understand and decode the messages they receive from both programmes and advertising, so as to become critical and well-informed media consumers.

In Canada, for instance, the organisation Mediawatch and the Federation of Women's Teachers' Associations have developed a curriculum for schools on stereotypes and gender issues. Media education can play a crucial role in counteracting the impact of these messages. Helping children to understand that media construct - as opposed to reflect - reality; that they communicate implicit and explicit values; and that they can influence the way we feel and think about ourselves and the world, are vitally important lessons.

In France, an initiative aimed at implementing the UN Convention, proposes ,associating adults and children to analyse and explain the programmes on television, iethe only medium generally accessible to children of all socio-cultural backgroundsla.' The ultimate objective is best summarised by George Gerbner again, who calls for media professionals to ,break the constraints that now bind them to markets that use but have little use for children': The need is for action towards creating a culture, and television system, that can afford to address itself to the nation's future, its children....Citizens, writers, actors and producers must work towards a system of popular storytelling whose culture-power cannot devalue and hurt children any more.

Impact of New Technologies

Advertising is also subject to a combination of legislation and self-regulation in the way it appeals to children. The Council of Europe experts noted that :

> Advertisers, in particular, have recently begun to rely on the impact of juvenile seduction, using it in the same way as iuconventionalli erotic advertising. In so doing, they may have the effect of encouraging those who wish to widen the choice of sexual partners by means of overtly paedophile propaganda.

Some notorious cases have sent shock waves through the advertising world, such as the Calvin Klein jeans advertisement, which President Clinton is said to have personally intervened to have withdrawn. In Europe, legislation focuses largely on banning pornography or protecting children. In Denmark, radio and TV advertising must respect ,decency'. Far more detailed are the self-regulatory codes, which tend to guarantee freedom of expression while at the same time affirming the responsibilities of advertisers.

Henry Danthan, Executive Manager of the World Federation of Advertisers, which represents national associations and multinational advertising companies, says the concept of self-regulation is largely European and North American, with mechanisms now existing in other countries such as Japan, Australia and South Africa. He believes that an ,anti-advertising climate' is being fostered in some parts of Europe because of a misguided moral panic about its influence on children. In other countries, says Danthan, children's role in society is so different that it is not perceived as a problem. irIt's a question which is less at the forefront of regulators' concerns than, for instance, tobacco or alcoholl,. Nevertheless, these days the advertising industry is, without doubt, sensitive about allegations over its use of children.

A report on Children and Television Commercials commissioned by the European Advertising Tripartite last year, condemned much research on children and advertising as ,politically motivated'. It concluded that advertising actually had positive effects on children, partly because it contained ,virtually no aggression and many examples of prosocial behaviour, breaking down stereotypes'. The European Advertising Standards Alliance, which brings together the self-regulatory bodies across Europe, carried out its own survey on the self-regulation of advertising and children, and in particular the use of naked children in adverts. It found that in nine of the 15 European Union countries, the screening of.20 naked children (including sexual organs) was permitted.

In Austria, Germany, Ireland and the UK, children had to be partially clothed. And in several of the other countries restrictions relating to taste and decency, and the age of the child, applied. The survey asked whether self-regulatory bodies had received any reaction from viewers to the use of naked children. Only four: Ireland, France, Portugal and the UK, reported any specific response, with viewers in the UK in particular complaining that such images would be regarded by paedophiles as erotic titillation. Henry Danthan believes advertisers now understand the need to adopt high standards in advertising for and by children. Yet the fact remains that shock adverts, like the Calvin Klein example, attract massive extra publicity.

In the end, there are two other problems with the concept of self-regulation, highlighted by Simon-Pierre De Coster, a legal advisor with the Belgian broadcaster RTBF. The first is that mechanisms are only equipped to deal with grave breaches of regulations. But it is not the grave cases that are the main problem, he points out. It is the accumulative effect of banal stereotypes that are used everyday without sanction.

Secondly, advertising codes rely on notions such as ,good taste', ,bad taste' and ,decency'. But how are these terms to be interpreted and implemented? 'What is the broadcaster to make of these texts? They should be defined somewhere'. Both media workers and the public have a crucial role to play in indicating where the bounds of acceptability are drawn, and consumer boycotts of products can have a powerful effect: The mere threat of such action is already effective insofar as a television station is very reluctant to risk seeing a source of advertising revenue diminish or disappear.

But while efforts continue to try to set standards in the existing world of media technology, the development of new forms of communication such as the Internet has opened up new opportunities for paedophiles and pornographers which have brought international concern. Men exchange pornographic accounts of their exploits as sex tourists, for example, supplying details of bars, brothels, and prices. In 1995, Thailand's Tourist Authority tried to take action to delete graphic details of sex venues and massage parlours from Netscape: The World Sex Guide. The

Internet contributor was identified as a 50-year-old American, Bruce Cassirer, who had also written a ,travel guide' on where to find young prostitutes. Cassirer was declared persona non grata by Thailand, and a warrant issued for his arrest. Governments have now discovered that the major problem in controlling material on the Internet, is that nobody controls it.

In France, net providers went on strike to obtain an assurance from the Ministry of Telecommunications that they were not to blame for child pornography. The Association of French Internet Professionals demanded a legal debate to establish who was responsible for the material. In the United States free-speech campaigners have won in recent days an injunction against officials attempts control content on the Internet. Whatever media strategies may emerge in the campaign for children's rights, they will have to be linked to this rapidly-changing media environment, and one that offers much less scope for control and regulation than before.

8

Ethical Challenges of Online Journalism

Online journalism is a new and growing field with a variety of ethical challenges and conflicts. So far, little research has been done in this field, and general ethical standards and protocols for online journalism have not yet been established. Ethics of online journalism can be regarded as a subdivision of media ethics, yet the openness of the Internet for all kinds of lay journalism and peer-to-peer journalism makes it difficult to establish binding professional norms. Although the basic forms and methods of the work process in online journalism are similar to any other type of journalism, different interpretations of the online journalist's professional role, as well as organizational structures and cultural differences can cause severe ethical conflicts.

Moreover, significant new challenges result from media specific characteristics, from technical difficulties, and from increased time pressure. In particular, the specific media logic of the Internet calls for the restructuring and redefinition of conventional journalistic forms of production and presentation. The online journalist has to make decisions on which media formats best tell a certain story (multimediality), has to allow room for options for the public to respond, interact or even customize certain stories (interactivity), and must consider ways to connect the story to other stories, archives, resources and so on through hyperlinks (hypertextuality).

Many of the ethical challenges and dilemmas of online journalism are unique-or at least more pronounced, intensified, or amplified than in other media-because of the distinctive media logic of the hybrid medium Internet and its conditions of use. In contrast to other mass media, the Internet combines and mingles interpersonal, group, and mass communication, because of its interactive, multimedia, and hypertextual features. These media-specific characteristics of the Internet shape the way online journalists do their research, and create and publish their work. In addition to these characteristics, computer speed and storage capacity can also cause new ethical challenges or at least amplify and extend existing ethical problems of conventional journalism.

Ethical Challenges of Online Journalism

The five main areas of ethical challenges and dilemmas specific to online journalism are;

— Gathering information for online media

— Producing journalistic content for online media

— Presenting and distributing online information

— Organizational structures and communications in online media

— Societal issues of converging media and global communication.

Gathering Information

Journalists' research practices have long been subject to attempts at ethical regulation. Protection of sources, respect for confidentiality and the private sphere, and refraining from using dishonest methods are highly valued in many media ethical codes, such as the Code of Ethics of the Society of Professional Journalists. Issues of data protection and invasion of privacy can constitute severe ethical conflicts in information gathering: Undercover research in online forums has become an easy way of obtaining personal information, yet it must be considered ethically questionable, particularly if the members of such a forum assume that their communications occur in a protected environment.

Invasion of privacy also occurs through unauthorized use of data networks and the improper combination of information from different databases. Online information technology simplifies and facilitates the information gathering process tremendously. Yet the overwhelming information flood, inadequate search instruments, suboptimal search strategies, and the lack of appropriate selection criteria often lead to superficial research and irrelevant results. As a rule, only the surface of the net is searched, whereas the deep web (such as database-generated dynamic web pages) is not included. The cut-and-paste culture of the Internet also invites inaccuracy, negligence, and plagiarism: Sources are often neither sufficiently evaluated nor correctly cited. Seemingly authorless online sources and readily available information from databases are copied without attribution and liberally altered.

Though this behaviour takes advantage of online technology, it is not limited to online media. The greatest long-term danger of online-based information gathering, however, may stem from the tunnel vision that results when the Internet becomes the primary instrument of research. Facts and events that are not to be found on the Internet will then escape the journalist's perception. Whereas the aforementioned ethical problems result from active violations of ethical norms and values, this tunnel vision effect is a rather passive form of negligence, caused by inertia and blindness toward the journalist's implicit selection criteria.

Producing Content

As in the case of information gathering, media ethical standards are crucial for producing high quality online content. Deadlines in online journalism are-similar to those in broadcast news-characterized by a permanent update requirement. This allows for more current and faster information delivery but also creates tremendous time pressure, yet ethical standards for coping with it are not available. Storage space, hypertextuality, and multimediality make it possible to replace the top-down writing format, known as the inverted pyramid, by networked, multi-layered, and context-oriented presentation of information. This permits a higher degree of freedom in writing online stories but also increases pressure to make decisions. This is particularly evident in the case of ethically questionable content, such as pictures of people jumping from the burning Twin Towers or bloody images from the Iraq war.

The fact that non-journalistic websites provide a plethora of such pictures actually represents a chance for online journalism to demonstrate its higher ethical standards by exercising restraint. Specific ethical conflicts are caused by the possibility of imperceptibly manipulating digital texts, sounds, and images: "To date, no industry-wide standards define the level of image or sound alteration that is acceptable within the bonds of ethical journalism," remarks Pavlik in his textbook on online journalism. Manipulation of images to augment their quality is an established journalistic practice, because digital technology allows for traceless enhancement and change.

The line between change and forgery, however, is thin, as was shown during the Iraq war by the photojournalist Brian Walski of the LA TIMES, who generated one digital picture from two different ones, allegedly "to enhance the composition." A similar issue is the practice of copying and plagiarizing. This ranges from unattributed copies of sentences and quotations to the illegitimate use of whole texts or multimedia documents without any attribution. Laziness, time pressure, and lack of easy access to sources often lead to stealing of quotes and themes and sometimes even to fabrication.

Plagiarism and violation of copyright can also occur when hyperlinks in combination with frames are used to include content from different web sources into a web site, because this makes the URL of the source invisible. The same is true for inline-linking of images and deep-linking into sub-pages of a website without linking to the main page. But even beyond blantant violations there will always be the question of "when to make the link. "Evaluation of sources, including fact and credibility checking, must happen before a hyperlink is created. Credibility issues may finally also arise from content sharing in joint operations when inflationary repurposing and recycling of content erodes the audience's trust in the integrity and originality of the journalistic product.

Presenting and Distributing Content

The uniform graphic user interface of the World Wide Web, its hypertextuality and interactivity, as well organizational constraints of production tend to dissolve the separation between editorial and paid content. Ad banners, sponsor logos, and ad links are often placed in the middle of editorial content or among navigational tools. This "tight intertwining of content and advertising" and the lack of binding rules for Internet publishing are frequently bemoaned. An additional conflict of interest arises if online journalists are at the same time expected to acquire ads for their product; this problem is exacerbated when editorial content merely provides a legitimizing environment for e-commerce. The fact that more and more non-journalistic entities (such as search engines, software companies, and portals) provide news only aggravates this problem.

A further ethical issue results from the volatility of the Internet. The advantage of almost unlimited storage is paid for with the virtuality and instability of the stored information. This palimpsest character of internet documents means that each document is only true until its next update and that its next version can differ greatly from the last one without any mention of the difference.

The changeability of online-based information also implies the additional complication that retractions can be done in a way that the original error just disappears. This may be an advantage when it comes to spelling and other minor errors, yet it causes severe ethical problems in case of research and factual errors. The traceless replacement of the error by a corrected update creates the illusion that the error never happened. Common standards for retractions are not yet established, but timeliness, visibility, clarity, publicity and explicitness can be considered as basic criteria for ethically acceptable retractions.

Communications in Online Media

Staff sizes, allocation of resources, and workloads for online employees are decisive elements of organizational ethics. In the past, online journalism has often been treated as a moonlighting business that was added to the journalist's normal workload. Competition with other departments can also be a severe stress factor. The lack of acknowledged organizational ethics and established standards of practice makes it difficult for online journalists to withstand intra-organizational pressure. Thus, they may be faced with the unattractive alternative of either becoming moral heroes without organizational support or behaving opportunistically.

In addition, networked workflow and a higher level of distribution of work in converging digital environments undermine clear-cut responsibility and accountability. Intraorganizational communication can be impeded when staff members and management have different backgrounds, sometimes even different nationalities. Extra-organizational communication can suffer when audiences and media workers have different cultural backgrounds.

Understanding across educational, departmental, technical, and cultural differences is a key factor in online journalism. Communication barriers and culturally different background assumptions can cause severe miscommunication and, consequently, social conflicts and unethical actions. As online media organizations internationalize, they have to deal with integrating disparate ethical standards and cultural expectations.

Societal Issues

The online journalist's role is strongly influenced by technical convergence, cross-media mergers, and the trend toward transnational media conglomerates. Moreover, economic imperatives and constraints of globalized media businesses can put new restrictions on journalistic freedom and free speech. Online journalists produce for a potentially global audience, which consists of members of many different cultures with sometimes radically different assumptions and world-views, even if they share a thematical interest as a specific target audience. Online journalists need to be prepared for their role as global communicators and the ethical challenges that this role implies.

Even though the Internet is widely disseminated in Western countries, people in economically depressed regions and in developing countries are often excluded from Internet access. Participation in and empowerment through the Internet require equal access in the first place, but also education toward web literacy and intelligent use. So far, the Internet has aggravated, rather than narrowed the already existing knowledge gap and the difference between the information poor and the information rich. In addition, access issues of gender, race, age and education repeat on the level of production of online content, too.

Global code of Online Journalism Ethics

Before elaborating points relate to the online journalism ethics, it would be necessary just in brief to explain why Many Voices, One World 1980 Report should be mentioned here. For those readers not enough familiar with the Report, it was prepared under the UNESCO auspices and inspired by at the time pressing issues of eliminating striking imbalances and disparities in communication and information flows. Underdeveloped and developing countries suffered badly such imbalance, not only in the communication and media sector, but in general. Sounds familiar, or what basically changed since then? Nothing.

What was said during the UN World Summit on the Information Society (WSIS) perfectly fits to the core of the Many Voices, One World's message, despite this Report could not anticipate entirely technical impact of the new Information and Communications Technologice (ICTs). Just to consider one single line: "Political and moral divide must be bridged before the digital divide", said World Association of Newspapers'(WAN) representative, which is an absolutely accurate remark The latest figures claim that Internet access worldwide is hitting half a billion people, but however, the digital divide is even still widening! It is indeed hypocrisy to claim that the Internet is spreading democracy, while one third of world population have never made a phone call, or Manhattan alone has still more phone lines than whole African continent!

Close to 1,5 billion people worldwide live on less than a dollar a day! And, of course, as a Consequence of their poverty, almost all of them have been deprived voice in decisions that affect their lives. To reduce poverty, implies the free access to information. People provided with more information are empowered to make better choices. Therefore, a free press is not a luxory. It is at the core of balanced development.

As a public watchdog, media should let people voice diverse opinions on government and politics, and help them to build public consensus over improtant economic, social, cultural, and related issues. Point was and still is to reduce significantly communication gap and digital divide. To that aim, Many Voices, One World document has to be reassessed in the context of new ICTs and its complex socio-cultural impacts.

Another burning issue is - how to regulate the Internet? Some scholars and media experts consider the cyberspace as a human rights frontier, implying that the Internet should be in a forefront of widening and strengthening of press freedoms. Of course, it should be put that way, but the Internet as the new medium must respect some postulates of traditional journalism, e.g., there is no absolute freedom of expression, including in the cyberspace communication.

Global Internet

Put in that context, it was very illustrative the case of Yahoo, France, of some three years ago, after the French courts banned the sale of Nazi memorabilia via Yahoo portals, under the pretext:"it offended France's collective memory". By many media watchdog and human rights groups, such move has been regarded as Yahoo's surrender, but they didn't understand that browsing can be an offense too, such as search for child porn. In brief, exercising of freedom of expression is strictly connected with duties and responsibilities. It mean also that Internet Service Providers (ISPs) must be responsible for their content posted. Naturally, it raised another issue: whose rules will govern or prevail in the cyberspace?

For example, what is illegal in one country may be legal in another country. Distinguished colleague, Jonathan Zitrrain, from the Berkman Center for Internet & Society at Harvard Law School, has been also overwhelmed with the Global Internet/Local Law dichotomy, i.e., how to reconcile it, or how to reduce problems in the context of fact that the Internet is global, and imposition of regulations is local? "These dilemmas of Internet jurisdiction and governance eliminate the originally cherished aspects of a global Internet, facing all of us with controversies over the

Internet's future", wrote Zittrain in one of his various original papers on this and related aspects of regulation of communications in the cyberspace. Seemingly that we must accept the cohabitation of both - light regulation and light censorship, despite how it might sound as deeply unprofessional and even unethical, but it is simply realpolitik. It requires a brief explanation.

An old belief that journalists "just reports the facts", can be only accepted in general, implying by that that wider context of the reported story has to be respected. Reporting the facts usually means to condense the facts/story in order to clarify, but to clarify often means to distort, and to distort is just one step to false reporting. It was the main reason why a simple rule has been introduced, making the clear distinction between news and opinion, put in all ethic codes.

Unfortunately, such rule, so far, remained an ethic creed only, which simply didn't fit the sad reality of this complex and imperfect world. This is in particular important in the context of distribution of digital content. The fact that practically anyone today can became a distributor of digital content at low expense online, suggests the way of decentralization of mass media, which should be regarded as a positive trend towards the democratization process, but at the same time many content- related pitfalls are standing by, in particular if put in the context of responsible journalism vs. freedom of non-accountability. Point is also to understand how the media convergence can be liberating and threatening at the same time.

Online Journalist

In this information age anyone can perform the role of a journalist. The World Wide Web allows anyone, anywhere, and timely to post piece of information, comments, opinions, pictures, etc., that can be viewed almost instantaneously around the globe. But it might be also a hate inspiring language onlined. If so, we have to care who gets called a journalist? And the key to that issue is ethics.

Since it is unlikely to reach an agreement over how to regulate the Internet worldwide, i.e., whose jurisdiction to apply, it would be fair at least to try to create a kind of Global Code of Online Journalism. To make thinks clear, it does not mean to strive for ethics in the cyberspace communications in general, or inside the Internet, but strictly reduced to online journalism. However, even self-regulation in this very reduced form of communication as is online journalism, might sound as an Utopian endeavor.

The first step should be to develop an umbrella code of conduct, mostly derived from existing codes applied to traditional mass media, but using step by step technique, some online journalism specifics will emerge. It is very important to understand the distinction between ethics and law. Just to remind, despite many of fundamental laws are based on ethical, or more precisely, on religious rules, but in reality, and unfortunately, many unethical actions are perfectly legal! Therefore, in a reduced definition, ethics are moral codes that people should live by. But to remind too, that ethics substantially differ between cultures and traditions.

However, moral codes we live by (part of Western civilization), have been derived from the Judeo-Christian tradition. But does it mean that such ethics have necessarily to be imposed to others? Certainly not. If so, if a consensus can be reached over basic ethic rules in journalism in general, then it would represent an important step in introducing process of self-regulation of the online journalism. Despite the online journalism is still in its infancy, but already plays increasingly important role, which means that it has to be properly self-regulated.

It should be admitted that self-regulation of the media worldwide doesn't work yet, but just facing the truth how important is the new medium, and how the world is shrinking thanks to the new ICTs, the communications in the cyberspace requires a proper self-regulation. Self-regulation, of course, doesn't exclude traditional or statutory regulation. Cohabitation already mentioned would be for the benefits of all people in the cyberspace, and for the benefits of those still outside the cyberspace.

It is perfectly known that regulation, in general, is not keeping up with technology, in particular not with new ICTs. If so, starting point should be - what is illegal offline should be illegal online. No need to mystify new medium. Disregard of communication technics applied, message matters, not the medium! In the very case of the Internet, it is not about the technology, per se, but it is about how it is used. If so, online journalists must extra sharpen the sense of responsibility, just bearing in mind the power new medium has.

9

Press Legislation in India

The mass media are converging, or coming together. This is due to the pace of technological change rather than any strategy on the part of media corporation managements. Recent developments in digital technology have resulted in improvements in the cost, quality and quantity of media outlets. Multimedia digital technologies have brought huge changes, over the last ten to fifteen years, in the way that computers are used. The CD-ROM, for example, has made large-scale data storage possible for computers; the growth of electronic communication networks has enabled the growth of the Internet; combining computer software and the CD-ROM with the MP3 data format has enabled people to obtain and share music via computers and the Internet in new ways; and video digitising cards, now beginning to be installed as standard in higher-powered computers, mean that more people will watch TV and video via their computer.

Over the next five to ten years most broadcast media will transfer to digital systems. As homes become connected to high-capacity broadband networks, computers and data appliances 2 will replace the separate telephones, radio, TV and computers that people use today. Interconnectivity between different media formats (video, audio and print) will enable wholly new approaches to the mass media, and to how people communicate and express themselves in society. There is a fear, however, that, as the media converge and ownership becomes concentrated in fewer and fewer hands, the media will cease to cover issues outside the mainstream. Pressures from sponsors or advertisers could limit editors' freedom to cover issues of concern to civil society campaigners. On the other hand, digital technology could enable new, low-budget forms of media based around Web radio and TV broadcasting. Those with interests within mainstream politics and the larger media corporations often perceive the rise of such alternative media as a threat to their hegemony.

Regulation of the media has traditionally been premised upon claims of "the public interest," a term that remains contested and ill-defined. In the context of ongoing trends of technological development, convergence, and corporate conglomeration, traditional "public service" values in British broadcasting are challenged by market values, and regualtors must, increasingly, justify their interventions. The commercialization and privatization of the communication industries poses a fundamental threat to democratic values.

Press Freedom

The freedom of the press is considered to be the most important right which must be protected in a democratic society. This freedom can only be available in a society where there is a right to free speech and expression. Similarly, the freedom of information can be enjoyed only if there are sources from which information can flow. These sources, again, would be available where there is a right to speech and expression. The freedom of expression and the freedom to receive and impart information are corollary of one another. In fact, there is an overlap between the freedom of expression and the freedom to receive or impart information. The freedom to impart information can be considered as an expression of an opinion, of the informant or of a third person. The seeking of information, on the other hand, precedes the formation of an opinion by the person who seeks the information, and consequently also its expression.

But with regard to the press, freedom of expression and information run parallel to each other. While the press might be the medium of expression, someone else might possess the information. Until and unless these two freedoms be exercised together both would be useless. In the case of information the only one who has the right of free distribution of that information is the party who is the author, originator or otherwise the intellectual owner of the information in question. In case of the press, however, the press can express opinions of others also, of course, held in good faith and believed to be true. It is incumbent on the press, with regard to the print media as well as audio-visual media, to impart information and ideas which the public has the right to receive. Otherwise, the press would not be able to play its role of 'public watch dog'. Thus for exercising the freedom of expression one must have the freedom of information.

The Press Council Act, 1978

This act establishes a press council for the purpose of preserving the freedom of the press and of maintaining the standards of newspapers and news agencies in India. Be it enacted by parliament in the 29th year of the Republic of India as follows.

Chapter I Preliminary

1. Short title and extent -

(1) This act may be called the Press Council Act, 1978.

(2) It extends to the whole of India.

2. Definitions - In this act, unless the context otherwise requires,-

(a) 'Chairman' means the chairman of the council;

(b) 'Council' means the Press Council of India established under section 4; (c) 'Member' means a member of the council and includes its chairman ;

(d) 'Prescribed' means prescribed by rules made under this act;

(e) The expressions 'editor' and 'newspaper' have the meaning respectively assigned to them in the Press and Registration of Books Act, 1867 (25 of 1867) and the expression 'working journalist' has the meaning assigned to it in the working Journalists and other Newspaper Employees (Conditions of Service) and Miscellaneous Provision Act, 1955 (45 of 1955).

3. Rule of construction respecting enactments not extending to the state of Jammu and Kashmir or Sikkim -

Any reference in this act to a law which is not in force in the state of Jammu and Kashmir or Sikkim shall, in relation to that state, be constructed as a reference to the corresponding law, if any inverse in that state.

Chapter II Establishment of the Press Council

4. Incorporation of the council -

(1) with effect from such date as the central government

may, by notification in the official gazette, appoint, there shall be established a council by the name of the press council of India.

(2) the said council shall be a body corporate having perceptual succession and a common seal and shall by the said name sue and bemused.

5. Composition of the council -

(1) The council shall consist of a chairman and 28 other members.

(2) The chairman shall be a person nominated by a committee consisting of the chairman of the council of states (Rajya Sabha), the speaker of the house of the people (Lok Sabha) and a person elected by the members of the council under sub-section (6) and the nomination so made shall take effect from the date on which it is notified by the central government in the official gazette.

(3) Of the other members -

(a) Thirteen shall be nominated in accordance with such procedure as may be prescribed from among the working journalists, of whom six shall be editors of newspapers and the remaining seven shall be working journalists other than editors; so, however that the number of such editors and working journalists other than editors in relation newspapers published in Indian languages shall be not less than three and four respectively;

(b) Six shall be nominated in accordance with such procedure as may be prescribed from among persons who own or carry on the business of management of newspapers, so, newspapers, so, however, that there shall be two representatives from each of the categories of big newspapers, medium newspapers and small newspapers;

(c) One shall nominated in accordance with such procedure as may be prescribed from among persons who manage news agencies;

(d) Three shall be persons having special knowledge or practical experience in respect of education and science, law and literature and culture of whom respectively one shall be nominated by the University Grants Commission one by the Bar Council of India and one by the Sahitya Academy;

(e) Five shall be members of Parliament of whom three shall be nominated by the speaker from among the members of the House of the People (Lok Sabha) and two shall be nominated by the chairman of the council of States (Rajya Sabha) from among its members: Provided that no working journalist who owns, or carries on the business of management of any newspaper shall eligible for nomination under clause (a): Provided further that the nominations under clause (a) and clause (b) shall be so made that among the persons nominated there is not more than one person interested in any newspaper or group of newspaper under the same control or management.

Explanation - for the purposes of clause (b), a 'newspaper' shall be deemed to be -

(i) 'Big newspaper' if the total circulation of all its editions exceeds 50,000 copies for each issue;

(ii) 'Medium newspaper' of the total circulation of all its editions exceeds 15,000 copies but does not exceed 50,000 copies for each issue;

(iii) 'Small newspaper' of the total circulation of all its editions does not exceed 15,000 copies for each issue.

(4) Before making any nomination under clause (a) clause (b) or clause (c) sub-section (3) the central government in the case of the first council and the retiring chairman of the previous council in the case of any subsequent council shall, in the prescribed manner, invite panels of names comprising twice the number to be nominated from such associations of persons of the categories referred to in the said clause (a) clause (b) or clause (c) as may be notified in this behalf by the central government in the case of the first council and by the council itself in the case of subsequent councils: Provided that where there is no association of persons of the category referred to in the said clause (c) the panels of names shall be invited from such news agencies as may be notified as aforesaid.

(5) The central government shall notify the names of persons nominated as members under sub-section (3) in the official gazette and every such nomination shall take effect from the date on which it is notify.

(6) The members of the council notified under sub-section (5) shall elect from among themselves in accordance with such procedure as may be prescribed, a person to be a member of the committee referred to in sub-section (2) and a meeting of the members of the council for the purpose of such election shall be prescribed over by a person chosen from among themselves.

6. Term of office and retirement of members -

(1) Save as otherwise provided in this section, the chairman and other members shall hold office for a

period of three years: Provided that the chairman shall continue to hold such office until the council is reconstituted in accordance with the provisions of section five for a period of six months whichever is earlier.

(2) Where a person nominated as a member under clause (a) clause (b) or clause (c) of sub-section (3) of section 5 if censured under the provisions of sub-section (1) of section 14, he shall cease to be a member of the council.

(3) The term of office of a member nominated under clause (e) of sub-section (3) of section 5 shall come to an end as soon as he ceases to be a member of the House from which he was nominated.

(4) A member shall be deemed to have vacated his seat if he is absent without excuse, sufficient in the opinion of the council, from three consecutive meetings of the council.

(5) The chairman may resign his office by giving notice in writing to the central government and any other member may resign his office by giving notice in writing to the chairman and upon such resignation being accepted by the central government, or as the case may be, the chairman, the chairman or the member shall be deemed to have vacated his office.

(6) Any vacancy arising under sub-section (2) sub-section (3) sub-section (4) or sub-section (5) or otherwise shall be filled, as soon as may be, nomination in the same manner in which the member vacating office was nominated and the member no nominated so nominated shall hold office for the remaining period in which the member in whose place he is nominated would have held office.

(7) A retiring member shall be eligible for re-nomination for not more than one term.

7. Conditions of service of members -

(1) The chairman shall be a whole-time officer and shall be paid such salary as the central government may think fit, and the other members shall receive such allowances of fees for attending the meetings of the council as may be prescribed.

(2) Subject to the provisions of sub-section (1) the condition of service of members shall be such as may prescribed.

(3) It is hereby declared that the office of a member of the council shall not disqualify its holder for being chooses, as or for being a member of either House of Parliament.

8. Committees of the council -

(1) For the purpose of performing its function under this act, the council may constitute from among its members such committees for general or special purposes as it may deem necessary and every committee so constituted shall perform such func-tions as are assigned to it by the council.

(2) The council shall have the power to co-opt as members of any committee con-stitute under sub-section (1) such other number of persons, not being members of the council, as it thinks fit.

(3) Any such member shall have the right to attend any meeting of the committee on which he is so co-opted and to take part in the dis-cussions thereat, but shall not have the right to vote and shall not be a member for any other purpose.

9. Meetings of the council and committees -

The council or any committee thereof shall meet at such times and places and shall observe such trolls of procedure in regard to the transaction of business at its meetings as may be provided by regulations made under this act.

10. Vacancies among members or defect in the constitution not to invalidate acts and proceedings of the council -

No act or proceeding of the council shall be deemed to be invalid by reason merely of the existence of any vacancy in, or any defect in the constitution of, the council.

11. Staff of the council -

(1) subject to such rules as may be made by the central government in this behalf, the council may appoint a secretary and such other employees as it may think necessary for the efficient performance of its function under this act.

(2) the terms and conditions of service of the employees shall be such as may be determined by regulations.

12. Authentication of orders and other instruments of the council -

All orders and decisions of the council shall be authenticated by the signature of the chairman or any other member authorised by the council in this behalf and other instruments issued by the council shall be authenticated by the signature of the secretary or any other officer of the council authorised in manner in this behalf.

Chapter III Powers and functions of the council

13. Objects and functions of the council -

(1) the objects of the Cancun shall be to preserve the

freedom of the press and to maintain and improve the standards of newspapers and news agencies in India.

(2) The council may, in furtherance of its objects, perform the following functions, namely -

(a) to help newspapers and news agencies to maintain their independence;

(b) to build up a code of conduct for newspapers news agencies and journalists in accordance with high professional standards;

(c) to ensure on the part of newspapers news agencies and journalists, the maintenance of high standards of public taste and foster a due sense of both the rights and responsibilities of citizenship;

(d) to encourage the growth of a sense of responsibility and public service aiming all those engaged in the profession of journalism;

(e) to keep under review any development likely to restrict the supply and dissemination of news of public interest and importance;

(f) to keep under review cases of assistance received by any newspaper or news agency in India from any foreign source including such cases as are referred to it by the central government or are brought to its notice by any individual, association of persons or any other organisation: Provided that nothing in this clause shall preclude the central government from dealing with any case of assistance received by a newspaper or news agency in India from any foreign source in any other manner it thinks fit;

(g) to undertake studies of foreign newspapers, including those brought out by any embassy or other representatives in India of a foreign state, their circulation and impact.

Explanation - For the purpose of this clause, the expression 'foreign state' has the meaning assigned to it in section 87A of the code of civil procedure, 1908 (5 of 1908);

(h) to promote a proper functional relationship among sell classes of persons engaged in the production or publication of newspapers or in news agencies: Provided that nothing in this Calais shall be deemed to confer on the council any functions in regard to dis-putes to which the Industrial Disputes Act, 1947 (14 of 1947) applies;

(i) to concern itself developments such as concentration of or other aspects of ownership of newspapers and news agencies which may affect the independence of the press;

(j) to indurate such studies as may be entrusted to the council and to espousers its opinion in regard to any matter referred to it by the central government;

(k) to do such other acts as may be incidental or conductive to the discharge of the above functions.

14. Power to censure -

(1) where on receipt of a complaint made to it or otherwise, the council has reason believe that a newspaper or news agency has offended against the standards or journalist ethics or public taste or that an editor or a working journalist has committed any professional; misconduct, the council may, after giving the newspaper, or news agency, the editor or journalist

concerned an opportunity of being heard, hold an inquiry in such annett as may be provided by regulations made under this act and, if it is satisfied that it is necessary so to do, it may, for reasons to be recorded in writing, warn, admonish or censure the newspaper, the news agency, the editor or the journalist or disapprove the conduct of the editor or the journalist, as the case may be: Provided that the council may not take cognisance of a complaint if in the opinion of the chairman there is no sufficient ground for holding an inquiry.

(2) If the council is of the opinion that it is necessary or expedient in the public interest so to do, it may require any newspapers to publish therein in such manner as the council thinks, fir any particulars relating to any inquiry under this section against a newspaper or news agency, an editor or a journalist working therein, including the name of such newspaper, news agency, editor or journalist.

(3) Nothing in sub-section (1) shall be deemed to empower the council to hold an inquiry into any matter in respect of which any proceeding is pending in a court of law.

(4) The decision of the council under sub-section (1) or sub-section (2) as the case may be shall be final and shall not be questioned in any court of law.

15. General powers of the council -

(1) For the purpose of performing its functions or holding any inquiry under this act, the council shall have the same powers throughout Indies are vested in a civil court while trying a suit under the code of civil

procedure 1908 (5 of 1908) in respect of the following matters, namely:

(a) summoning and enforcing the atten-dance of persons and examining them on oath;

(b) requiring the discovery and inspection of documents;

(c) receiving evidence on affidavits;

(d) requisitioning any public record or copies thereof from any court or office;

(e) issuing commissions for the examination of witness or documents; and (f) any other matter which may be prescribed.

(2) Nothing in sub-section (1) shall be deemed to compel any newspaper news agency editor or journalist to disclose the source of any news ore in-formation published by that newspaper or received or reported be that news agency editor or journalist.

(3) Every inquiry held by the council shall be deemed to be a judicial proceeding within the meaning of sections 193 and 228 of the Indian Penal Code (45 of 1860).

(4) The council may, it if considers Ir.necessary for the purpose of carrying out its objects or for the performance of any of its function under this act, make such observation as it may think, fir, in any of its decisions or reports, respecting the conduct of any authority, including government.

16. Levy of fees -

(1) The council may, for the purpose performing its functions under this act, levy such fees, at such rates and in such manner as my be prescribed from

registered newspapers and news agencies and different rates may be prescribed for different newspapers banging regard to their circulation and other matters.

(2) Any fees payable to the council under sub-section (21) may be recovered as an areas of land revenue.

17. Payments to the council -

The central government may after due appropriation made by Parliament by law in this behalf, pay to the council by way of grants such sums of money as the central government may consider necessary for the performance of the functions of the council under this act.

18. Fund of the council -

(1) The council shall have its own fund; and the fees collected by it all such sums as may from time to time be paid to it by the central government and all grants and advances made to it by any other authority or person shall be credited to the fund and all payments by the council shall be made therefrom.

(2) All moneys belonging to the fund shall be deposited in such banks or invested in such manner as may subject to the approval of the central government, be decided by the council.

(3) The council may spend such sums as it thinks fit or for performing its functions under this act, and such sums shall be treated as expenditure payable out of the fund of the council.

19. Budget -

The council shall prepare, in such form and at such time each year as may be prescribed a budget in respect of the financial year next ensuing showing the stimulated receipts and expenditure and copies thereof shall be forwarded to the central government.

20. Annual report -

The council shall prepare once every year, in such form and at such time as may be prescribed an annual report giving summary of its activities during the previous year, and giving an account of the standards of newspapers and news agencies and factors affecting them, and copies thereof, together with the statement of accountants audited in the manner prescribed under section 22 shall be forwarded to the central government and the government shall cause the same to be laid before both houses of Parliament.

21. Interim reports -

Without prejudice to the provisions of Section 20, of the council may prepare at any time during the course or a year a report giving a summary of such of its activities during the year as it considers to be of public impor-tance and copies thereof shall be forwarded to the central government and the government shall cause to be laid before both Houses of Parliament.

22. Accounts and audit -

The accounts of the council shall be maintained and audited in such as may in consultation with the comptroller and auditor of India be prescribed.

Chapter IV Miscellaneous

23. Protection of action taken in good faith -

(1) No suit or other legal proceeding shall lie against the

council or any member thereof or any person acting under the direction of the council in respect of anything which is in good faith done intended to be done under this act.

(2) No suit or other legal proceeding shall lie against any newspaper in respect of the publication of any matter therein under the authority of the council.

24. Members, etc., to be public servants -

Every member of the council and every officer or other employee appointed by the council shall be deemed to be a public servant within the meaning of section 21 of the Indian Penal code (45 of 1860).

25. Power to make rules -

(1) The central government may, be notification in the official gazette, make rules to carry out the purposes of this ct. Provided that when the council has been established no such rules shall be made without consulting the council.

(2) In particular and without prejudice to the generality of the foregoing power such rules may provide for all or any of the following matters, namely: (a) the procedure for nomination of members of the council under clauses (a) (b) and (c) of sub-section 5;

(b) the manner in which panels of names may be invited under sub-section (4) of section 5;

(c) the procedure for election of a number of the committee referred to in sub-section (2) of section 5 under sub-section (6) of that section;

(d) the allowances of fees to be paid to the members of the council for attending the meetings of the council, and other conditions of service of such members under sub-section 91) and (2) of section 7;

(e) the appointment of the secretary and other employees of the council under section 11;

(f) the matters referred to in clause(f) of sub-section (1) of section 15;

(g) the rates at which fees may be levied by the council under section 16 and the manner in which such fees any be levied;

(h) the form in which and the time within which the budget and annual report are to be prepared by the council under section 19 and 20 respectively;

(i) the manner in which the accounts of the council are to be maintained and audited under sections (3) every rule made under this section shall be laid as soon as may be after it is made, before each house of parliament while it is in session for a total period of 30 days which may be comprised in one session or into or more successive sessions, and if before the expiry of the session immediately following the session or the successive sessions aforesaid, both houses agree in making any modification in the rule or both houses agree that the rule should not be made the rule shall thereafter have effect only in such modified form or be of no effect, as the case may be; so however that any such modification or annulment shall be without prejudice to the validity of anything done under that rule.

26. Power to make regulations -

The council may make regulations not inconsistent with this act and the rules made thereunder for -

(a) regulating the meeting of the council or any committee thereof and the procedure for conducting the business thereat under section 9;

(b) specifying the terms and conditions of service of the employees, appointed by the council under sub-section (2) of section 11;

(c) regulating the manner of holding any inquiry under this act;

(d) delegating to the chairman or the secretary of the council, subject to such conditions as it may think fit to impose, any of its powers under sub-section (3) of section 18;

(e) any other matter for which provision any be made by regulations under this act; Provided that the regulations made under clause (b) shall be made only with the price approval of the central government.

27. Amendment of Act 25 of 1867 -

In sub-section (1) of section 8C of the Press and Registration of Books Act, 1867, for the words 'consisting of a chairman and another member to be appointed by the central government', the words and figures 'consisting of a chairman and another member to be nominated by the Press Council of India, established under section 4 of the Press Council Act 1978, from among its members' shall be substituted.

THE PRESS COUNCIL OF INDIA'S NORMS OF JOURNALISTIC CONDUCT

The Press Council of India has been established with the objects of preserving the freedom of the press and of maintaining and improving the standards of newspapers and news agencies in the country. It is to further these objects, that the council is required among other things, to help newspapers and news agencies to maintain independence; to build up a code of conduct for newspapers agencies and journalists in accordance with high professional standards to ensure on their part the maintenance of high standards of public taste and to foster a due sense of the rights and responsibilities of citizenship and to foster the growth of a sense of responsibility and public service among all those engaged in the profession of journalism.

To discharge these functions entrusted to it, the council has to frame a code of ethics for those engaged in journalism and to enforce it. The council over the years has built up a code of ethics covering aspects of journalism which came to the fore from time to time and which needed to be dealt with at its end, keeping in mind the objects with which it has been established and the role it is expected to perform.

Since its last publication, there have been some additions to the ethical code on important aspects such as financial journalism and pre-poll and exit poll surveys. The council decided to publish and update code and the result is the present publication. This publication has been designed to be a trim and at the same time a comprehensive treatment on the subject.

Besides the ethics, the publication also contains references to the provisions of the constitution and of the various statute laws which have a bearing on the print media. It is hoped that it will be found useful by all concerned. The council hopes to publish its translation in regional languages in due course, for the council is of the view that the education in the code of ethics of journalists connected particularly with the small and regional language newspapers is very necessary if the code is to be effective.

We have no doubt that we will succeed in getting assistance in this task from public-spirited individuals and associations.

Principles and ethics

The fundamental objective of journalism is to serve the people with news, views, comments and information on matters of public interest in a fair, accurate, unbiased, sober and decent manner. Towards this end, the press is expected to conduct itself in keeping with certain norms of professionalism universally recognised. The norms enunciated below and other specific guidelines appended thereafter, when applied with due discernment and adaptation to the varying circumstance of each case, will help the journalist to self-regulate his or her conduct.

1. *Accuracy and fairness*: The press shall eschew publication of inaccurate, baseless, graceless, misleading or distorted material. All sides of the core issue or subject should be reported. Unjustified rumours and surmises should not be set forth as facts.

2. *Pre-publication verification*: On receipt of a report or article of public interest and benefit containing imputations or comments against a citizen, the editor should check with due care and attention its factual accuracy - apart from other authentic sources with the person or the organisation concerned to elicit his / her or its version, comments or reaction and publish the same with due amendments in the report where necessary. In the event of lack or absence of response, a footnote to that effect should be appended to the report.

3. *Caution against defamatory writings*: A newspaper should not publish anything which is manifestly defamatory or libellous against any individual organisation unless after due care and checking, they have sufficient reason to believe that it is true and its publication will be for public good.

4. Truth is no defence for publishing derogatory, scurrilous and defamatory material against a private citizen where no public interest is involved.

5. No personal remarks which may be considered or construed to be derogatory in nature against a dead person should be published except in rare cases of public interest, as the dead person cannot possibly contradict or deny those remarks.

6. The press shall not rely on objectionable past behaviour of a citizen for basing the scathing comments with reference to fresh action of that person. If public good requires such reference, the press should make pre-publication inquiries from the authorities concerned about the follow-up action, if any, in regard to those adverse actions.

7. The press has a duty, discretion and right to serve the public interest by drawing reader's attention to citizens of doubtful antecedents and of questionable character but as responsible journalists they should observe due restraint and caution in hazarding their own opinion or conclusion in branding these persons as 'cheats' or 'killers' etc. The cardinal principle being that the guilt of a person should be established by proof of facts alleged and not by proof of the bad character of the accused. In the zest to expose, the press should not exceed the limits of ethical caution and fair comments.

8. Where the impugned publication are manifestly injurious to the reputation of the complainant, the onus shall be on the respondent to show that they were true or to establish that they constituted for comment made in good faith and for public good.

9. Parameters of the right of the press to comment on the acts and conduct of public officials. So far as the government, local authority and other organs/ institutions exercising governmental power are concerned, they cannot maintain a suit for damages for acts and conduct relevant to the discharge of their official duties unless the official establishes that the publication was made with reckless disregard for the truth. However, the judiciary which is protected by the power to punish for contempt of court and the parliament and legislatures, protected as their privileges are by Articles 105 and 194 respectively, of the constitution of India, represent exception to this rule.

10. Publication of news or comments / information on public officials conducting investigations should have a tendency to help the commission of offences or to impede the prevention or detection of offences or prosecution of the guilty. The investigative agency is also under a corresponding obligation not to leak out or disclose such information or indulge in disinformation.

11. The Official Secrets Act, 1923 or any other similar enactment or provision having the force of law equally bind the press or media though there is no law empowering the state or its officials to prohibit, or to impose a prior restraint upon the press / media.

12. Cartoons and caricatures in depicting good humour are to be placed in a special category of news that enjoy more liberal attitude.

13. *Right to privacy*: The press shall not intrude or invade the privacy of an individual unless outweighed by genuine overriding public interest, not being a prurient or morbid curiosity. So, however, that once a matter becomes a matter of public record, the right to privacy no longer subsists and it becomes a legitimate subject for comment by press and media among others. Explanation: Things concerning a person's home, family, religion, health, sexuality, personal life and private affairs are covered by the concept of privacy excepting where any of these impinges upon the public or public interest.

14. *Caution against identification*: While reporting crime involving rape, abduction or kidnap of women / females or sexual assault on children, or raising doubts and questions touching the chastity, personal character and privacy of women, the names, photographs of the victims or other particulars leading to their identity shall not be published.

15. Minor children and infants who are the offspring of sexual abuse or 'forcible marriage' or illicit sexual union shall not be identified or photographed.

16. *Recording interviews and phone conversation*: The press shall not tape-record anyone's conversation without that person's knowledge or consent, except where the recording is necessary to protect the journalist in a legal action, or for other compelling good reason.

17. The press shall, prior to publication, delete offensive epithets used by an interviewer in conversation with the pressperson.

18. Intrusion through photography into moments of personal grief shall be avoided. However, photography of victims of accidents or natural calamity may be in larger public interest.

19. *Conjecture, comment and fact*: A newspaper should not pass on or elevate conjecture, speculation or comment as a statement of fact. All these categories should be distinctly stated.

20. *Newspapers to eschew suggestive guilt*: Newspapers should eschew suggestive guilt by association. They should not name or identify the family or relatives or associates of a person convicted or accused of a crime, when they are totally innocent and a reference to them is not relevant to the matter reported.

21. It is contrary to the norms of journalism for a paper to identify itself with and project the case of any one party in the case of any controversy / dispute.

22. *Corrections*: When any factual error or mistake is detected or confirmed, the newspaper should publish the correction promptly with due prominence and with apology or expression of regrets in a case of serious lapse.

23. *Right of reply*: The newspaper should promptly and with due prominence, publish either in full or with due editing, free of cost, at the instance of the person affected or feeling aggrieved / or concerned by the impugned publication, a contradiction / reply / clarification or rejoinder sent to the editor in the form of a letter or note. If the editor doubts the truth or factual accuracy of the contradiction / reply / clarification or rejoinder, he shall be at liberty to add separately at the end a brief editorial comment

doubting its veracity, but only when this doubt is reasonably founded on unimpeachable documentary or other evidential material in his / her possession. This is a concession which has to be availed of sparingly with due discretion and caution in appropriate cases.

24. However, where the reply / contradiction or rejoinder is being published in compliance with the discretion of the Press Council, it is permissible to append a brief editorial note to that effect.

25. Right of rejoinder cannot be claimed through the medium of press conference, as publication of a news of a conference is within the discretionary powers of an editor.

26. Freedom of the press involves the readers' right to know all sides of an issue of public interest. An editor, therefore, shall not refuse to publish the reply or rejoinder merely on the ground that in his opinion the story published in the newspaper was true. That is an issue to be left to the judgement of the readers. It also does not behove an editor to show contempt towards a reader.

27. *Letters to editor*: An editor who decides to open his columns for letters on a controversial subject, is not obliged to publish all the letters received in regard to that subject. He is entitled to select and publish only some of them either in entirety or the gist thereof. However, in exercising this discretion, he must make an honest endeavour to ensure that what is published is not one-sided but represents a fair balance between the views for and against with respect to the principal issue in controversy.

28. In the event of rejoinder upon rejoinder being sent by two parties on a controversial subject, the editor has the discretion to decide at which stage to close the continuing column.

29. *Obscenity and vulgarity to be eschewed*: Newspapers / journalists shall not publish anything which is obscene, vulgar or offensive to public good taste.

30. Newspapers shall not display advertisements which are vulgar or which, through depiction of a woman in nude or lewd posture, provoke lecherous attention of males as if she herself was a commercial commodity for sale.

31. Whether a picture is obscene or not, is to be judged in relation to three tests; namely:

    i) Is it vulgar and indecent?

    ii) Is it a piece of mere pornography?

    iii) Is its publication meant merely to make money by titillating the sex feelings of adolescents and among whom it is intended to circulate? In other words, does it constitute an unwholesome exploitation for commercial gain. Other relevant considerations are whether the picture is relevant to the subject matter of the magazine. That is to say, whether its publication serves any preponderating social or public purpose, in relation to art, painting, medicine, research or reform of sex.

32. *Violence not to be glorified*: Newspapers / journalists shall avoid presenting acts of violence, armed robberies and terrorist activities in a manner that glorifies the perpetrators' acts, declarations or death in the eyes of the public.

33. Glorification / encouragement of social evils to be eschewed Newspapers shall not allow their columns to be misused for writings which have a tendency to encourage or glorify social evils like sati pratha or ostentatious celebrations.

34. *Covering communal disputes / clashes*: News, views or comments relating to communal or religious disputes / clashes shall be published after proper verification of facts and presented with due caution and restraint in a manner which is conducive to the creation of an atmosphere congenial to communal harmony, amity and peace. Sensational, provocative and alarming headlines are to be avoided. Acts of communal violence or vandalism shall be reported in a manner as may not undermine the people's confidence in the law and order machinery of the state. Giving community-wise figures of the victims of communal riot, or writing about the incident in a style which is likely to inflame passions, aggravate the tension, or accentuate the strained relations between the communities / religious groups concerned, or which has a potential to exacerbate the trouble, shall be avoided.

35. Headings not to be sensational / provocative and must justify the matter printed under them. In general and particularly in the context of communal disputes or clashes - a. Provocative and sensational headlines are to be avoided; b. Headings must reflect and justify the matter printed under them; c. Headings containing allegations made in statements should either identify the body or the source making it or at least carry quotation marks.

36. *Caste, religion or community references*: In general, the caste identification of a person or a particular class should be avoided, particularly when in the context it conveys a sense or attributes a conduct or practice derogatory to that caste.

37. Newspapers are advised against the use of word 'scheduled caste' or 'harijan' which has been objected to by some persons.

38. An accused or a victim shall not be described by his caste or community when the same does not have anything to do with the offence or the crime and plays no part either in the identification of any accused or proceeding, if there be any.

39. Newspapers should not publish any fictional literature distorting and portraying religious characters in an adverse light, transgressing the norms of literary taste and offending the religious susceptibilities of large sections of society who hold those characters in high esteem, invested with attributes of the virtuous and lofty.

40. Commercial exploitation of the name of prophets, seers or deities is repugnant to journalistic ethics and good taste.

41. *Reporting on natural calamities*: Facts and data relating to spread of epidemics or natural calamities shall be checked up thoroughly from authentic sources and then published with due restraint in a manner bereft of sensationalism, exaggeration, surmises or unverified facts.

42. *Paramount national interest*: Newspapers shall, as a matter of self-regulation, exercise due restraint and caution in presenting any news, comment or

information which is likely to jeopardise, endanger or harm the paramount interests of the state and society, or the rights of individuals with respect to which reasonable restrictions may be imposed by law on the right to freedom of speech and expression under clause (2) of Article 19 of the constitution of India.

43. Publication of wrong / incorrect map is a very serious offence, whatever the reason, as it adversely affects the territorial integrity of the country and warrants prompt and prominent retraction with regrets.

44. Newspapers may expose misuse of diplomatic immunity. The media shall make every possible effort to build bridges of co-operation, friendly relations and better understanding between India and foreign states. At the same time, it is the duty of a newspaper to expose any misuse or undue advantage of the diplomatic immunities.

45. Investigative journalism, its norms and parameters. Investigative reporting has three basic elements. a. It has to be the work of the reporter, not of others he is reporting; b. The subject should be of public importance for the reader to know; c. An attempt is being made to hide the truth from the people.

(i) The first norm follows as a necessary corollary from (a) that the investigative reporter should, as a rule, base his story on facts investigated, detected and verified by himself and not on hearsay or on derivative evidence collected by a third party, not checked up from direct, authentic sources by the reporter himself.

(ii) There being a conflict between the factors which require openness and those which necessitate secrecy, the investigative journalist should strike and maintain in his report a proper balance between openness on the one hand and secrecy on the other, placing the public good above everything.

(iii) The investigative journalist should resist the temptation of quickies or quick gains conjured up from half-baked incomplete, doubtful facts, not fully checked up and verified from authentic sources by the reporter himself.

(iv) Imaginary facts, or ferreting out or conjecturing the non-existent should be scrupulously avoided. Facts, facts and yet more facts are vital and they should be checked and cross-checked whenever possible until the moment the paper goes to press.

(v) The newspaper must adopt strict standards of fairness and accuracy of facts. Findings should be presented in an objective manner, without exaggerating or distorting, that would stand up in a court of law, if necessary.

(vi) The reporter must not approach the matter or the issue under investigation, in a manner as though he were the prosecutor or counsel for the prosecution. The reporter's approach should be fair, accurate and balanced. All facts properly checked up, both for and against the core issues, should be distinctly and separately stated, free from any one-sided inferences or unfair comments. The tone and tenor of the report and its language should be sober, decent and dignified, and not needlessly offensive, barbed, derisive or castigatory, particularly while commenting on the version of the person whose alleged activity or misconduct is being investigated. Nor should the investigative reporter conduct the proceedings and pronounce his verdict of guilt or innocence against the person whose alleged criminal acts and conduct were investigated, in a manner as if he were a court trying the accused.

(vii) In all proceedings including the investigation, presentation and publication of the report, the investigative journalist's newspaper should be guided by the paramount principle of criminal jurisprudence, that a person is innocent unless the offence alleged against him is proved beyond doubt by independent, reliable evidence.

(viii) The private life, even of a public figure, is his own. Exposition or invasion of his personal privacy or private life is not permissible unless there is clear evidence that the wrong-doings in question have a reasonable nexus with the misuse of his public position or power and has an adverse impact on public interest.

(ix) Though the legal provisions of criminal procedure do not in terms, apply to investigating proceedings by a journalist, the fundamental principles underlying them can be adopted as a guide on grounds of equity, ethics and good conscience.

46. *Confidence to be respected*: If information is received from a confidential source, the confidence should be respected. The journalist cannot be compelled by the Press Council to disclose such source; but it shall not be regarded as a breach of journalistic ethics if the source is voluntarily disclosed in proceedings before the council by the journalist who considers it necessary to repel effectively a charge against him / her. This rule requiring a newspaper not to publish matters disclosed to it in confidence, is not applicable where:

(a) consent of the source is subsequently obtained; or

(b) the editor clarified by way of an appropriate footnote that since the publication of certain matters were in the public interest, the information in question was being published although it had been made 'off the record'.

47. *Caution in criticising judicial acts*: Excepting where the court sits 'in-camera' or directs otherwise, it is open to a newspaper to report pending judicial proceedings, in a fair, accurate and reasonable manner. But it shall not publish anything --which, in its direct and immediate effect, creates a substantial risk of obstructing, impeding or prejudicing seriously the due administration of justice; or -- is in the nature of a running commentary or debate, or records the paper's own findings, conjectures, reflection or comments on issues, sub judice and which may amount to arrogation to the newspaper the functions of the court; or -- regarding the personal character of the accused standing trial on a charge of committing a crime. The newspaper shall not as a matter of caution, publish or comment on evidence collected as a result of investigative journalism, when, after the accused is arrested and charged, the court becomes seized of the case. Nor should they reveal, comment upon or evaluate a confession allegedly made by the accused.

48. While newspapers may, in the public interest, make reasonable criticism of a judicial act or the judgement of a court for public good; they shall not cast scurrilous aspersions on, or impute improper motives, or personal bias to the judge. Nor shall they scandalise the court or the judiciary as a whole, or make personal allegations of lack of ability or integrity against a judge.

49. The newspaper shall, as a matter of caution, avoid unfair and unwarranted criticism which, by innuendo, attributes to a judge extraneous consideration for performing an act in due course of his / her judicial functions, even if such criticism does not strictly amount to criminal contempt of court.

50. *Newspapers to avoid crass commercialism*: While newspapers are entitled to ensure, improve or strengthen their financial viability by all legitimate means, the press shall not engage in crass commercialism or unseemly cut-throat commercial competition with their rivals in a manner repugnant to high professional standards and good taste.

51. Predatory price wars / trade competition among newspapers, laced with tones disparaging the products of each other, initiated and carried on in print, assume the colour of unfair 'trade' practice, repugnant to journalistic ethics. The question as when it assumes such an unethical character, is one of the fact depending on the circumstances of each case.

52. *Plagiarism*: Using or passing off the writings or ideas of another as one's own, without crediting the source, is an offence against the ethics of journalism.

53. *Unauthorised lifting of news*: The practice of lifting news from other newspapers publishing them subsequently as their own, ill-comports the high standards of journalism. To remove its unethicality, the 'lifting' newspaper must duly acknowledge the source of the report. The position of features articles is different from 'news'. Feature articles shall not be lifted without permission and proper acknowledgement.

54. The press shall not reproduce in any form offending portions or excerpts from a proscribed book.

55. *Non-return of unsolicited material*: A paper is not bound to return unsolicited material sent for consideration of publication. However, when the same is accompanied by a stamped envelope, the paper should make all efforts to return it.

56. *Advertisements*: Commercial advertisements are information as much as social, economic or political information. What is more, advertisements shape attitude and ways of life at least as much as other kinds of information and comment. Journalistic propriety demands that advertisements must be clearly distinguishable from editorial matters carried in the newspaper.

57. A newspaper shall not publish anything which has a tendency to malign wholesale or hurt the religious sentiments of any community or section of society.

58. Advertisements which offend the provisions of the Drugs and Magical Remedies (Objectionable Advertisement) Act, 1954, should be rejected.

59. Newspapers should not publish an advertisement containing anything which is unlawful or illegal, or is contrary to good taste or to journalistic ethics or proprieties.

60. Newspapers while publishing advertisements, shall specify the amount received by them. The rationale behind this is that advertisements should be charged at rates usually chargeable by a newspaper since payment of more than the normal rates would amount to a subsidy to the paper.

61. Publication of dummy advertisements that have neither been paid for, nor authorised by the advertisers, constitute breach of journalistic ethics.

62. Deliberate failure to publish an advertisement in all the copies of a newspaper offends against the standards of journalistic ethics and constitutes gross professional misconduct.

63. There should be no lack of vigilance or a communication gap between the advertisement department and the editorial department of a newspaper in the matter of considering the propriety or otherwise of an advertisement received for publication.

64. The editors should insist on their right to have the final say in the acceptance or rejection of advertisements, specially those which border on or cross the line between decency and obscenity.

65. An editor shall be responsible for all matters, including advertisements published in the newspaper. If responsibility is disclaimed, this shall be explicitly stated beforehand.

Guidelines on specific issues

A) Guidelines for observance by the press in the wake of communal disturbances 1969

Recognising that the press which enjoys the utmost freedom of expression has a great and vital role to play in educating and moulding public opinion on correct lines in regard to the need for friendly and harmonious relations between the various communities and religious groups forming the fabric of Indian political life and in mirroring the conscience of the best minds of the country to achieve national solidarity, the Press Council of India considers that this object would be defeated, communal peace and harmony disturbed and national unity disrupted if the press does not strictly adhere to proper norms and standards in reporting on or commenting on matters which bear on communal relations.

Without attempting to be exhaustive, the council considers the following as offending against journalistic proprieties and ethics:

1. Distortion or exaggeration of facts or incidents in relation to communal matters or giving currency to unverified rumours, suspicions or inferences as if they were facts and base their comments on them.

2. Employment of intemperate or unrestrained language in the presentation of news or views, even as a piece of literary flourish or for the purpose of rhetoric or emphasis.

3. Encouraging or condoning violence even in the face of provocation as a means of obtaining redress of grievances whether the same be genuine or not.

4. While it is the legitimate function of the press to draw attention to the genuine and legitimate grievances of any community with a view to having the same redressed by all peaceful, legal and legitimate means, it is improper and a breach of journalistic ethics to invent grievances, or to exaggerate real grievances, as these tend to promote communal ill-feeling and accentuate discord.

5. Scurrilous and untrue attacks on communities, or individuals, particularly when this is accompanied by charges attributing misconduct to them as due to their being members of a particular community or caste.

6. Falsely giving a communal colour to incidents which might occur in which members of different communities happen to be involved.

7. Emphasising matters that are not to produce communal hatred or ill-will, or fostering feelings of distrust between communities.

8. Publishing alarming news which are in substance untrue or make provocative comments on such news or even otherwise calculated to embitter relations between different communities or regional or linguistic groups.

9. Exaggerating actual happenings to achieve sensationalism and publication of news which adversely affect communal harmony with banner headlines or in distinctive types.

10. Making disrespectful, derogatory or insulting remarks on or reference to the different religions or faiths or their founders.

Guidelines issued by the Press Council for observance by the state governments and the media in relation to communal disturbances 1991

i. The state government should take upon themselves the responsibility of keeping a close watch on the communal writings that might spark off tension, destruction and death, and bring them to the notice of the council;

ii. The government may have occasion to take action against erring papers or editors. But it must do so within the bounds of law. If newsmen are arrested, or search-and-seizure operations become necessary, it would be healthy convention if such developments could be reported to the Press Council within 24 to 48 hours followed by a detailed note within a week;

iii. Under no circumstances must the authorities resort to vindictive measures like cut in advertisements, cancellation of accreditation, cut in newsprint quota and other facilities;

iv. Provocative and sensational headlines should be avoided by the press;

v. Headings must reflect and justify the master primed under them;

vi. Figures of casualties given in headlines should preferably be on the lower side in case or doubt about their exactness and where the numbers reported by various sources differ widely;

vii. Headings containing allegations made in statements should either identify the person / body making the allegation or, at least, should carry quotation marks;

viii. News reports should be devoid of comments and value judgement;

ix. Presentation of news should not be motivated or guided by partisan feelings, nor should it appear to be so;

x. Language employed in writing the news should be temperate and such as may foster feelings or amity among communities and groups;

xi. Corrections should be promptly published with due prominence and regrets expressed in serious cases; and

xii. It will help a great deal if in-service training is given to journalists for inculcation of all these principles.

Guidelines issued by the Press Council on January 21-22, 1993 in the wake of the Ram Janambhoomi - Babri Masjid dispute

Guidelines for guarding against the commission of the following journalistic improprieties and unethicalities

1. Distortion or exaggeration of facts or incidents in relation to communal matters or giving currency to unverified rumours, suspicions or inferences as if they were facts and base their comment on them.

2. Employment of intemperate or unrestrained language in the presentation of news or views, even as a piece of literary flourish or for the purpose of rhetoric or emphasis.

3. Encouraging or condoning violence even in the face of provocation as a means of obtaining redress of grievance whether the same be genuine or not.

4. While it is the legitimate function of the press to draw attention to the genuine and legitimate grievances of any community with a view to having the same redressed by all peaceful legal and legitimate means, it is improper and a breach of journalistic ethics to invent grievances, or to exaggerate real grievances, as these tend to promote communal ill-feeling and accentuate discord.

5. Scurrilous and untrue attacks on communities, or individuals, particularly when this is accompanied by charges attributing misconduct to them as due to their being memoers of a particular community or caste.

6. Falsely giving a communal colour to incidents which might occur in which members of different communities happen to be involved.

7. Emphasising matters that are apt to produce communal hatred or ill-will, or fostering feelings of distrust between communities.

8. Publishing alarming news which are in substance untrue or make provocative comments on such news or even otherwise calculated to embitter relations

between different communities or regional or linguistic groups.

9. Exaggerating actual happenings to achieve sensationalism and publication of news which adversely affect communal harmony with banner headlines or distinctive types.

10. Making disrespectful, derogatory or insulting remarks on or reference to the different religions or faiths or their founders.

B) Coverage of handouts of militants / terrorists

Guiding principles arising out of a complaint against the publication of some ULFA handouts / threat notes by a newspaper of Assam

The Press Council has enunciated some general principles for the guidance of the press. These are in tune with the recommendations of the Press Council of India Report on Punjab and Jammu and Kashmir, adopted by the Press Council in January, 1991. These guiding principles considered by the council in September 1992, are as follows:

Dictates or 'press notes' commanding newspapers to publish them, under duress or threats of dire consequence, emanating from elements wedded to violence, constitute "the gravest assault on the freedom of the press which is one of the surest guarantors of a democratic and plural society".

Generally, such dictates or notes are not newsworthy per se. Their publication tends to demoralise the public and to affect adversely public, police and security. The publication not only compromises the freedom and independence of the newspaper concerned, but also constitutes an offence against the standards of journalistic ethics and professional responsibility.

This is not to say that if there is anything newsworthy in a 'press note' emanating from any source, it should be blacked-out altogether, because 'self-censorship' may be "no less dangerous for being insidious". The essential point is that editors must exercise due caution and circumspection in considering the dissemination of such press notes.

If the whole of the note is not pernicious, then it may be edited, its objectionable portions removed and language toned down so that whatever is truly newsworthy gets disseminated in a balanced manner. However, where the 'news' and the objectionable portions are inextricably mixed up, violating the entire warp and woof of the 'press note', it will be prudent to withhold its publication altogether.

This is not an easy way out, as the media's experience of militancy in Punjab has amply demonstrated. More than 50 media personnel have lost their lives in terrorist attacks and ignoring a militant press note can lead and has often led, to death of innocent and defenceless media persons.

Any show of editorial defence and courage is likely to be seen by defenceless employees of newspapers as exposing them to avoidable dangers. Editors and proprietors under these circumstances have little room for manoeuvres. A workable expedient that proved useful in Punjab, is for the government to be in close touch with newspapers so that objectionable and anti-national press notes from groups swearing by violence could be removed from newspapers before publication.

Even though this may be seen as a form of pre-censorship, this arrangement saved lives and spared newspapers from difficult and delicate choices. There is however a danger of a wilful administration using this process to muzzle the press and misuse its authority under the law to define 'objectionable material' on its own terms.

Strict procedures must therefore be laid down. Orders passed under any legislation in this regard from time to time in relation to publication of allegedly 'objectionable matter' should be subjected to some kind of appellate review so as to curb any propensity to arbitrary action. The principal legislation and rules made thereunder should also be periodically reviewed in the light of changing circumstances. These safeguards should be built into all such press legislation.

C) Aids and the media

The mass media should help set an agenda for the country to fight the Aids pandemic in co-ordination with the government, the medical profession and the voluntary agencies. So far, the media in India have treated Aids more as news than as a growing menace and scourge threatening both human lives and dignity.

An exploratory content-analysis study conducted by the Operations Research Group during 1989-90 revealed the inadequacy of print media coverage on Aids in India. The coverage of prominent urban dailies focussed more on clinical diagnostic research on Aids in western countries, and little on the Aids problem in India and its social implications.

There were very few independent reports on Aids and the sources of most stories were international agencies. Further, most stories were located in inside pages or in supplements, and, content-wise were superficial in nature. Since the disclosures of the survey, until 1992, the quality and quantity of newspaper coverage on Aids in India has not changed much while the relative quantity of Aids coverage is on the rise, and while a greater recognition exists on the part of the print media about the problem of Aids in India, newspapers are to quote experts, still 'reactive' rather than 'proactive'.

Dos and don'ts

From sporadic news, Aids must become a campaign target for our mass media with the following components of dos and don'ts:

— The media must inform and educate the people, not alarm or scare them. The emphasis must be on the fact that HIV (Human immunodeficiency virus) can be prevented from going into unaffected humans. Aids takes around 10 years to develop and HIV is a virus which does not survive for long outside a body. Thus, it is not spread by casual contact, hugging or kissing or through food or water or through insects.

— The media must hammer home the point that Aids, through sexual transmission or blood infection, can be prevented. Minimum precaution of the use of condoms in sex, and sterilisation of skin-piercing instruments and their prompt disposal after use.

— The media must report every case pertaining to Aids, be it positive or negative. There must be a constant liaison between the media and the medical profession to report on latest developments and research findings.

— The media must highlight and crusade against such practice as quarantine, isolation and ostracism of Aids patients. Besides being an affront to human dignity, those practices will not help minimise Aids infection, and are injurious to public health as 'they give a false sense of security to people outside the stigmatised group that the threat of infection has been removed and the need for precaution minimised.' Also, such practices will drive the Aids problem underground and make the campaign against the scourge more difficult. Community education, using all the latest expertise of mass education and behavioural scientists and media experts, has to play a crucial role in spreading the message about preventing this dreaded infection. Option builders of the society (political and religious leaders, movie and sports personalities, other famous persons) must take the leadership in educating the public about Aids and how to avoid contracting this infection. The innovative use of media and a positive reporting attitude of the media will go a long way in making the Aids awareness campaign a success.

— The media must force the authorities to impose rigorous blood-testing norms on prostitutes and professional women and issue periodical warnings to the public about areas where the incidence of Aids has high probability.

— The media must help the authorities in eliminating commercial blood collection and pre-testing of all blood donors for HIV and other diseases.

— The media must as a role respect the right to privacy of Aids patients and must not subject them to needless exposure and social stigma.

— Every mass medium must observe the terms of the final document of the international consultation of Aids and human rights, and promptly report the violation of such rights protecting the basic human rights to life and liberty, privacy and freedom of movement.

D) Guidelines for financial journalists

1. The Press Council of India has counselled reporters / financial journalists / newspaper establishments to refrain from receiving any gifts / grants / concessions / facilities, etc., either in cash or kind which are likely to compromise free and unbiased reporting on financial matters.
2. The council in its report has observed that financial journalists today enjoy considerable influence over readers' minds and, therefore, they owe it to them to present a balanced and objective view of the financial dealings, status and prospects of a company. It observed that some companies are given excessive news coverage in the newspapers / magazines because they have issued advertisements to that print media. Sometimes, adverse reports are published of those companies which do not give advertisements to the newspapers or magazines. Again, when a media is not happy with any company / management for whatever reason, the negative aspects of the company are highlighted, while in the reverse situation, no negative aspects are brought to light. Some companies are also known to give gifts, loans, discounts, preferential shares, etc., to certain financial journalists to receive favourable and positive reports of the companies. At the same time, there is no mechanism for investors' education or for raising public opinion against such unhealthy practices.
3. The council feeling concerned over the malpractice in the corporate sector and after holding detailed deliberations and discussions with the representatives of financial institutions and journalists, has recommended the guidelines enumerated below for observance by the financial journalists:

— The financial journalists should not accept gifts, loans, trips, discounts, preferential shares or other considerations which compromise or are likely to compromise his position.

— It should be mentioned prominently in the report about any company that the report is based on information given by the company or the financial sponsors of the company.

— When the trips are sponsored for visiting establishments of a company, the author of the report who has availed of the trip must state invariably that the visit was sponsored by the company concerned and that it had also extended the hospitality as the case may be.

— No matter related to the company should be published without verifying the facts from the company and the source of such report should also be disclosed.

— A reporter who exposes a scam or brings out a report for promotion of a good project, should be encouraged and awarded.

— A journalist who has financial interests such as share holdings, stock holdings, etc., in a company, should not report on that company.

— The journalist should not use for his own benefit or for the benefit of his relations and friends, information received by him in advance for publication.

— No newspaper owner, editor or anybody connected with a newspaper should use his relations with the newspaper to promote his other business interests.

— Whenever there is an indictment of a particular advertising agency or advertiser by the Advertising Council of India, the newspaper in which the advertisement was published must publish the news of indictment prominently.

E) Guidelines expected to be observed by the newspapers, journalists, etc., while publishing reports on elections

General elections are a very important feature of our democracy and it is imperative that the media transmits to the electorate fair and objective reports of the election campaign by the contesting parties. Freedom of the press depends to a large measure on the press itself behaving with a sense of responsibility.

It is, therefore, necessary to ensure that the media adheres to this principle of fair and objective reporting of the election campaign. The Press Council has, therefore, formulated the following guidelines to the media for observance during elections:

— It will be the duty of the press to give objective reports about elections and candidates. The newspapers are not expected to indulge in unhealthy election campaigns, exaggerated reports about any candidate / party or incident during the elections. In practice, two or three closely contesting candidates attract all the media attention. While reporting on the actual campaign, a newspaper may not leave out any important point raised by a candidate and make an attack on his or her opponent.

— Election campaign along communal or caste lines is banned under the election rules. Hence, the press should eschew reports which tend to promote feelings of enmity or hatred between people on the ground of religion, race, caste, community or language.

— The press should refrain from publishing false or critical statements in regard to the personal character and conduct of any candidate or in relation to the candidature or withdrawal of any candidate or his candidature, to prejudice the prospects of that candidate in the elections. The press shall not publish unverified allegations against any candidate / party.

— The press shall not accept any kind of inducement, financial or otherwise, to project a candidate / party. It shall not accept hospitality or other facilities offered to them by or on behalf of any candidate / party.

— The press is not expected to indulge in canvassing of a particular candidate / party. If it does, it shall allow the right of reply to the other candidate / party.

— The press shall not accept / publish any advertisement at the cost of public exchequer regarding achievements of a party / government in power.

— The press shall observe all the directions / orders / instructions of the election commission / returning officers or chief electoral officer issued from time to time.

Guidelines for pre-poll / exit-poll survey

The Press Council of India having considered the question of desirability or otherwise of publication of findings of pre-poll surveys and the purpose served by them, is of the view that the newspapers should not allow their forum to be used for distortions and manipulations of the elections and should not allow themselves to be exploited by interested parties.

— The Press Council, therefore, advises that in view of the crucial position occupied by the electoral process in a representative democracy like ours, the newspapers should be on guard against their precious forum being used for distortions and manipulations of the elections. This has become necessary to emphasise today since the print media is sought to be increasingly exploited by the interested individuals and groups to misguide and mislead unwary voters by subtle and not-so-subtle propaganda on casteist, religious and ethnic basis as well as by the use of sophisticated means like the alleged pre-poll surveys. While the communal and seditious propaganda is not difficult to detect in many cases, the interested use of the pre-poll survey, sometimes deliberately planted, is not so easy to uncover. The Press Council, therefore, suggests that whenever the newspapers publish pre-poll surveys, they should take care to preface them conspicuously by indicating the institutions which have carried such surveys, the individuals and organisations which have commissioned the surveys, the size and nature of the sample selected, the method of selection of the sample for the findings and the possible margin of error in the findings.

— Further in the event of staggered poll dates, the media is seen to carry exit-poll surveys of the polls already held. This is likely to influence the voters where the polling is yet to commence. With a view to ensure that the electoral process is kept pure and the voters' minds are not influenced by any external factors, it is necessary that the media does not publish the exit-poll surveys till the last poll is held.

— The Press Council, therefore, requests the press to abide by the following guideline in respect of the exit-polls.

10

Broadcast Regulation in India

THE BROADCASTING BILL, 1997

The bill is to provide for an independent authority to be known as the Broadcasting Authority of India for the purpose of facilitating and regulating broadcasting services in India. The authority will have a perpetual succession and a common seal with powers to enter into a contract and can sue and can be sued in its name. It consists of a chairperson who will be appointed by the President of India on recommendation from the chairman of the states who will be the chairman of the committee, the information and broadcasting minister and the Press Council of India. It will also consist of a maximum of 11 part-time members to be appointed by the central government, a secretary to the government in charge of the department of telecommunications and a secretary general.

The chairperson will be a whole-time member and will hold office for a term of five years. He will be appointed from amongst the persons of eminence with more than 15 years of experience in administration, law, broadcasting and public relations. The functions of authority will be:

1. To carry out frequency planning of such frequencies or band of frequencies assigned to it by the wireless

adviser to the government for the purpose of ING services.

2. To grant licences for broadcasting services.

3. To ensure that a wide range of broadcasting services are available throughout India.

4. To ensure services of high quality and offer a wide range of programmes to appeal to a variety of tastes and interests.

5. To determine the programme code and standard.

6. To take necessary action for violation of code, violation of condition of licence.

7. To set technical and other quality standards to ensure a reasonable quality of reception.

The authority can appoint a committee of experts to advise on:

1. Practices to be followed in connection with unjust and unfair treatment to any person in programmes, unwarranted infringement of privacy included in programmes.

2. Practices to be followed in connection to portrayal of violence, sexual conduct in the programmes i.e., to set standards of decency for programmes, with regard to the attitude of the public at large.

Licences

No person is entitled to provide broadcasting services without obtaining a licence, after commencement of this act. The authority can grant licences for the following broadcasting services, namely:

1. Terrestrial radio broadcasting
2. Terrestrial television broadcasting
3. Satellite radio broadcasting
4. Satellite television broadcasting
5. Direct-to-home broadcasting
6. Local delivery sevices
7. Such other services as may be prescribed.

The terrestrial broadcasting services can be further categeorised into analogue and digital and also into national, regional, local, restricted local services or any other similar service for the purposes of the licences and prevention of their accumulation.

The licence shall be provided subject to following conditions:

1. The person granted the licence will ensure that nothing is included in the programmes of the licensee which is likely to encourage crime or lead to disorder or will be offensive to public feeling.
2. The licensee will ensure that news given in the programme will be presented with due accuracy and impartiality.
3. The licensee has to ensure that due impartiality is maintained with respect to social or political issues or matters relating to public policy.
4. The licensee will ensure that due responsibility is exercised with respect to religious programmes with a view to avoiding improper exploition of religious susceptibilities and offence to the religious views and beliefs of those belonging to a particular religion.

5. The licensee will ensure that due emphasis is given to promote national integration, Indian culture in his programmes.

6. The licensee will have to ensure that time, detemined by the authority, is earmarked for broadcasting of -- children's programmes, educational programmes, programmes of Indian origin, a range of diversity of independent production.

7. The licensee will have to follow the programme codes and standards and codes set by the authority.

8. The licensee will pay the licence fees in the same manner as may be determined by the regulations.

9. The licensee will not carry out networking of local or regional broadcasting services without prior approval of the authority.

10. The conditions of the licence can be changed by the authority after giving to the licensee a reasonable opportunity of being heard.

The licence granted for direct-to-home service or local delivery service shall be subject to the following conditions in addition to the conditions referred above:

1. The licensee will have to provide a tier basic service which may include a number and type of terrestrial broadcasting for every permitted service and also of the public service broadcaster.

2. The licensee will include only licensed services or permitted services in his delivery package for the purpose of distribution and also he will not use more than that number of channels as determined by the authority out of the total channel capacity of the system for providing his own programming.

The period of licence for each category will be for a period not exceeding 10 years. The licence is not transferable and it will lapse prior to its normal expiry in case of insolvency or death of the licensee. No person will be given the number of licences for a category of service. There are restrictions on cross media ownership between the newspaper and the broadcasting service. The government can modify any limit on interest or equity holding in the body corporate or companies by notification in the official gazette.

Grant of licence for satellite broadcasting services

1. Any person desirous of obtaining a satellite broadcasting licence will have to apply to the authority.
2. If the authority is satisfied that the applicant:
   a) has acquired transponder on an Indian satellite system or on a foreign satellite system.
   b) has obtained technical clearance for transponders from the wireless adviser.
   c) has fulfilled all other conditions laid down in the act; the authority may grant a licence to such person on payment of fees; if the authority refuses to grant a licence it will have to give the applicant an opportunity to be heard.

Provide further that such a person providing his broadcasting services immediately before the commencement of the act may continue to do so without a licence for a period of one month from such commencement.

Grant of licence for direct-to-home service

The authority will invite bids for grant of licence and it will be granted to the highest bidder if he fulfils all the conditions for the grant of such licence. The authority grants such number of licences (not less than two) as may be prescribed.

Special provisions for satellite broadcasting and direct-to-home services

The wireless adviser will give technical clearance for licensing (the clearance can be refused on technical or security reasons). In cases where operations of the services are permitted with foreign satellite system, while giving technical clearance for relicensing or renewal of such services, give priority for their operation with Indian satellite system. The licensee shall carry out the uplinking of satellite broadcasting services or direct-to-home will grant two licences for local delivery service for each telecom circle as identified by the central government. The authority will invite bids and licence will be granted to the highest bidder. The wireless adviser shall assign frequencies for MMDS for providing local delivery service, wherever it is required.

The authority may exempt the non-commercial establishments under common ownership from obtaining a licence for the purpose of providing cable television services for the exclusive use of their members. The government can by notification confer upon the licensee of the local delivery services, such rights and obligations as it may consider necessary in respect of the placing and maintaining of his cable networks as available to the telegraph authority.

Enforcement of licences

The authority can take any of the following actions in case of breach of any terms of the licence:

1. Direct licensing to correction or apology or not to repeat a programme;

2. To impose a penalty which may extend up to Rs 50 lakh.
3. Suspend the licence for a specified period.
4. Curtail the period of the licence.
5. Revoke the licence.

Any aggrieved person may prefer an appeal and action of the authority in the high court having jurisdiction within 30 days of such action. The proceeds of the licence fee will be credited to the consolidated fund of India. The authority will have its own fund and all receipts of the authority will be credited to the fund and all payments by the authority will be from them. The authority will submit a report at the end of each financial year to the central government.

Offence and punishments

A person who provides, distributes or receives any broadcasting service which is neither a licensed service nor a permitted service or abets or assists transmission of such service in any manner which may include collection of subscription for his principal, issuing of advertisements to such service, dealing in or distribution of decoders or dish antennas, shall be guilty of committing an offence of illegal broadcasting and on conviction, shall be punishable with imprisonment which may extend up to five years, or with fine which may extend up to Rs 10 lakh and in subsequent offence such fine may extend to rupees Rs 50 lakh, or with both.

Special provisions for certain foreign satellite broadcasting services

The authority after receiving a request in this regard, may grant permission for reception of an unlicensed foreign satellite broadcasting service in India, if such broadcasting is service:

1. Is free to air broadcasting service;
2. Does not carry any advertisements; or carries advertisements for the duration as may be fixed by the authority and the service is devoted solely to sports or international news and current affairs;
3. Fulfils the programme standard with respect to permitted service. Provided that the authority may revoke such permission, if it feels that the service has contravened any of the above conditions.

No licensee shall carry a live broadcast of any sporting or other event of national or international interest held in India, without the consent of the authority unless the public service broadcasters have also been given the broadcasting right for carrying the same.

Procedure and powers of the authority

1. The authority will be guided by principles of natural justice and subject to the other provisions of this act and of any rules, the authority will have powers to regulate its own procedure including the fixing of places and times of its inquiry.
2. The authority will have for the purpose of discharging its functions under this act, the same powers as are vested in a civil court under the code of civil procedure, while trying a suit, in respect of the following matters, namely:
   a) Summoning and enforcing the attendance of any peron and examining him on oath;
   b) Receiving evidence on affidavits;

c) Issuing commissions for the examination of witnesses or documents;

d) Any other matter which may be prescribed.

In event of any war or a natural calamity of national magnitude, the central government may, in public interest, take over the control and management of any broadcasting service or any facility connected therewith, suspend its operation or entrust the public service broadcaster to manage it in the manner directed by the government for such period as it deems fit.

The government, if it considers necessary or expedient to do so, may, in public interest, at any time require the authority to direct any licensee to:

1. Transmit in his broadcasting service such announcement in such a manner as may be considered necessary;

2. Stop any broadcasting service which is considered prejudicial to friendly relations with a foreign country, public order, security of state, or communal harmony. The central government may in public interest, issue such other directions, to the authority, from time to time as considered necessary.

Powers of the authority to seek information conduct enquires, take evidence, etc

1. The licensee will have to start his service within the period specfied by the authority and maintain documents, records and transmission schedules as may be specified and allow inspection of such records to the authority.

2. The authority can call for information from the licensee which it considers in the public interest and necessary

for the transparency and ascertaining the true ownership of the licensee. The authority will have all the powers of an inspecting officer. If the licensee defaults with any conditions, the authority can cancel the licence. The application of this law is in addition to and not in derogation of the provisions of any other law.

Power to make rules

The central government can by notification make rules for carrying out provisions of this act. The rules will provide for all or any of the following matter:

1. Provide for circumstances for communication.
2. Salaries and allowances payable to the chairperson and other part-time members.
3. The functions to be performed by the authority.
4. Number of licences more than which can't be given.

Power to make regulations

The authority can make regulations and rules made their underby notification. The rules will provide for all or any of the following matter:

1. The time and place of the meetings, the procedure of transaction of business.
2. The manner of appointment of officers and employees and their salary.
3. The quality of reception and the programme code and standard.
4. The manner in which the licence fee should be paid by the licensee and the conditions of granting licence.

5. The minimum number and type of ING service of public service broadcaster and of terrestrial broadcasting services for every permitted service.

6. The number of channels to be used and the period of licence to the licensee.

7. The criteria subject to which the uplinking from outside India will be permitted in respect of these services for coverage of live events taking place outside India.

8. Restricted area under which permission may be granted.

9. Any sporting or other event of national or international interest of which live telecast shall be carried out without the authority's permission.

10. The documentary record and transmission schedule to be maintained.

Every rule and regulation is to be laid before the parliament. The central government can make provisions in the act within three years of commencemant of this bill and not after that, to remove any difficulties that arise.

Repeal and saving

The Cable Television Networks (Regulation) Act 1995 is repealed. The cable operators registered under this act can make an application to the authority for grant of licence within six months of commencement of this act. The authority may grant or refuse the licence to the operator. No licence will be granted to any cable TV network which provides such service to more than 5000 households and from more than one location. No refusal can be made unless the applicant has a chance to present the case. The authority will authorise a district magistrate to look in to the complaints of the public, give notice to the operators, make enquiries and take necassary action.

Restrictions on the holding of licences

Part — I

A disqualification for holding of licences

The following persons will be disqualified for the purpose of grant of licence:

General disqualification:

(a) An individual who is not an Indian national.

(b) A partnership firm all of whose partners are not citizens of India.

(c) Companies not incorporated in India.

(d) Companies incorporated in India but with:

— foreign equity in case of terrestrial broadcasting services.

— foreign equity exceeding 49 per cent in case of other services not mentioned in (i) above and management control not with Indian shareholders.

(e) Governments and local authorities.

(f) Any person convicted of an offence under this act or convicted under the Representation of the Peoples Act or declared as insolvent.

(g) A body, which is controlled by a person, referred to in any of clause (a) to (e) above.

(h) A body corporate, in which a body referred to in clause (g) above, is a participant with more than five per cent interest.

Foreign equity for this part will be notified to the government from time to time.

Disqualification of religious bodies

1. A body which is or is controlled by, a body or controls a body whose objectives are wholly or mainly of a religious nature.
2. A body corporate in which the body referred to above is a participant with more than five per cent interest.
3. A person who is an officer of the body.

Disqualification of political bodies

1. A body which is or affiliated to or is a participant with more than five per cent interest to a body whose objects are or mainly of political nature.
2. An individual who is an officer of the body.

Disqualification of publicly funded bodies

1. A body (other than a local authority) which has in its last financial year received more than half its income from public funds.
2. A body which is controlled or a corporate which has more than five per cent interest in the abovementioned body.

Disqualification of advertising agencies

1. An advertising agency, its associate or a body corporate having more than five per cent interest in an ad agency.

Part — II

Restriction to prevent accumulation of interest in licensed services

1. A person will be allowed to hold licences in only one of the following category of services:

[a] Terrestrial radio broadcasting

[b] Terrestrial television broadcasting

[c] Satellite television or radio broadcasting

[d] Direct-to-home broadcasting

[e] Local delivery services

[f] Any other category of services which may be notified by the central government.

2. Any restriction on participation imposed as above on the holder of a licence shall apply to him as if he and every person connected with him were one person.

Part — III

Restrictions on controlling interest in both newspapers and licensed services

1. No proprietor of a newspaper will either be a participant with more than 20 per cent interest in or control a body corporate which is the holder of a licence to provide a licensed service under this act.

2. No proprietor of a newspaper who is a participant with more than five per cent but less than 20 per cent interest in a body corporate and not controlling such a body corporate, holding a licence will be a participant with more than five per cent interest in any other such body corporate.

3. No person who is the holder of a licence to provide licensed service under this act will be either a participant with more than 20 per cent interest in or control a body corporate which controls a newspaper.

4. No person who is the holder of a licence and is a participant with more than five per cent but less than

20 per cent interest in a body corporate and not controlling such a body corporate which runs a national newspaper, shall be a participant with more than five per cent interest in any other such corporate.

5. For the purpose of this part, a person controls a newspaper if :

   [a] He is the proprietor of such newspaper; or

   [b] He controls a body which is the proprietor of such newspaper.

6. Any restriction on participation imposed as above on the proprietor of any newspaper or on the holder of licence shall apply to him as of he and every person connected with him were one person.

Part — IV

1. (1) For the purpose of this schedule,

'Advertising agency' means an individual or a body corporate who carries on business as an advertising agent (whether alone or in partnership) or has control over any body corporate which carries on business as an advertising agent, and any reference to an advertising agency includes a reference to an advertising agency includes a reference to an individual who-

a) is a director or officer of any body corporate who carries on such a business, or

b) is employed by any person who carries on such a business.

Associate' -

a) in relation to a body corporate, means a director of that body corporate or a body corporate interconnected with that body corporate.

b) in relation to the partner of the firm, means a relative of such partner and includes any other person of such firm;

c) in relation to the trustee of a trust, means any other trustee of such trust; and

d) in relation to an individual, shall be construed in accordance with subclause (3);

e) where a person or a body corporate is an associate of another person or body corporate, the latter shall also be deemed to be an associate of the former.

'Control' -

a) in relation to the body corporate, shall be construed in accordance with subclause (3); and

b) in relation to any body other than a body corporate, means the power of a person to secure, by virtue of the rules regulating that or any other body, that the affairs of the first mentioned body are conducted in accordance with the wishes of that person, and would include control as a result of, or by means of, trusts, agreements, arrangements, understandings and practices, whether or not having legal or equitable force and whether or not based on legal or equitable rights.

'Newspaper' means as defined under the Press and Registration Act, 1867 (25 of 1867).

(2) For the purpose of determining the persons who are an individual's associates for the purposes of this schedule, the following persons shall be regarded as associates of each other, namely:

a) any individual and that individual's husband or wife of a relative, of that individual or of that individual's husband or wife;

b) any individual or any body corporate of which that individual is a director;

c) any person in his capacity as trustee of a settlement and the settlor or grantor and any person associated with the settlor and grantor;

d) persons carying on business in partnership and the husband or wife and relatives of any of them;

e) any two or more persons acting together to secure or exercise control of a body corporate or any other associates or to secure control of any enterprise or assets; and in this sub-paragraph 'relative' means as defined under the Companies Act, 1956.

(3) A person controls a body corporate if:

a) he has a controlling interest in the body, or

b) (although not having such an interest in the body) he is able, by virtue of the holding of shares or the possession of voting power in or in relation to the body or any other body corporate, to secure that the affairs of the body are conducted in accordance with his wishes, or

c) he has the power, by virtue of any powers conferred by the articles of association or other document regulating the body or any other body corporate, to secure that the affairs of the body are so conducted, and for this purpose, in the absence of proof to the contrary, a person has a controlling interest in a body corporate if he holds, or is beneficially entitled to, more than 20 per cent, of the voting power in it.

(4) it is hereby declared that a person may be regarded as controlling a body corporate by virtue of clause (b) of sub-clause (3) despite the fact that:

a) he does not have a controlling interest in any such other body corporate as is mentioned in that paragraph, or

b) any such other body corporate does not have a controlling interest in the body in question, or

c) he and any such body corporate together do not have a controlling interest in that body.

(5) For the purpose of any provision of this schedule which refers to a body controlled by two or more persons or bodies of any description taken together, the persons or bodies in question shall not be regarded as controlling the body by virtue of paragraph (b) and sub-paragraph (3) unless they are acting together in concert.

(6) In this schedule any reference to a participant with more than a five per cent, or, as the case may be, 20 per cent interest in a body corporate is a reference to a person who:

a) holds or is beneficially entitled to more than five or, as the case may be, 20 per cent of the shares in that body or,

b) possesses more than five or, as the case may be, 20 per cent of the voting power in that body, and, where any such reference has been amended by an order under this schedule varying the percentage in question, this sub-paragraph shall have effect in relation to its subject to the necessary modifications.

2. (1) Any reference in paragraph 1 to a person:

a) holding or being entitled to shares, or any amount of the shares or equity share capital, in a body corporate, or

b) possessing voting power, or any amount of the voting power, in a body corporate, is a reference to his doing so, or being so entitled, whether alone or jointly with one or more other persons and whether directly or through one or more nominees.

(2) 'Inter connected undertakings or corporate bodies' shall have the same meaning as assigned in the Monopolies and Restrictive Trade Practices Act, 1969 (54 of 1969).

3. For the purpose of this schedule, the following persons are connected with each other in relation to a particular licence, namely:

a) the license holder;

b) a person who controls the holder;

c) an associate of the license holder or of a person referred to in clause (b), and

d) a body which is controlled by the license holder or by an associate of the license holder.

Statement of objects and reasons

1. The broadcasting scenario, especially in the realm of satellite broadcasting, has undergone a revolution during the last few years. A large number of satellite television channels have been beaming their programmes through the Indian skies to our people. All these channels are foreign entities and their programmes are uplinked from outside the country without any regulation through the law of our land, while Indian enrtepreneurs and Indian companies are not at present permitted to own either radio or television stations.

2. Concern has been voiced both inside parliament and outside about the implications of these unregulated

television programmes and the denial of a level playing field to Indian entities. The only legal instrument available is the Indian Telegraph Act, 1885, which is considered totally inadequate to govern modern broadcasting media. All leading democratic countries have enacted laws specifically regarding the broadcasting media. The introduction of the broadcasting bill is a step in this direction.

3. It is felt that the public service broadcaster alone will not be able to meet the needs and urges of the people in terms of variety and plurality of programmes required in different regions by different sections of society in our vast country. Keeping in view our great democratic traditions, it is imperative that our citizens are all informed and given wider choice in matters of information, education and entertainment. This can be provided by facilitating private broadcasting in the country.

4. The bill needs to establish an autonomous broadcasting authority for the purposes of facilitating and regulating broadcasting services in India so that they become competitive in terms of quality of services, cost of services and use of new technologies, apart from becoming a catalyst for social change, promotion of values of Indian culture and shaping of a modern vision. It will also curb monopolistic trends in this sensitive field, so that people are provided with a wide range of news and views.

NOTES ON CLAUSES

Clause 2 defines the various expressions occuring in the bill.

Clause 3 provides for the establishment of the broadcasting authority of India.

Clause 4 provides that the President may on the grounds provided under article 317 of the constitution may remove or suspend the chairperson and members.

Clause 5 provides detailed provisions regarding the conduct of the meetings of the authority.

Clause 6 provides procedure for appointment of secretary-general of authority and empowers the authority to appoint other officers.

Clause 7 provides function of the authority and empowers the authority to appoint committees of experts to advise on matters considered necessary.

Clause 8 provides prohibition on broadcasting service without licence by any person.

Clause 9 specifies the different services for which licences may be granted by the authority.

Clause 10 specifies the conditions for granting licences for broadcasting services licences.

Clause 11 provides for the period of broadcasting licence and other conditions.

Clause 12 specifies the eligibility and restrictions for licences to be granted by the authority.

Clause 13 gives procedure for grant of licence for satellite broadcasting services.

Clause 14 provides procedure for grant of licence for direct-to-home services.

Clause 15 provides for special provisions for satellite broadcasting and direct-to-home services.

Clause 16 provides procedure for grant of licence for terrestrial broadcasting services.

Clause 17 provides procedure for grant of licence for local delivery services by the authority.

Clause 18 gives the details of actions which can be taken by the authority for enforcement of licences.

Clause 29 provides that licence fee shall be credited to the Consolidated Fund of India and also specifies the maintainance of the accounts, budget and audit by the comptroller-auditor-general of India by the authority.

Clause 20 provides for furnishing of the annual report to the central government which shall be laid before the parliament.

Clause 21 prescribes offence and punishment.

Clause 22 provides special provisions for certain foreign satellite broadcasting services.

Clause 23 empowers the authority to refuse licence for live broadcasting of certain events of national and international importance.

Clause 24 enumerates the procedure and powers of the authority.

Clause 25 specifies the powers of the central government in event of war or natural calamities.

Clause 26 provides powers of the authority to seek information, conduct enquiries, take evidence, for operation and regulation licences and also empowers the authority to give directions to licences.

Clause 27 provides that the chairperson and members of the authority shall be deemed to be a public servant within the meaning of section 21 of the Indian Penal Code.

Clause 28 provides for usual provisions relating to the protection of action taken in good faith by the authority or chairperson or members or officers and other employees of the authority.

Clause 29 provides for delegation of powers to the authority to chairperson or other member or other officers.

Clause 30 provides that application of other laws are not barred and in case of an offence committed under this act and also under another act, and also under another act, the offender shall be punished under this act.

Clause 31 confers on the central government powers to make rules for carrying out the provisions of the bill.

Clause 32 confers on the authority the powers to make regulation consistent with provision of this bill and rules made by the central government thereunder before each house of parliament.

Clause 33 provides laying of the rules and regulations before parliament.

Clause 34 empowers the central government to remove difficulties which may arise in giving effect to the provisions of the bill.

Clause 35 provides for repeal of the Cable Television Networks (Regulation) Act, 1995 and for licencing and regulations of cable networks registered under that act on the date of commencement of this act.

Lok Sabha

A bill to provide for the establishment of an independent authority to be known as the broadcasting authority of India, for the powers of developing, promoting, facilitating and regulating broadcasting services in India and to provide for matters connected therewith or incidental thereto.

The Prasar Bharati (Broadcasting Corporation of India) Act, 1990

(Act No. 25 of 1990)

(September 12, 1990)

An Act to provide for the establishment of a Broadcasting Corporation for India, to be known as Prasar Bharati, to define its composition, functions and powers and to provide for matters connected therewith or incidental thereto. Be it enacted by Parliament in the Fourty-first Year of the Republic of India as follows:-

Chapter I Preliminary

1. *Short title, extent and commencement,*

1) This Act may be called the Prasar Bharati (Broadcasting Corporation of India) Act, 1990
2) It extends to the whole of India.
3) It shall come into force on such date as the Central Government may, by notification, appoint.

2. *Definitions*: In this Act, unless the context otherwise requires,

a) "Akashvani" means the offices, stations and other establishments, by whatever name called, which, immediately before the appointed day, formed part or were under the Director-General, All India Radio of the Union Ministry of Information and Broadcasting;
b) "appointed day" means the date appointed under Section 3;
c) "broadcasting" means the dissemination of any form of communication like signs, signals, writing, pictures, images and sounds of all kinds by transmission of

electro-magnetic waves through space or through cables intended to be received by the general public either directly or indirectly through the medium of relay stations and all it's grammatical variations and cognate expressions shall be construed accordingly;

d) "board" means the Prasar Bharati Board;

e) "Broadcasting Council" means the council established under Section 14;

f) "Chairman" means the Chairman of the Corporation appointed under Section 3;

g) "Corporation" means the "Prasar Bharati (Broadcasting Corporation of India) established under Section 3;

h) "Doordarshan" means the offices, kendras and other establishments, by whatever name called, which, immediately before the appointed day, formed part of or were under the Director-General, Doordarshan of the Union Ministry of Information and Broadcasting;

I) "elected Member" means a Member elected under Section 3;

j) "Executive Member" means the Executive Member appointed under Section 4;

k) "kendra" means any telecasting centre with studios or transmitters or both and includes a relay station.

l) "Member" means a Member of the Board;

m) "Member (Finance)" means the Member (Finance) appointed under Section 4;

n) "Member (Personnel)" means the Member (Personnel) appointed under Section 4;

o) "Nominated Member" means the Member nominated by the Union Ministry of Information and Broadcasting under Section 3;

p) "Non-lapsable Fund" means the Fund created from the commercial revenues of Akashvani and Doordarshan to meet expenditure on certain issues;

q) "notification" means a notification published in the Official Gazette;

r) "Part-time Member" means a Part-time Member of the Board appointed under Section 4, but does not include an ex-officio Member, the Nominated Member or an elected Member; s) "prescribed" means prescribed by rules made under this Act;

t) "Recruitment Board" means a board established under sub-section (1) of Section 10;

u) "regulations" means regulations made by the Corporation under this Act;

v) "station" means any broadcasting station with studios or transmitters or both and includes a relay station;

w) "Whole-time Member" means the Executive Member, Member (Finance) or Member (Personnel);

x) "year" means the financial year.

CHAPTER II PRASAR BHARATI (BROADCASTING CORPORATION OF INDIA)

3. *Establishment and composition of Corporation*:

1) With effect from such date as the Central Government may by notification appoint in this behalf, there shall be established for the purposes of this Act a Corporation, to be known as Prasar Bharati (Broadcasting Corporation of India).

2) The Corporation will be a body corporate by the name aforesaid, having perpetual succession and a common seal with power to acquire, hold and dispose of property, both moveable and immovable, and to contract, and shall by the said mane sue or be sued.

3) The Headquarters of the Corporation shall be at New Delhi and the corporation may establish offices, kendras or stations at other places in India and, with the previous approval of the Central Government outside India.

4) The general superintendence, direction and management of affairs of the Corporation shall vest in the Prasar Bharati Board which may exercise all such powers and do all such acts and things as may be exercised or done by the Corporation under this Act.

5) The Board shall consist of :

a) a Chairman;

b) one Executive Member;

c) one Member (Finance);

d) one Member (Personnel);

e) six Part-time Members;

f) Director-General (Akashvani), ex officio;

g) Director-General (Doordarshan), ex officio;

h) one representative of the Union Ministry of Information and Broadcasting, to be nominated by that Ministry;

I) two representatives of the employees of the Corporation, of whom one shall be elected by the engineering staff from amongst themselves and one shall be elected by the other employees from amongst themselves.

6) The Corporation may appoint such Committees as may be necessary for the efficient performance, exercise and discharge of its functions, powers and duties; Provided that all or a majority of the members of each committee shall be Members and a member of any such committee who is not a Member shall have only the right to attend meetings of the committee and take part in the proceedings thereof, but shall not have a right to vote.

7) The Corporation may associate with itself, in such manner and for such purposes as may be provided by regulations, any person whose assistance or advice it may need in complying with any of the provisions of this Act and a person so associated shall have the right to take part in the discussions of the Board relevant to the purposes for which he has been associated, but shall not have the right to vote.

8) No Act or proceeding of the Board or of any committee appointed by it under sub-section (6) shall be invalidated merely by reason of -

   a) any vacancy in, or any defect in the constitution of, the Board or such committee; or

   b) any defect in the appointed of a person acting as a Member or a member of such committee; or

   c) any irregularity in the procedure of the Board or such committee not affecting the merits of the case.

4. *Appointment of a Chairman and other members*

1) The Chairman and the other members, except the ex officio Members, the Nominated Member and the

elected Members shall be appointed by the President of India on the recommendation of a committee consisting of -

a) the Chairman of the Council of States, who shall be the Chairman of the Committee.

b) the Chairman of the Press Council of India established under Section 4 of the Press Council Act, 1978 (37 of 1978); and

c) one nominee of the President of India.

2) No appointment of a Member shall be invalidated merely by reason of any vacancy in, or any defect in the constitution of, the committee appointed under sub-section (1)

3) The Chairman and the Part-time Members shall be persons of eminence in public life; the Executive Member shall be a person having special knowledge or practical experience in respect of much matters as administration, management, broadcasting, education, literature, culture, arts, music, dramatics or journalism; the Member (Finance) shall be a person having special knowledge or practical experience in respect of financial matters and the Member (Personnel) shall be a person having special knowledge or practical experience in respect of personnel management and administration.

4) The recommendations made by the committee constituted under sub-section (1) shall be binding for the purposes of appointments under this Section.

5. *Powers and functions of executive Member:* The executive Member shall be the Chief Executive of the Corporation and shall, subject to the control and supervision of the Board,

exercise such powers and discharge such functions of the Board as it may delegate to him.

6. *Term of office, conditions of service, etc., of Chairman and other Members*

1) The Chairman shall be Part-time Member and shall hold office for a term of six years from the date on which he enters upon his office.

2) The Executive Member, the Member (Finance) and the Member (Personnel) shall be Whole-time Members and every such Member shall hold office for a term of six years from the date on which he enters upon his office or until he attains the age of sixty-two years, whichever is earlier.

3) The term of office of Part-time Members shall be six years, but one-third of such Members shall retire on the expiration of every second year.

4) The term of office of an elected Member shall be two years or till he ceases to be an employee of the Corporation, whichever is earlier.

5) As soon as may be after the establishment of the Corporation, the President of India may, by order, make such provision as he thinks fit for curtailing the term of office of some of the Part-time Members then appointed in order that one-third of the Members holding office as such Part-time Members shall retire in every second year thereafter.

6) Where before the expiry of the term of office of a person holding the office of Chairman, or any other Member, a vacancy arises, for any reason whatsoever, such vacancy shall be deemed to be a casual vacancy and the person appointed or elected to fill such

vacancy shall hold office for the unexpired period of the term for which his predecessor in office would have held office if such vacancy had not arisen.

7) The Whole-time Members shall be the employees of the Corporation and as such shall be entitled to such salaries and allowances and shall be subject to such conditions of service in respect of leave, pension (if any), provident fund and other allowances and other matters as may be prescribed: Provided that the salaries and allowances and the conditions of service shall not be varied to their disadvantage after their appointment.

8) The Chairman and Part-time Members shall be entitled to such allowances as may be prescribed.

7. *Removal and suspension of Chairman and Members*:

1) Subject to the provisions of sub-section (3), the Chairman or any other Member, except an ex officio Member, the Nominated Member and an elected Member, shall only be removed from his office by order of the President of India on the ground of misbehavior after the Supreme Court, on a reference being made to it by the President, has, on inquiry held in accordance with such procedure as the Supreme Court may by rules provide, reported that the Chairman or such other Member, as the case may be, ought, on such ground, be removed.

2) The President may suspend from office the Chairman or any other Member, except an ex officio member, the Nominated Member or an elected member, in respect to whom a reference has been made to the Supreme Court under sub-section (1) until the President has passed orders on receipt of the report of the Supreme Court on such reference.

3) Notwithstanding anything contained in sub-section (1), the President may, by order, remove the Chairman or any Whole-time Member from his office if such Chairman or such Whole-time Member-

   a) ceases to be a citizen of India.;or

   b) is adjudged as insolvent; or

   c) engages during his term of office in any paid employment outside the duties of his office; or

   d) is convicted of any offence involving moral turpitude; or

   e) is, in the opinion of the President, unfit to continue in office by reason of infirmity of body or mind:

   Provided that the President may, by order, remove any Part-time Member from his office if he is adjudged an insolvent or is convicted of any offence involving moral turpitude or where he is, in the opinion of the President, unfit to continue in office by reason of infirmity of body or mind.

4) If the Chairman or any Whole-time Member, except any ex officio Member, the Nominated Member or any elected Member, is, or becomes in any way concerned or interested in any contract or agreement made by or on behalf of the Corporation or the Government of India or the Government of a State or, participates in any way in the profit thereof, or in any benefit or emolument arising therefrom than as a member, and in common with other members of an incorporated company, he shall, for the purposes of sub-section (1), be deemed to be guilty of misbehavior.

5) If a Part-time Member is, or becomes in any way concerned, or interested in any contract or agreement

made by or on behalf of the Corporation, he shall, for the purposes of sub-section (1), be deemed.

6) The Chairman or any other Member may resign his office by giving notice thereof in writing to the President of India and on such resignation being accepted, the Chairman or any other Member shall be deemed to have vacated his office.

8. *Meetings of Board*

1) The Board shall meet at such times and places and shall observe such rules of procedure in regard to the transaction of business at its meetings (including the quorum at meetings) as may be provided by regulations: Provided that there shall not be less than six meetings every year but three months shall not intervene between one meeting and the next meeting.

2) A Member shall be deemed to have vacated his office if he absents himself for three consecutive meetings of the Board without the leave of the Chairman.

3) The Chairman shall preside at the meetings of the Board and if for any reason he is unable to attend any meeting, the Executive member and in the absence of both, any other Member elected by the Members present at such meeting, shall preside at the meeting.

4) All questions which come up before any meeting of the Board shall be decided by a majority of the votes of the Members present and voting and, in the event of an equality of votes, the Chairman, or in his absence, the person presiding, shall have and exercise a second or casting vote.

9. *Officers and other employees of Corporation*

1) Subject to such control, restrictions and conditions as

may be prescribed, the Corporation may appoint, after consultation with the Recruitment Board, the Director-General (Akashvani), the Director-General (Doordarshan) and such other officers and other employees as may be necessary.

2) The method of recruitment of such officers and employees and all other matters connected therewith and the conditions of service of such officers and other employees shall be such as may be provided by regulations.

10. *Establishment of Recruitment Boards*

1) The Corporation shall, as soon as may be, after the appointed day and in such manner and subject to such conditions and restrictions as may be prescribed, establish for the purpose of Section 9, one or more Recruitment Boards consisting wholly of persons other than Members, officers and other employees of the Corporation : Provided that for the purposes of appointment to the posts carrying scales of pay which are not less than that of a Joint Secretary to the Central Government, the Recruitment Board shall consist of the Chairman, other Members, the ex officio Members, the Nominated Member and the elected Members.

2) The qualifications and other conditions of service of the members constituting the Recruitment Board and the period for which such Members shall hold office, shall be such as may be prescribed.

11. *Transfer of service of existing employees to Corporation*

1) Where the Central Government has ceased to perform any functions which under Section 12 are the functions of the Corporation, it shall be lawful for the Central Government to transfer, by order and with effect from

such date or dates as may be specified in the order, to the Corporation any of the officers or other employees serving in the Akashvani or Doordarshan and engaged in the performance of those functions:

Provided that no order under this sub-section shall be made in relation to any officer or other employee in the Akashvani or Doordarshan who has, in respect of the proposal of the Central Government to transfer such officer or other employee to the Corporation, intimated within such time may be specified in this behalf by the Central Government, his intention of not becoming an employee of the Corporation.

2) The provisions of sub-section (1) shall also apply to the members of the Indian Information Service, the Central Secretariat Service or any other service or to persons borne on cadres outside Akashvani and Doordarshan who have been n working in Akashvani and Doordarshan immediately before the appointment day: Provided that where any such member intimates, within the time specified in sub-section (1), his intention of not becoming an employee of the Corporation but to continue on deputation, he may be allowed to continue on deputation in accordance with such terms and conditions as may be prescribed.

3) In making an order under sub-section (1), the Central Government shall, as far as may be, take into consideration the functions which the Akashvani or, as the case may be, Doordarshan has ceased or ceases to perform and the area in which such functions have been or are performed.

4) An officer or other employee transferred by an order under sub-section (1) shall, on and from the date of transfer cease to be an employee of the Central

Government and become an employee of the Corporation may determine and shall, subject to the provisions of sub-sections (5) and (6), be governed by such regulations as may be made as respects remuneration and other conditions of service including pension, leave and provident fund and shall continue to be an officer or any other employee of the Corporation unless and until his employment is terminated by the Corporation.

5) Every officer or other employee transferred by an order made under sub-section (1) shall, within six months from the date of transfer, exercise his option, in writing, to be governed -

a) by the scale of pay applicable to the post held by him in the Akashvani or Doordarshan immediately before the date of transfer or by the scale applicable to the post under the Corporation to which he is transferred.

b) by the leave, provident fund, retirement or other terminal benefits admissible to employees of the Central Government in accordance with the rules or orders of the Central Government, as amended from time to time, or the leave, provident fund or other terminal benefits admissible to the employees of the Corporation under the regulations, and such option once exercised under this Act shall be final:

Provided that the option exercised under clause (a) officer or other employee shall be applicable only in respect of the post under the Corporation to which such officer or other employee is transferred and on appointment to a higher post under the Corporation he shall be eligible only for the scale of pay applicable to such higher post.

Provided further that if immediately before the date of his transfer and such officer or other employee is officiating in a higher post under the Government either in a leave vacancy or any other vacancy of a specified duration, his pay on transfer shall be protected for the unexpired period of such vacancy and thereafter he shall be entitled to the scale of pay applicable to the post under the Government to which he would have reverted or to the scale of pay applicable to the post under the Corporation to which he is transferred, whichever he may opt:

Provided also that an officer or other employee serving in the Union Ministry of Information and Broadcasting or in any of its attached or subordinate offices subsequent to the transfer to the Corporation of any other officer or employee senior to him in that Ministry or office before such transfer, the officer or other employee who is promoted of officiate in such higher post shall, on transfer to the Corporation, be entitled only to the scale of pay applicable to the post he would have held but for such promotion or the scale of pay applicable to the post under Corporation to which he is transferred, whichever he may opt.

6) No officer or other employee transferred by an order made under sub-section (1) or sub-section (2),

   a) shall be dismissed or removed by an authority subordinate to that competent to make a similar or equivalent appointment under the Corporation as may be specified in the regulation.

   b) shall be dismissed or removed or reduced in rank except after an inquiry in which he has been informed of the charges against him and given a reasonable opportunity of being heard in respect of those charges:

Provided that where it is proposed after such inquiry to impose upon him any such penalty, such penalty may be imposed on the basis of evidence adduced during such inquiry and it shall not be necessary to give such person an opportunity of making representation on the proposed penalty : Provided further that clause (b) shall not apply where an officer or other employee is dismissed or removed or reduced in rank on the ground of conduct which has led to his conviction on a criminal charge.

12. *Functions and powers of Corporation*

1) Subject to the provisions of this Act, it shall be the primary duty of the Corporation to organize and conduct public broadcasting services to inform, educate and entertain the public and to ensure a balanced development of broadcasting on radio and television. Explanation: For the removal of doubts, it is hereby declared that the provisions of this section shall be in addition to, and not in derogation of, the provisions of the Indian Telegraphic Act, 1885 (13 or 1885)

2) The Corporation shall, in the discharge of its functions, be guided by the following objectives, namely

    a) upholding the unity and integrity of the country and the values enshrined in the Constitution;

    b) safeguarding the citizen's right to be informed freely, truthfully and objectively on all matters of public interest, national or international, and presenting a fair and balanced flow of information including contrasting views without advocating any opinion or ideology of its own.

    c) paying special attention to the fields of education and spread of literacy, agriculture, rural development, environment, health and family welfare and science and technology;

d) providing adequate coverage to the diverse cultures and languages of the various regions of the country by broadcasting appropriate programmes;

e) providing appropriate coverage to sports and games so as to encourage healthy competition and the spirit of sportsmanship;

f) providing appropriate programmes keeping in view the special needs of the youth;

g) informing and stimulating the national consciousness in regard to the status and problems of women and paying special attention to the upliftment of women;

h) promoting social justice and combating exploitation, inequality and such evils as untouchability and advancing the welfare of the weaker sections of the society;

i) safeguarding the rights of the working classes and advancing their welfare;

j) serving the rural and weaker sections of the people and those residing in border regions, backward or remote areas;

k) providing suitable programmes keeping in view the special needs of the minorities and tribal communities;

l) taking special steps to protect the interests of the children, the blind, the age, the handicapped and other vulnerable Sections of the people;

m) promoting national integration by broadcasting in a manner that facilitates communication in the languages in India; and facilitating the distribution of regional broadcasting services in every State in the languages of that State;

n) providing comprehensive broadcast coverage through the choice of appropriate technology and the best utilization of the broadcast frequencies available and ensuring high quality reception;

o) promoting research and development activities in order to ensure that radio and television broadcast technology are constantly updated; and

p) expanding broadcasting facilities by establishing additional channels of transmission at various levels.

3) In particular, and without prejudice to the generality of the foregoing provisions, the Corporation may take such steps as it thinks fit -

a) to ensure that broadcasting is conducted as a public service to provide and produce programmes;

b) to establish a system for the gathering of news for radio and television;

c) to negotiate for the purchase of, or otherwise acquire, programmes and rights or privileges in respect of sports and other events, films, serials, occasions, meetings, functions or incidents of public interest, for broadcasting and to establish procedures for the allocation of such programmes, rights or privileges to the services;

d) to establish and maintain a library or libraries of radio, television and other materials;

e) to conduct or commission, from time to time, programmes, audience research, market or technical service, which may be released to such persons and in such manner and subject to such terms and conditions as the Corporation may think fit;

f) to provide such other services as may be specified by regulations.

4) Nothing in sub-sections (2) and (3) shall prevent the Corporation from managing on behalf of the Central Government and in accordance with such terms and conditions as may be specified by that Government the broadcasting of External Services and monitoring of broadcasts made by organizations outside India on the basis of arrangements made for reimbursement of expenses by the Central Government.

5) For the purposes of ensuring that adequate time is made available for the promotion of the objectives set out in this Section, the Central Government shall have the power to determine the maximum limit of broadcast time in respect to the advertisement.

6) The Corporation shall be subject to no civil liability on the ground merely that it failed to comply any of the provisions of this Section.

7) The Corporation shall have power to determine and levy fees and other service charges for or in respect of the advertisements and such programmes as may be specified by regulations: Provided that the fees and other service charges levied and collected under this sub-section shall not exceed such limits as may be determined by the Central Government, from time to time.

13. *Parliamentary Committee* :

1) There shall be constituted a Committee consisting of twenty-two Members of Parliament, of whom fifteen

of the House of the People to be elected by the Members thereof and seven from the Councils of States to be elected by the Members thereof in accordance with the system of proportional representation by means of single transferable vote, to oversee that the Corporation discharges its functions in accordance with the provisions of this Act and, in particular, the objectives set out in Section 12 and submit a report thereon to Parliament.

2) The Committee shall function in accordance with such rules as may be made by the Speaker of the House of the People.

14. *Establishment of Broadcasting Council, term of office and removal, etc., of members thereof*

1) There shall be established, by notification, as soon as may be after the appointed day, a Council, to be known as the Broadcasting Council, to receive and consider complaints referred to in Section 15 and to advise the Corporation in the discharge of its functions in accordance with the objectives set out in Section 12.

2) The Broadcasting Council shall consist of

a) a President and ten other members to be appointed by the President of India from amongst persons of eminence in public life;

b) four Members of Parliament, of whom two from the House of the People to be nominated to the Speaker thereof and two from the Council of States to be nominated by the Chairman thereof.

3) The President of the Broadcasting Corporation shall be a Whole-time member and every other member shall be a Part-time member and the President or the Part-time member shall hold the office as such for a term

of three years from the date on which he enters upon his office.

4) The Broadcasting Council may constitute such number of Regional Councils as it may deem necessary to aid assist the Council in the discharge of its function.

5) The President of the broadcasting Council shall be entitled to such salary and allowances and shall be subject to such conditions of service in respect of leave, pension (if any), provident fund and other matters as may be prescribed: Provided that the salary and allowances and the conditions of service shall not be varied to the disadvantage of the President of the Broadcasting Council after his appointment.

6) The other members of the Broadcasting Council and the Members of the Regional Councils constituted under sub-section (4) shall be entitled to such allowances as may be prescribed.

15. *Jurisdiction of, and the procedure to be followed by Broadcasting Council*

1) The Broadcasting Council shall receive and consider complaints from:

   a) any person or group of persons alleging that a certain programme or broadcast or the functioning of the Corporation in specific cases or in general is not in accordance with the objectives for which the Corporation is established.

   b) any person (other than an officer or employee of the Corporation) claiming himself to have been treated unjustly or unfairly in any manner (including unwarranted invasion of privacy, misinterpretation, distortion or lack of objectivity) in connection with any programme broadcast by the Corporation.

2) A complaint under sub-section (1) shall be made in such a manner and within such period as may be specified by regulations.

3) The Broadcasting Council shall follow such procedure as it thinks fit for the disposal of complaints received by it.

4) If the complaint is found to be justified either wholly or in part, of the Broadcasting Council shall advise the Executive Member to take appropriate action.

5) If the executive Member is unable to accept the recommendation of the Broadcasting Council, he shall place such recommendation before the Board for its decision thereon.

6) If the Board is also unable to accept the recommendation of the Broadcasting Council, it shall record its reasons therefor and inform the Broadcasting Council accordingly.

7) Notwithstanding anything contained in sub-section (5) and (6),where the Broadcasting Council deems it appropriate, it may, for reasons to be recorded in writing, require the Corporation to broadcast its recommendations with respect to a complaint in such manner as the Council may deem fit.

Chapter III Assets, Finances and Accounts

16. *Transfer of certain assets, liabilities, etc., of Central Government to Corporation*:

As from appointed day,

a) all property and assets (including the Non-lapsable Fund) which immediately before that day vested in the Central Government for the purpose of Akashvani or

Doordarshan or both shall stand transferred to the Corporation on such terms and conditions as may be determined by the Central Government and the book value of all such property and assets shall be treated as the capital provided by the Central Government to the Corporation;

b) all debts, obligations and liabilities incurred, all contracts entered into and all matters and things engaged to be done by, with or for the Central Government immediately before such day for or in connection with the purposes of Akashvani or Doordarshan or both shall be deemed to have been incurred, entered into and engaged to be done by, with or for the Corporation;

c) all sums of money due to the Central Government in relation to the Akashvani or Doordarshan or both immediately before each day shall be deemed to be due to the Corporation;

d) all suits and other legal proceedings instituted or which could have been instituted by or against the Central Government immediately before such day for any matter in relation to the Akashvani or Doordarshan or both may be constituted or instituted by or against the Corporation.

17. *Grants, etc., by the Central Government*: For the purposes of enabling the Corporation to discharge its functions effectively under this Act, the Central Government may, after due appropriation made by Parliament by law this behalf, pay to the Corporation in each financial year,-

a) the proceeds of the broadcast receiver license fees, if any, as reduced by the collection charges; and

b) such other sums of money as that Government considers necessary, by way of equity, grand-in-aid or loan.

18. *Fund of Corporation*

1) The Corporation shall have its own Fund and all the receipts of the Corporation (including the amounts which stand transferred to the Corporation under Section 16) shall be credited to the Fund and all payments by the Corporation shall be made therefrom.

2) All moneys belonging to the fund shall be deposited in one or more nationalised banks in such manner as the Corporation may decide.

3) The Corporation may spend much sums as it thinks fit for performing its functions under this Act and such sums shall be treated expenditure payable out of the Fund of the Corporation.

Explanation

For the purposes of this Section, "nationalized bank" means a corresponding new bank specified in the First Schedule to the Banking Companies (Acquisition and Transfer of Undertakings) Act, 1980 (40 of 1980).

19. *Investment of moneys*: The Corporation may invest its moneys in the securities of the Central Government or any State government or in any such other manner as may be prescribed.

20. *Annual Financial Statement of the Corporation*:

1) The Corporation shall prepare, in each financial year, an Annual Financial Statement for the next financial year showing separately;

a) The expenditure which is proposed to be met from the internal resources of the Corporation; and

b) the sums required from the Central Government to meet other expenses, and distinguishing;

(1) revenue expenditure from other expenditure; and

(2) non-plan expenditure from plan expenditure.

2) The Annual Financial Statement shall be prepared in such form and forwarded at such time to the Central Government for its approval as may be agreed to by that Government and the Corporation.

21. *Accounts and audit of Corporation*:

1) The Corporation shall maintain proper accounts and other relevant records and prepare an annual statement of accounts in such forms and in such manner as may be prescribed.

2) The accounts of the Corporation shall be audited by the Comptroller and Auditor-General of India at such intervals as may be specified by him and any expenditure incurred in connection with such audit shall be payable by the Corporation to the Comptroller and Auditor-General.

3) The Comptroller and Auditor-General and any person appointed by him in connection with the audit of the accounts of the Corporation shall have the same rights and privileges and authority in connection with such audit as the Comptroller and Auditor-General has with the audit of the government accounts, and in particular, shall have the right to demand the production of books, accounts, connected vouchers and other documents and papers and to inspect any of the offices of the Corporation.

4) The accounts of the Corporation as certified by the Comptroller and Auditor-General of India or any other person appointed by him in this behalf together with the audit report thereon shall be forwarded annually to the Central Government and that Government shall cause the same to be laid before each House of Parliament.

22. *Corporation not liable to be taxed*: Notwithstanding anything contained in the Income Tax Act, 1961 (43 of 1961), or any other enactment for the time being in force relating to income-tax or any other tax on income, profits or gains, the Corporation shall not be liable to pay any income-tax or any other tax in respect of -

a) any income, profits or gains, accruing or arising out of the Fund of the Corporation or any amount received in that Fund; and

b) any income, profits or gains, derived or any amount received, by the Corporation.

Chapter IV Miscellaneous

23. *Power of Central Government to give directions*:

1) The Central Government may, from time to time as and when occasion arises, issue to the Corporation such directions as it may think necessary in the interests of the sovereignty, unity and integrity of India or the security of the State or preservation of public order requiring it not to make a broadcast on any matter of public importance specified in the direction.

2) Where the Corporation makes a broadcast in pursuance of the direction issued under sub-section (1), the fact that such broadcast has been made in pursuance of such direction may also be announced

along with such broadcast, if the Corporation so desires.

3) A copy of every direction issued under sub-section (1) shall be laid before each House of Parliament.

24. *Power of Central Government to obtain information*: The Central Government may require the Corporation to furnish such information as that Government may consider necessary.

25. *Report to Parliament in certain matters and recommendations as to action against the Board*:

1) Where the Board persistently makes default in complying with any directions issued under Section 23 or fails to supply the information required under Section 24, the Central Government may prepare a report thereof and lay it before each House of Parliament for any recommendation thereof as to any action (including super-session of the Board) which may be taken against the Board.

2) On the recommendation of the Parliament, the President may by notification supersede the Board for such period not exceeding six months as may be specified in the notification:: Provided that before issuing the notification under this sub-section, the President shall give a reasonable opportunity to the Board to show cause as to why it should not be superseded and shall consider the explanations and objections, if any, of the Board.

3) Upon the publication of the notification under sub-section (2),

   a) all the Members shall, as from the date of supersession, vacate their offices as such;

b) all the powers, functions and duties which may, by or under the provisions of this Act, be exercised and discharged by such person or persons as the President may direct.

4) On the expiration of the period of supersession specified in the notification issued under sub-section (2), the President may reconstitute the Board by fresh appointments, and in such a case any person who had vacated his office under clause (a) of sub-section (3) shall not be disqualified for appointment: Provided that the President may, at any time before the expiration of the period of supersession, take action under this sub-section.

5) The Central Government shall cause the notification issued under sub-section (2) and a full report of the action taken under this Section to be laid before each House of Parliament.

26. *Office of member not to disqualify a Member of Parliament*: It is hereby declared that the office of the member of the Broadcasting Council or of the Committee constituted under Section 13 shall not disqualify its holder for being chosen as, or for being, a Member of either House of Parliament.

27. *Chairman, Members, etc., to be public servants*: The Chairman and every other Member, every officer or other employee of the Corporation and every member of a Committee thereof, the President and every member of the Broadcasting Council or every member of a Regional Council or a Recruitment Board shall be deemed to be a public servant within the meaning of Section 21 of the Indian Penal Code (45 of 1860).

28. *Protection of action taken in good faith*: No suit or other legal proceeding shall lie against the Corporation, the

Chairman or any Member or officer or other employee thereof or the President or a member of the Broadcasting Council or a member of a Regional Council or a Recruitment Board for anything which is in good faith done or intended to be done in pursuance of this Act or of any rules or regulations made thereunder.

Good Faith Defined

The words "good faith" are not defined in the Act. They are, however defined in other Acts. Nothing is said to be done or believed in good faith which is done or believed without due care and attention - Section 52 of the IPC. A thing shall be deemed to be done in good faith where it is done honestly, whether it is done negligently or not - Section 3(22) of the General Clauses Act, 1897. Nothing shall be deemed to be done in good faith which is not done with due care and attention - Section 2 (7) of the Indian Limitation Act, 1908.

Good Faith in criminal law is different from good faith as understood in civil law. If an act is not done with due care and attention, it cannot so far as criminal law is concerned be said to be done in good faith - Pagla Baba v. State, AIR 1957 Ori 130 : 1950 Cri LJ 769. Nothing can be said to have been done in good faith when it is done without care and caution - Public Prosecutor v. Rajammal, 12 Cri LJ 566 : 12 IC 654.

29. *Authentication of orders and other instruments of Corporation*:

All orders and decisions of the Corporation shall be authenticated by the signature of the Chairman or any other Member authorized by the Corporation in this behalf and all other instruments executed by the Corporation shall be authenticated by the signature of the Executive Member or by any officer of the Corporation authorized by him in this behalf.

Where powers and duties are interconnected and it is not possible to separate one from the other in such in such case the powers may be delegated while duties are retained and vice versa, the delegation of powers takes with it the duties.

30. *Delegation of Powers*

The Corporation may, by general or special order, delegate to the Chairman or any other Member or to any officer of the Corporation, subject to such conditions and limitations, in any, as may be specified therein, such of its powers and duties under this Act as may deem fit.

31. *Annual Report*:

1) The Corporation shall prepare once in every calendar year, in such form and within such time as may be prescribed, an annual report giving a full account of its activities (including the recommendations and suggestions made by the Broadcasting Council and the actions taken thereon) during the previous year and copies thereof shall be forwarded to the Central Government and that Government shall cause the same to be laid before each House of Parliament.

2) The Broadcasting Council shall prepare once in every calendar year, in such form and within such time as may be prescribed, an annual report giving a full account of its activities during the previous year and copies thereof shall be forwarded to the Central Government and that Government shall cause the same to be laid before each House of Parliament.

32. *Power to make rules*:

1) The Central Government may, by notification, make rules for carrying out the provisions of this Act.

2) In particular, and without prejudice to the generality of the foregoing power, such rules may provide for all or any of the following matters, namely :-

   a) the salaries and allowances and conditions of service in respect of leave, pension (if any), provident fund and other matters in relation to the Whole-time Members under sub-section (7) of Section 6;

   b) the allowances payable to the Chairman and Part-time Members under sub-section (8) of Section 6;

   c) the control restrictions and conditions subject to which the Corporation may appoint officers and other employees under sub-section (1) of Section 9;

   d) the manner in which the conditions and restrictions subject to which a Recruitment Board may be established under sub-section (1) of Section 10;

   e) the qualifications and other conditions of service of the members of a Recruitment Board and their period of office under sub-section (2) of Section 10;

   f) the terms and conditions in accordance with the deputation may be regulated under sub-section (2) of Section 11;

   g) the salary and allowances and conditions of service in respect of leave, pension (if any), provident fund and other matters in relation to the President of the Broadcasting Council under sub-section (5) of Section 14;

h) the allowances payable to other members of the Broadcasting Council and the members of the Regional Councils under sub-section (6) of Section 14;

i) the manner in which the Corporation may invest its moneys under Section 19;

j) the form and the manner in which the annual statement of accounts shall be prepared under sub-section (1) of Section 21;

k) the form in which, and the time within which, the Corporation and the Broadcasting Council shall prepare their annual report under Section 31;

l) any other matter which is required to be, or may be, prescribed.

31. *Power to make regulations*:

1) The Corporation may, by notification, make regulations not inconsistent with this Act and the rules made thereunder for enabling it to perform its functions under this Act.

2) Without prejudice to the generality of the foregoing power such regulations may provide for all or any of the following matters, namely:

   a) the manner in which and the purposes for which the Corporation may associate with itself any person under sub-section (7) of Section 3;

   b) the times and places at which meetings of the Board shall be held, and the procedure to be followed thereat, and the quorum necessary for the transaction of the business at a meeting of the Board under sub-section (1) of Section 8;

c) the methods of recruitment and conditions of service, including pension, leave and provident fund in relati0on to an officer or other employee of the Corporation under sub-section (4) of Section 11;

d) the authority competent to make certain appointments referred to in clause (a) of sub-section (3) of Section 12;

e) the determination and levy of fees and other service charges in respect of advertisements and other programmes under sub-section (7) of Section 12;

f) the manner in which and the period within which complaints may be made under sub-section (2) of Section 15;

g) any other matter in respect of which provision is, in the opinion of the Corporation, necessary for the performance of its functions under this Act:
Provided that the regulations under clause (c) or clause (d) shall be made only with the prior approval of the Central Government.

The rules and regulations do not lose their character as rules and regulations, even though they are to be of the same effect as if contained in the Act. They continue to be rules subordinate to the Act, and though for certain purposes, including the purpose of construction, they are to be treated as if contained in the Act, their true nature as subordinate rules is not lost. Therefore, with regard to the effect of a repeal of the Act, they continue to be subject to the operation of Section 24 of the General Clauses Act. Chief Inspector Mines v. K.G.Thapar, (1962) 1 SCR 9 : AIR 1961 SC 838 : (1961) 2 SCA 86 : (1961) 2 Lab LJ 146 : 1961 (3) FLR 241.

Where the regulations are changed for particular cases, there will be violation of Equality Clause. Rain Prasad v.

State of Binar, 1953 SCR 1129 : AIR 1953 SC 215 : 1953 SCA 578 : 32 Pat 375 : 8 DLR (SC) 289 : 1953 BLJR 318. Rules and regulations have the force of law. Therefore, writ if mandamus will be available against administrative or quasi-judicial authority, which refuses to follow the rules. State of U.P. v. Baburam, (1961) 2 SCR 679 : AIR 1961 SC 751.

34. *Rules and regulations to be laid before Parliament*

Every rule and every regulation made under this Act shall be laid, as soon as may be after it is made, before each House of Parliament, while it is in session for a total period of thirty days which may be comprised in one session or in two or more successive sessions, and if, before the expiry of session immediately following the session or the successive sessions aforesaid, both Houses agree that the rule or regulation should not be made, the rule or regulation shall thereafter have effect only in such modified form or be of no effect, as the case may be; so, however, that any such modification or annulment shall be without prejudice to the validity of anything previously done under that rule or regulation.

35. *Power to remove difficulties*

If any difficulty arises in giving effect to the provisions of this Act, the Central Government may, by order, published in the Official Gazette, make such provisions, not inconsistent with the provisions of this Act, as it may deem necessary, for the removal of the difficulty: Provided that no such order shall be made after the expiry of a period of three years from the appointed day.

Bibliography

Arant, David, ed. *Perspectives: Ethics, Issues and Controversies in Mass Media.* St. Paul, MN: Coursewise Publishing, 1999.

Atkins, Joseph B., ed. *The Mission: Journalism, Ethics, and the World: International Topics in Media.*Ames: Iowa State University Press, 2002.

Berkman, Robert I. and Christopher A. Shumway. *Digital Dilemmas: Ethical Issues for Online Media Professionals.* Ames: Iowa State Press, 2003.

Berry, David, ed. *Ethics and Media Culture.* Woburn, MA: Focal Press, 2000.

Bertrand, Claude-Jean. *An Arsenal for Democracy: Media Accountability Systems.* Cresskill, NJ: Hampton Press, 2003. [Originally publ. in French (Economica, 1999), translated in Brazil (2002), Japan (2002)]

____________. *Media Ethics and Accountability Systems.* New Brunswick, NJ: Transaction Publishers, 2000. [Originally published in French, translated in Armenia, Brazil, Greece, Italy, Korea, Portugal, Romania & Turkey. Arabic & Chinese translations in progress.]

Black, Jay. *Mixed News.* Mahwah, NJ: L. Erlbaum Associates, 1997.

Bovee, Warren G. *Discovering Journalism.* Westport, CT: Greenwood Press, 1999.

Bugeja, Michael J. *Living Ethics.* Needham Heights, MA: Allyn and Bacon, 1995.

Christians, Clifford G. *Good News*. New York: Oxford University Press, 1993.

______________, et al. *Media Ethics*. White Plains, NY: Longman Publishing Group, 2001.

Clark, Roy Peter and Cole C. Campbell, eds.*The Values and Craft of American Journalism*.Gainesville: University Press of Florida, 2002.

Cohen, Elliot D. and Deni Elliott, eds. *Journalism Ethics: A Reference Handbook*. Santa Barbara, CA: Abc-Clio, 1998.

Cote, William and Roger Simpson. *Covering Violence*. New York: Columbia University Press, 2000.

Day, Louis A. *Ethics in Media Communications*, 4th ed. Belmont, CA: Wadsworth, 2003.

De Vries, Paul, et al. *Ethics Applied*. Boston: Pearson Education, 2000.

Downie, Jr. Leonard and Robert G. Kaiser. *The News About the News*. New York: Knopf, 2002.

Fallows, James. *Breaking the News: How the Media Undermine American Democracy*. New York: Pantheon, 1996.

Fuller, Jack. *News Values: Ideas for an Information Age*. Chicago: University of Chicago Press, 1996.

Giles, Robert and Robert W. Snyder, eds. *What's Fair?: The Problem of Equity in Journalism*. New Brunswick, NJ: Transaction Publishers, 2000.

Good, Howard. *Desperately Seeking Ethics*. Lanham, MD: Scarecrow, 2003.

______________and Michael Dillon. *Media Ethics Goes to the Movies*. Westport, CT: Praeger, 2002.

Goodwin, H. Eugene, Ron F. Smith, Gene Goodwin.*Groping for Ethics in Journalism*.Ames: Iowa State University Press, 1999.

Gordon, A. David, et al. *Controversies in Media Ethics*. White Plains, NY: Longman Publishers, 1999.

Gross, Larry, John Stuart Katz and Jay Ruby, eds. *Image Ethics in the Digital Age*. Minneapolis: University of Minnesota Press, 2003.

Hausman, Carl. *Crisis of Conscience: Perspectives on Journalism Ethics.* New York: Harper Collins, 1992.

Herbert, John. *Journalism and Broadcast Ethics*. Woburn, MA: Focal Press, 2002. Iggers, Jeremy. *Good News, Bad News: Journalism Ethics and the Public Interest*. Boulder, CO: Westview Press, 1998.

Keeble, Richard. *Ethics for Journalists.* New York: Routledge, 2001.

Knowlton, Steven R. *Moral Reasoning for Journalists.* Westport, CT: Praeger, 1997.

____________ and Patrick R. Parsons, eds. *The Journalist's Moral Compass.* Westport, CT: Praeger, 1995.

Kovach, Bill and Tom Rosenstiel. *The Elements of Journalism: What Newspeople Should Know and the Public Should Expect.*New York: Crown Publishers, 2001.

LaMay, Craig L. *Journalism and the Debate over Privacy*. Mahwah, NJ: Lawrence Erlbaum, 2003.

Lambeth, Edmund. *Committed Journalism: An Ethic for the Profession.* Bloomington: Indiana University Press, 1992.

Lee, M. and N. Solomon. *Unreliable Sources: A Guide to Detecting Bias in News Media.* New York: Carol Publishing Group, 1990.

Leslie, Larry Z. *Mass Communication Ethics: Decision Making in Postmodern Culture*. Boston, MA: Houghton Mifflin, 2000.

Lester, Paul Martin. *Images That Injure: Pictorial Stereotypes in the Media.* Westport, CT: Praeger, 1996.

____________. *Photojournalism: An Ethical Approach*. Hillsdale, NJ: Lawrence Erlbaum Associates, 1991.

Limburg, Val E. *Electronic Media Ethics.* Boston: Focal Press, 1994.

MacDonald, Barrie and Michel Petheram.*Keyguide to Information Sources in Media Ethics*. London: Mansell Publishing, 1998.

Matelski, Marilyn J. *TV News Ethics*. Boston: Focal Press, 1991.

Merrill, John C. *Journalism Ethics: Philosophical Foundations for News Media*. New York: St. Martin's Press, 1997.

Moore, Roy L. *Mass Communication Law and Ethics*. Hillsdale, NJ: Lawrence Erlbaum Associates, 1999.

Patterson, Philip and Lee Wilkins, 4th ed. *Media Ethics: Issues and Cases*. Boston, MA: McGraw Hill, 2002.

Pritchard, David, ed. *Holding the Media Accountable: Citizens, Ethics, and the Law*. Bloomington: Indiana University Press, 2000.

Rosenstiel, Thomas and Amy Mitchell. *Thinking Clearly: Cases in Journalistic Decision-Making*. New York: Columbia University Press, 2003.

Russell, Nick. *Morals and the Media: Ethics in Canadian Journalism*. Vancouver: University of British Columbia Press, 1994.

Sanders, Karen. *Ethics & Journalism*. London: Sage Publications, 2003.

Seib, Philip. *Campaigns and Conscience: The Ethics of Political Journalism*. Westport, CT: Praeger, 1994.

Seib, Philip and Kathy Fitzpatrick. *Journalism Ethics*. Fort Worth: Harcourt Brace, 1997.

Weaver, Paul H. *News and the Culture of Lying: How Journalism Really Works*. New York: The Free Press, 1995.

Wheeler, Tom. *Phototruth or Photofiction?* Manwah, NJ: Lawrence Erlbaum, 2002.

Index

Media, Ethics and Law

Naval Prabhakar
Narendra Basu

Commonwealth

Media, Ethics and Law

Edition : 2019

ISBN 81-311-0023-5

Published by :
COMMONWEALTH PUBLISHERS PVT. LTD.
e-mail : commonwealthbooks@gmail.com

Distributed by :
CAMPUS BOOKS INTERNATIONAL
ARPAN PUBLICATIONS
4831/24, Prahlad Street,
Ansari Road, Darya Ganj,
New Delhi - 110002
Ph. : 23275511, 23257835
e-mail : arpanpublications@gmail.com
campusbooks@hotmail.com

Typesetting by :
Rishu Computers
Delhi

Printed at :
Divine Digital Press
Delhi